Nashville Architecture

NASHVILLE ARCHITECTURE

A Guide to the City

CARROLL VAN WEST

Support provided by The Metro Nashville Historical Commission, AIA Middle Tennessee, and MTSU Center for Historic Preservation.

THE UNIVERSITY OF TENNESSEE PRESS / Knoxville

Library of Congress Cataloging-in-Publication Data

West, Carroll Van, 1955–
Nashville architecture : a guide to the city / Carroll Van West. — First Edition.
pages cm
ISBN 978-1-57233-920-0 (paperback)
1. Architecture—Tennessee—Nashville—Guidebooks.
2. Historic buildings—Tennessee—Nashville—Guidebooks.
3. Nashville (Tenn.)—Buildings, structures, etc.—Guidebooks.
4. Nashville (Tenn.)—Guidebooks. I. Title.

NA735.N24W47 2015
720.9768'55—dc23   2015002926

Contents

Illustrations

Foreword

Several years ago, The Metro Historical Commission (MHC) of Nashville and Davidson County, AIA Middle Tennessee, a Chapter of The American Institute of Architects (AIA), and the Center for Historic Preservation at Middle Tennessee State University decided to join together on a book venture. Individually we had each written extensively on the subjects of architecture, the history of Nashville, and urban planning in the Middle Tennessee region, and we realized it would be incredibly rewarding to come together and elaborate on the work we had already done. Through many challenges over the years, we are thrilled to finally present the finished product: *Nashville Architecture: A Guide to the City.*

In 1974, the MHC published a book simply titled *Nashville: A Short History and Selected Buildings.* It was a remarkable accomplishment for a group of volunteers who operated with almost no money or staff. With concise text and black and white photographs, the book was designed to be a guide to the "typical as well as superlative" among the city's buildings, in the words of Margaret Lindsley Warden, then commission chair. It was published at a time when few Nashvillians were aware of the richness and diversity of the city's built environment. They were familiar with the architectural icons—historic ones such as The Hermitage, the Tennessee State Capitol, Union Station, and Belle Meade Plantation, and newer ones such as the L & C Tower. But there was little appreciation for the architectural fabric that formed a 200-year-old city, or for the history that wove it together.

Nashville: A Short History and Selected Buildings was the first publication in the city to look at more than the grand structures, to reflect the architecture of all genres, styles and periods, in all corners of the county. For the first time, neighborhoods, modest commercial and industrial structures, civic buildings such as district fire halls and branch libraries, rural stone bridges, and schools were all considered important enough to be in a book about architecture. In making the guidebook so inclusive, the commission was reflecting a national awareness that the view of what and whose history was significant had been too limited for too long. That recognition had been codified with the passage of the National Historic Preservation Act in 1966, the same year in which the Historical Commission was established. To the great credit of those first commissioners, they saw the need for taking inventory of the city's built environment and bringing their findings to the public.

In 1986 AIA Middle Tennessee, under the guidance of architects Frank Orr, AIA, Charles Warterfield, FAIA, Elbridge White, AIA and then AIA Middle TN Executive Director Polly Fitts, began working on *Notable Nashville Architecture 1930–1980*. Like MHC, with almost no money and a part time staff, they entered the literary world. This book was possibly the local community's first introduction into architectural criticism, where Orr describes the purpose as "illumination and education over flattery." His criticism urges the architect to grow beyond self-set boundaries. AIA's purpose for *Notable Nashville Architecture 1930–1980* could be expressed in the words "interest, history and information." It was printed to pique the interest of the public inhabiting the spaces and to enlighten them with the process the architect used to answer the challenges the projects were expected to overcome.

It is a new Millennium, but many of the goals of the original books by MHC and AIA are reintroduced as the purpose for this joint publication, *Nashville Architecture: A Guide to the City*. Nashville is far more conscious now of historic preservation, architecture, and urban design. This book aims to be the successor to the 1974 and 1989 books in its broad scope and comprehensive nature, yet small enough to store in one's car. Appropriately, as awareness of the importance of the built environment and the intertwining of history and architecture has grown, it is the result of collaboration between the MHC and the AIA. In bringing our goal to fruition we handed over our initial research and property list to Dr. Carroll Van West, noted historian and author at the Center for Historic Preservation at Middle Tennessee State University, who added his own research, fieldwork investigations and stock of knowledge about Nashville to produce the manuscript.

Architecture is social art with people in its focus. It is well known that you cannot move forward without knowing where you have been, where you have originated and where you want to be. Our rich Nashville history has and we hope always will be told by our city's wonderful architecture and built environment. We believe that architecture extends beyond image making; it affects and influences our quality of life. Architecture is quite simply about people and their need for shelter, identity, inspiration, and sense of being. These are global concerns regarding common issues that affect us all. The architect for centuries has addressed these challenges, and the end result, the architecture, develops a multicultural language spanning generations and cultures.

By publishing the book we intend to raise awareness of the immense value of the architecture and history of Nashville. We seek to make the public and our youth aware of the significant architectural legacy we leave to our community and the citizens. Our story and our history are reflected in the way that these buildings and spaces are designed and built. Furthermore, we should all help protect these buildings and spaces because they are our visual storytellers.

Please pledge to help us protect our architectural legacy for the future, by promoting the historic preservation, restoration and conservation of our built environment. Although changes will continue and will be recorded in the future, for now, thanks to the University of Tennessee Press, Dr. Carroll Van West, MHC, and AIA, we have marked our place in time with this book.

ANN REYNOLDS ROBERTS
Director Emeritus of the Metro Historical Commission

TIM WALKER
Executive Director of the Metro Historical Commission

CAROL PEDIGO
Hon. AIA; Executive Director of AIA Middle Tennessee,
A Chapter of the American Institute of Architects

Acknowledgments

This book has been a fascinating and challenging collaborative project, involving the Metropolitan Historical Commission (MHC), the Middle Tennessee Chapter of the American Institute of Architects, and the University of Tennessee Press. I especially thank Ann Roberts, the former MHC Executive Director and Tim Walker, the current MHC Executive Director, for presenting me with this opportunity. Also I must acknowledge the research and assistance of Margaret Slater, Laura Rost, Ophelia Paine, Anne-Leslie Owens, Jeanne Holder, Blythe Semmer and Tara Mitchell Mielnik of the MHC staff. Always there with kind words of encouragement, Margaret, Laura, and Ophelia created the initial research files for this book. Tara kept my feet to the fire, pushing me the last couple of years to finish the project. Nashville is extremely lucky, and blessed, to have such a dedicated and gifted history office as the Metropolitan Historical Commission.

Next, the wonderful photography of Gary Layda enhances the volume, making this book a comprehensive document of the city's architecture after two hundred years of growth and change.

Many people served in an advisory capacity and helped to develop the list of places included in the book. Invaluable assistance came from Glenn Oxford, Carol Pedigo, Charles Warterfield, Jr., Christine Kreyling, Michael Emrick, Manuel Zeitlin, Gary Everton, Curt Garrigan, Susan Crew, George Gause, Bill Kelly, Tim Walker, Linda Center, Anne-Leslie Owens, Tara Mitchell Mielnik and the entire MHC staff in compiling the properties chosen for the book.

I also thank the librarians at the Nashville Room of the Ben West Library (now the Public Library of Nashville and Davidson County) for their friendly and efficient help. Several former graduate students in historic preservation at Middle Tennessee State

University left me with important research about Nashville's architectural evolution. I especially thank Trina Binkley, Mike Fleenor, Jane Laub, Lauren Batte, Teresa Douglass, Philip Thomason, Sarah J. Martin, David Price, Brenda Colladay, Robbie Jones, Katie S. Randall, James Draeger, Tammy Sellers, Holly Barnett, and Martha Carver. Claudette Stager at the Tennessee Historical Commission patiently answered questions about the city's many National Register properties. Margaret Beasley, the assistant editor of the *Tennessee Encyclopedia of History and Culture*, gave me valuable comments on the early draft of this manuscript. Elizabeth Moore Humphreys, a former colleague at the Center for Historic Preservation, helped guide me through Nashville modernism.

But my biggest debt belongs to my wife, Mary Hoffschwelle, and son, Owen West, and daughter, Sara West, for their support and encouragement in seeing the book completed. Mere words cannot express the contributions they bring to my work.

How to Use this Book

Nashville Architecture: A Guide to the City documents 277 properties including hundreds of buildings and places significant to the architectural and historical evolution of Nashville and Davidson County. As the city continues to grow and develop in the twenty-first century, it is time to document what remains of the historic architectural legacy of Nashville and to record its modern architectural landmarks.

The introduction, "Nashville's Architecture over Two Centuries," is a thematic overview of the city's history and key architectural landmarks. This chapter establishes historic, geographic, and architectural context that helps to interpret the wider significance of the many individual properties.

The inventory of properties is divided into ten sections, beginning with the downtown business district and Capitol Hill. Maps are provided for each of these zones to locate individual properties. If you want to find one building or district immediately, turn to the index; it lists people, places, events, and institutions in alphabetical order.

As you experience Nashville's architecture, please respect private property rights and boundaries. Many of the guide's properties are public buildings, historic sites, or commercial businesses that welcome visitors. But many are privately owned and should be viewed only from public rights of way. Remember, you should never enter private property without owner consent.

Key Map

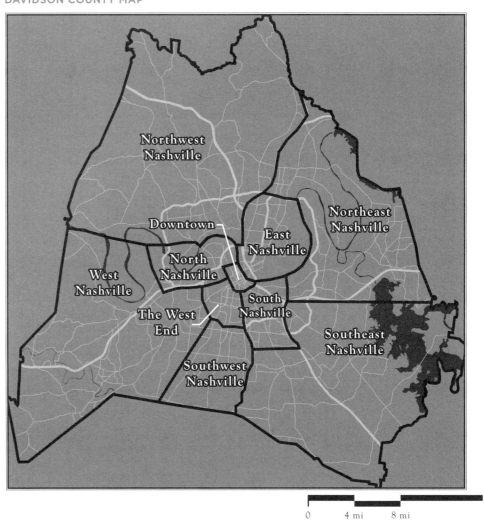

Northwest
Nashville

Northeast
Nashville

Downtown

East
Nashville

West
Nashville

North
Nashville

South
Nashville

The West
End

Southeast
Nashville

Southwest
Nashville

0   4 mi   8 mi

Nashville's Architecture Over Two Centuries

Architecture represents more than the design ideas of architects and the cultural tastes of patrons. It also has significant social and historical meaning. "Social function, not physical function," observes architectural historian Alan Gowans, "is what determines the form and significance of a visual metaphor, hence what architecture is."[1] The size, ornamentation, design, technology, location, and function of a building hold important clues about the people who designed it, who lived or worked there, and who profited from it. As we change over time, so our buildings change, as does the corresponding interconnected fabric of buildings, bridges, fences, roads, signs, and structures that make up our urban landscape.

Over the last two hundred years, Nashville has evolved from a place of unadorned wooden and stone outposts at the end of the southwestern frontier to a major urban center, with recent growth in size and population propelled by both downtown and suburban expansion. The co existence of a faded yet still inspiring architectural past with the postmodern monuments of the present defines the urban landscape of Nashville, and, in large part, defines our own identity and sense of place at this particular point in history.

THE GEOGRAPHICAL SETTING

Nashville rests in the middle of Tennessee's central basin, a region called the "garden" of Tennessee by nineteenth century residents. In general, Davidson County is blessed with rich top soil and in its western, southern, and eastern corners, the land is flat and rolling, easily adaptable for agriculture. The land also is well watered by the Cumberland, Stones, and Harpeth rivers, along with numerous flowing creeks. But within Davidson County are places quite different in soil quality and topography. Parts of the southern border with Rutherford County are hilly, still forested, and full of limestone outcroppings. Limestone, in fact, would often be used in constructing foundations, fences, and some buildings. The land of the northern and western borders, near the boundaries with Montgomery and Robertson counties, is even more rugged, with abundant outcroppings, steep hills, and thick woods. This is where the Central Basin of Tennessee meets the different countryside of the Western Highland Rim, a region that residents once called the "barrens" of Middle Tennessee. The northern reaches of the county are clearly marked by rural settlement patterns and rural ways of life.

NATIVE AMERICANS AND EARLY SETTLERS, 1700–1820

Due to the ruggedness of the surrounding countryside, the first people to use the region's resources concentrated their efforts along the rivers. Native Americans during the Mississippian culture, from about 1000 to 1400 AD, established permanent villages adjacent to the rivers, where they raised maize and other vegetables while taking advantage of the good hunting opportunities. During the early historic period, hunting parties of Cherokees, Chickasaws, and Shawnees crossed the region repeatedly.

By the early 1700s, the resources of the rivers, especially the buffalo, deer, and elk who came there to drink, attracted fur traders to the region. French Canadian trader Charles Charleville established the first trading post around 1710. During the early 1700s, the Davidson County area served as a southern outpost in the international Great Lakes fur trade network. By the 1760s, another French Canadian, Timothy Demonbreun, chose to locate a post near a prominent salt spring that had attracted wild game for centuries. His post became known as French Lick, which became the initial focal point for the county's early settlement following the American Revolution.

When Nashville was permanently established as a frontier station from the winter of 1779 to the spring of 1780 by James Robertson and John Donelson, the fledgling settlement was centered on the banks of Cumberland River. The first settlers came in two parties. Robertson brought a group of men and women from East Tennessee, across the Wilderness Road, and through Kentucky to reach the French Lick area. Donelson led a flotilla on the Holston, Tennessee, Ohio, and Cumberland rivers during the spring of 1780 to bring men, women, and children to the settlement. Both groups brought along African American slaves. Even though the river route was an extremely roundabout way, the settlers learned that access to the river was a necessity. The Cumberland River was the settlers' lifeline to eastern states and served as a trade outlet to already established French and Spanish settlements on the Mississippi River, especially the international trading bases of Natchez and New Orleans.

Nashville's history as a transportation hub for commerce in Middle Tennessee dates to these early patterns of exchange between Native Americans and colonial hunters. Several Native American trails—then nothing more than rough paths through the forests and countryside—connected French Lick to other southern locations. Later roads, highways, railroads, and even interstates would parallel those initial trails, shaping Nashville in distinctive ways as a transportation crossroads, which benefited from surrounding rich natural resources.

From 1780 to 1810, Nashville became the jumping off point for the settlement and development of Middle Tennessee as families moved from the fort on the Cumberland to establish separate frontier stations, farms, plantations, and towns. Today little remains downtown from those first years of urban growth. In 1784, Thomas Molloy prepared Nashville's initial town plat, laying out 165 one-acre square lots, with four reserved for a public square, on the bluffs overlooking the Cumberland. From an interpretive overlook at the Davidson County Courthouse, discerning eyes can find the faint outlines of a town square plan that modern planners and engineers sacrificed to make way for different urban renewal and traffic improvement schemes. Otherwise, one looks to the suburban and the remaining rural areas of Davidson County for traces of the city's earliest architectural beginnings.

The massive logs of the Stump Tavern (1789) on Brick Church Pike are representative of the most common and readily used building material during the frontier generation. Average settlers as well as the rich and politically powerful, as evident in the initial Hermitage cabins of Andrew Jackson, constructed log homes. Evidence of the log building tradition may be found in several Davidson County homes, sometimes hidden behind new facades of brick or wood siding.

Another persistent trait of many early dwellings was the central hall plan, where two rooms of roughly equal size flanked a typically spacious central hall. The three to five bay symmetrical facades of the central hall house became a distinguishing characteristic of early Davidson County residences, a tradition that continued to the time of the Civil War.

The red brick and Federal style of Devon Farm (c. 1798), the Hays-Kiser House (c. 1800, or Locust Hill), the May-Granbery House (c. 1807), and the Craighead House (c. 1811) signify how quickly a planter elite distinguished itself by means of its elegant two-story houses built of brick. African American slave carpenters typically made and fired the bricks and built many of the houses. Compared to neighboring Sumner County and earlier settlements in East Tennessee, limestone proved not so popular for building complete buildings in early Nashville and Davidson County. Limestone was readily used in fences—and surviving stone walls from the nineteenth and early twentieth century are significant components of the rural landscape throughout the county—and for outbuildings and building foundations, but Davidson County was a settlement landscape largely of wood and brick. An exception can be found at the Nashville City Cemetery. Established in 1822, the cemetery contains many finely carved limestone buildings and gravestones, bordered by a stone wall.

THE ANTEBELLUM ERA, 1820–1860

The year 1827 marks the beginning of a new chapter in the city's development. The state capital was temporarily moved from Murfreesboro to Nashville. Not coincidentally, a branch of the Bank of the United States also was established in the city. Mercantile activity increased as did the amount of steamboat traffic on the Cumberland River, up from thirty-three arrivals in 1824 to 112 five years later. Merchants and professionals took center stage in the development of Nashville. This new socio-economic order was matched by a new order in the architecture of Nashville, the language of classicism, best articulated perhaps in the temple form and the two-story classical portico of the Bank of the United States and emulated in new public buildings such as the State Penitentiary, designed by David Morrison (neither building is extant). Nashville's elite, such as then-President Andrew Jackson at the Hermitage, soon called upon Morrison to give an updated classical look to their dwellings. Nashville architects, builders, and clients joined fully in the national movement of Greek Revival architecture.

The 1830s witnessed a push for internal improvements, largely aimed at improving Nashville's commercial connections with surrounding Middle Tennessee county seats at Gallatin, Spring-field, Franklin, Murfreesboro, Charlotte, and Lebanon. The city's first macadamized road led to Franklin; by 1846, Nashville was not only an important river port, but a transportation hub of some 410 miles of turnpikes, connecting its merchants and financiers to the rich farmlands of Middle Tennessee. The basic paths of these antebellum turnpikes serve Nashvillians today as Hillsboro Pike, Franklin Pike, Old Murfreesboro Pike, Gallatin Pike, Lebanon Pike, White's Creek Pike, Charlotte Pike, and Brick Church Pike.

Classicism was codified as the dominant architectural expression of the age in 1845 when the cornerstone was laid for the new State Capitol, the Tennessee General Assembly having chosen Nashville as the permanent capital two years earlier. The architect was William Strickland, who was already well-known for Greek Revival landmarks in Philadelphia and New Orleans. On Cedar Knob, the highest point in downtown Nashville, a few blocks west of the public square, Strickland took Tennessee marble and limestone and composed a monumental Greek temple, interlocked by four Ionic porticoes, and crowned with a Corinthian-style cupola. Long before the building finally was completed in 1859, the new capitol established a standard for downtown buildings. In 1844–47, for example, German engineer and builder Adolphus Heiman designed St. Mary's Catholic Church in a Greek Revival style similar enough to Strickland's capitol that for decades architectural scholars assumed that Strickland was the church's architect. Just south of the capitol, James M. Hughes designed a Cornithian-portico mansion (not extant) for President James K. Polk in 1848–49. The capitol's classical style accentuated the city's embrace of the national Greek Revival movement and established a classical tradition for public buildings that lasted into the twentieth century.

In addition, the location of the new capitol west of the Cumberland River further encouraged Nashville's expansion from the town square and riverfront to continue a westward course. Politicians, merchants, and professionals built gracious townhouses on large landscaped lots near the new capitol. Almost none of these survive today because they gave way to office, commercial, and government pressures that largely replaced the initial downtown residential areas during the twentieth century. Only the Italianate-styled Savage House (1859) is left; the remainder eventually gave way to the construction of large office, commercial, and public buildings during the twentieth century.

By 1850, three key forces had shaped Nashville's urban fabric—the state government, the transportation system of the river and turnpikes, and the agricultural prosperity of surrounding plantations, farms, and towns. The following year, the Nashville and Chattanooga Railroad made its presence felt; on its iron rails rode a remarkable decade of economic growth and prosperity. With better and quicker access to markets and consumer goods, the planter and merchant elite gained greater prosperity and built new churches, schools, houses, businesses, and public buildings. For example, prominent citizens commissioned William Strickland to design a new First Presbyterian Church in the then fashionable Egyptian Revival style. The merchant and planter elite built or expanded imposing two-story classically-styled mansions, like at Belle Meade in 1853. The different architectural styles associated with the Victorian era in architecture also made their distinctive appearance. With its gardens, sculptures, and many outbuildings, Belmont (1850s), designed by Adolphus Heiman, created the city's best example of a Victorian domestic landscape. Clover Bottom (1858) and Two Rivers (1859) blended Italianate style and elements of classicism within the framework of the traditional central hall plan house. Heiman's Literary Department for the University of Nashville (1850s, now known as Lindsley Hall) and his Central State Hospital for the Insane (1849–51, not extant) were Gothic

Revival in style as was the Holy Trinity Episcopal Church (1852–53) by New York-based architects Frank Wills and Henry Dudley.

This expansion of architectural expressions beyond the traditional vernacular of the central hall plan house and the dominant classical style reflected a broader cultural trend toward urban maturation and Victorian sophistication in Nashville. Another significant trend of the 1850s was the impact of recent immigrants, such as the German engineer Adolphus Heiman, who became an important architect in Middle Tennessee. A growing German neighborhood north of the capitol later became known as "Germantown." Here Jacob Geiger, a German master mason, designed the Gothic-styled Church of the Assumption in the late 1850s. German Jews built the elaborate, assymmetrical Reform Temple (not extant) on what is now Seventh Avenue North in the 1880s. In the next decade, Irish immigrants established St. Patrick's Church (c. 1890) on Second Avenue South.

Throughout the 1850s, the Louisville and Nashville and the Nashville and Decatur railroads joined the Nashville and Chattanooga in creating a new engineered, industrial landscape within the city. A corridor of iron, coal piles, railroad roundhouses, terminals, and warehouses emerged west of the capitol. Railroad lines directly connected the city to the Ohio River at Louisville and the Tennessee River at Chattanooga and Decatur, Alabama. The tracks soon eclipsed the once dominant riverfront as Nashville's key commercial thoroughfare. The modern technology and distinctive landscape represented by the railroad signaled the dawn of a new age. In both cultural and economic contexts, as

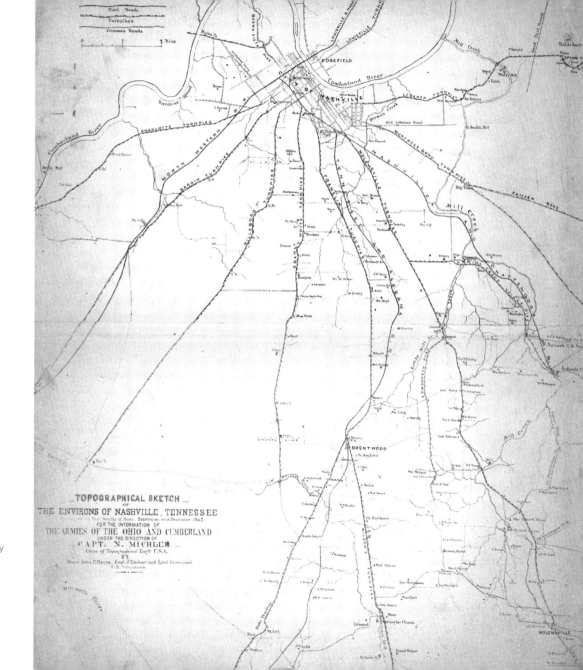

1862 Map of Nashville, Library of Congress, Maps Division.

historian Anita Shafer Goodstein observed, "Nashville was a mature urban society by 1860."[2]

CIVIL WAR AND RECONSTRUCTION, 1860–1875

That new age was delayed and changed by the American Civil War. From February 1862 to the end of the war, Nashville was an occupied city. Union soldiers and African American laborers built a ring of forts protecting the city, Fort Negley (1862) being most prominent. The war closed many Nashville stores and businesses. But since the city also served as a major supply depot for the Union army during most of these months, many other Nashville merchants benefited from the war. While armies on both sides invaded the countryside, leaving many plantations as devastated wastelands, the railroads, especially the Louisville and Nashville, became more powerful.

The war years left little in the way of an architectural legacy. Besides the forts, temporary military structures, and expanded railroad facilities, the only substantial building was the St. Cecilia Convent (1860–62), an Italianate building completed by the Dominican Sisters at the beginning of the war. But the social and economic reconstruction of the defeated South after the war soon brought a dramatic new look to Nashville.

The most significant change involved the tremendous expansion in the number of freed people in Nashville. Free blacks residing in Nashville totaled 719 in 1860. With emancipation, however, this community immediately expanded by thousands, with more freed people arriving weekly in search of better oppor-

National Trust for Historic Preservation conference, 2009, at Van Vechten Gallery, Fisk University, Carroll Van West, photographer.

tunities. African Americans quickly established their own homes, churches, cemeteries, and schools. Bishop Daniel Payne of the African Methodist Episcopal (AME) church, for example, worked with local African Americans to organize St. Paul's AME Church in 1863. Wooden army hospital barracks served as the initial home of the Fisk Free Colored School, located in what are now railroad

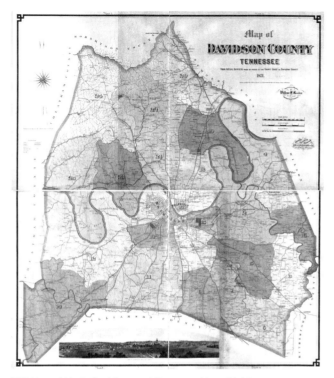

1871 Map of Nashville, Library of Congress, Maps Division.

yards near Union Station. After a successful national fund-raising concert tour by the Fisk Jubilee Singers, a new, permanent campus was located in north Nashville, at the site of Fort Gillem, a former "contraband" camp, where former slaves lived during and after the Civil War. This area became the heart of the post-Reconstruction black community in Nashville. By the 1890s, Fisk University itself

would house such distinguished examples of Victorian architecture as Jubilee Hall (1873–75), the Gymnasium (1888, now the Carl Van Vechten Gallery), and Fisk Memorial Chapel (1892).

NASHVILLE IN THE NEW SOUTH, 1875-1900

The 1877 dedication ceremonies for the new Victorian Gothic-styled U.S. Custom House in downtown Nashville, attended by President Rutherford B. Hayes, marked a symbolic end of the Reconstruction period. New civic and business leaders led Nashville's development in the following years. An economic future, grounded in manufacturing, finance, insurance, and education, was pursued by an "ambitious crowd of 'new men,'" in the words of historian Don H. Doyle, "whose vision and entrepreneurial skill propelled Nashville into a leading position in the emerging economic structure of the South." These civic capitalists tied their own economic self-interest to the boosting of the city itself; as Doyle concludes, "they set the tone of the times, creating a vigorous climate of enterprise that opened the city to new ideas—and new money."[3]

The architectural legacy funded by Nashville's civic capitalists from 1875 to 1900 ranged from modern educational facilities to a performing arts auditorium to modern engineering marvels, like the Union Station Trainshed (1900, no longer extant) and the Arcade (1900–03), a glass-covered shopping area. Nashville's changing appearance mirrored its improved transportation systems. The large multiple-story warehouses along Second Avenue and the new canal locks along the Cumberland River marked the height of Nashville's steamboat trade. The construction of the massive Richardsonian Romanesque-styled Union Station in 1900 symbolized the L&N's monopoly control on local railroad traffic as well as Nashville's full integration into the national railroad system.

Residential patterns were changing too. Soon after the Civil War, streetcars, first powered by mules, then steam railroad engines, and finally electricity in 1888, allowed the wealthy then the middle class to move out of the increasingly crowded and industrial downtown core to suburban homes. Nashville, like other American cities during this age, lost its antebellum character as a "walking city," where the classes and races lived in relatively close proximity. In 1872, the Nashville and Edgefield Street Railroad Company, and a modern iron bridge over the Cumberland River, accelerated the development of the town of Edgefield, on the east side of the river in what is known now as East Nashville; Edgefield was incorporated into the City of Nashville in 1880. Residential expansion westward came quickly once the McGavock and Mount Vernon Company built a wooden viaduct over the railroad tracks and gulch west of Tenth Avenue and extended a streetcar line to the Vanderbilt University area in the 1880s. The electric streetcar suburbs of the 1890s and early 1900s remain today, with most preserved as historic districts. They contain the city's best range of Victorian and early twentieth century domestic architecture, from the picturesque Queen Anne style to the brick and stone of Romanesque and the stylistic eclecticism of the bungalow.

At the same time that wealthy and middle-class whites carved new lives in neighborhoods west of downtown, African Americans experienced a significant decline in their economic opportunities, and their residential choices, as the harsh hand of Jim Crow segregation created invisible, but very real, spatial boundaries between the races within the city. The dictates of Jim Crow meant that African American neighborhoods were lacking in public services and had substandard schools. The Fisk University area remained a center of activity; another was in South Nashville, within the industrial belt along the railroad tracks.

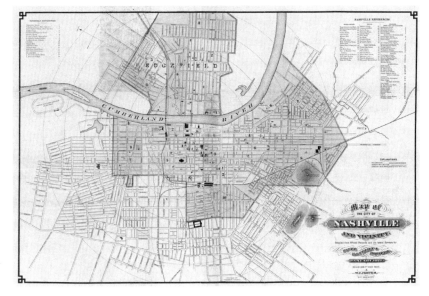

1877 Map of Nashville, Library of Congress, Maps Division.

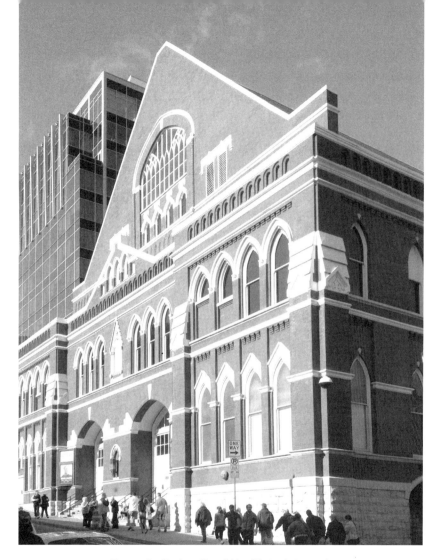

Ryman Auditorium, Carroll Van West, photographer.

The Cameron-Trimble neighborhood emerged as another center for African American families in the early twentieth century.

Within the downtown commercial district, race and gender created both visible and invisible boundaries. Many restaurants and stores refused any service to African Americans while other businesses offered only the indignity of second-class service. In response, Jefferson Street in North Nashville developed as the commercial heart of the African American community. The infamous Men's Quarter sought patronage from white middle class professionals and elite businessmen. Summer Street (now Fifth Avenue North) was home to dress shops, piano stores, and department stores, whose primary customers were white women. The YWCA (1907) provided a respectable haven for working women in the downtown.

The expansion of Nashville in the late 1800s coincided with the further development of the city's architectural profession. Peter J. Williamson is credited with several important buildings, including the Vanderbilt Gymnasium (1880). His disciple Hugh C. Thompson designed the Ryman Auditorium (1892), along with many fine homes in the suburban neighborhoods. Commissions for some late Victorian landmarks went to non-residents like federal architects W. A. Potter and James Knox Taylor (U.S. Customs House) and railroad engineer Richard Montfort (Union Station).

THE PROGRESSIVE ERA, 1900–1930

Nashville's architectural profession became permanently established from 1900 to 1930. The city's population almost doubled in size, from 80,865 to 153,866, and its historic built environment took the general appearance it retains today. In 1919, Nashville architects created the first local chapter of the American Institute of Architects. Christian Asmus, Henry Hibbs, Donald Southgate, Edwin Keeble, and George D. Waller, along with such local firms as Hart Freeland Roberts; Marr and Holman; and McKissack and McKissack, left a distinguished architectural record in their regional interpretations of Classical Revival, Tudor Revival, Colonial Revival, and Art Deco styles. In fact, McKissack and McKissack was recognized as one of the first African American owned and controlled architectural firms in the nation. From this point forward, the Nashville architectural profession was firmly established and would increasingly gain a national reputation.

Many commissions came for new downtown businesses, offices, and apartments as commercial activity rapidly shifted from the public square to Fifth, Sixth, and Seventh Avenues and the intersecting streets of Commerce and Church. These new buildings quickly replaced the once large downtown residential neighborhood. In 1903, Nashville capitalist Daniel C. Buntin commissioned the Arcade; that same year, the first Cain-Sloan department store opened on Fifth Avenue North. In 1906, Charles Castner and William Knott opened a new Castner-Knott department store at the corner of Seventh and Church, where the grand Demoville family mansion once stood. This same decade also witnessed the innovative reinforced concrete construction of Cummins Station and the concrete trusses of the Shelby Street Bridge.

Nashville became more dependent on the growth of a distinctive service economy, especially in finance, insurance, medicine, and education. By 1916, the Doctors' Building, designed by Edward Dougherty and Thomas Gardner, stood at 710 Church Street. To the northeast was the new Beaux-Arts masterpiece, the Hermitage Hotel (1910), designed by Edwin Carpenter. Across the street, in 1924–25, the state government built the first major state office building since the State Capitol. The War Memorial Building was designed in the Classical Revival style by Dougherty and Gardner, in association with the noted New York City firm of McKim, Mead, and White. Along Union Street developed the city's financial district, centered around the Classical Revival-styled Stahlman Building (1906–7), designed by Edwin Carpenter. This early Nashville skyscraper would soon be surrounded by Marr and Holman's Federal Reserve Bank Building (1922); Henry Hibbs' American Trust Building (1909, 1926); and Asmus and Clark's Nashville Trust Building (1925–26). At the corner of Charlotte Avenue and Fourth Avenue North was the Morris Memorial Building (1924–25), a Classical Revival design by McKissack and McKissack. It often housed African American professionals and leading business institutions.

The construction of new college campuses in the suburbs matched the downtown boom. For its new school along Twenty-first Avenue South, administrators of the George Peabody College for Teachers purchased land from Vanderbilt University and Roger Williams University (an African American Baptist institution that closed its campus in 1905 and relocated to a Whites Creek Pike location in 1908). Peabody's replication of Thomas Jefferson and Benjamin Henry Latrobe's famous plan for the

Auditorium, Tennessee Centennial Exposition, 1897, Library of Congress, Prints and Photographs Division.

Centennial Park, Carroll Van West, photographer.

University of Virginia immediately made the campus the grandest collegiate landscape in the city, with individual buildings designed during the 1910s and 1920s by local architects such as Henry Hibbs and such national architects as Ludlow and Peabody; McKim, Mead, and White; and New York architect Raymond Hood. As the last major buildings were under construction at Peabody, Henry Hibbs designed the adjacent Scarritt College for Christian Workers (mid-1920s, now the Scarritt-Bennett Center), using native Crab Orchard stone in his exquisite Collegiate Gothic design.

INTRODUCTION

In the 1920s, city boosters commissioned Hart Freeland Roberts to build a concrete replica of the Parthenon in the middle of Centennial Park. The original Parthenon replica, constructed of plaster, had been the most popular building of the Tennessee Centennial Exposition of 1897. This replica, along with Nashville's institutions of higher education and Classical Revival architecture, firmly established the city's self-proclaimed reputation as the "Athens of the South." Choosing to make the Parthenon a permanent part of the cityscape signified a desire to equate the city's institutions and images with classical values and traditions.

The image of a classical Athens was even shared, albeit in an understated form, by the emerging campus of Tennessee Agricultural and Industrial College (now Tennessee State University) in northwest Nashville. Although given rocky, rough land on the road to the State Penitentiary, and inadequate state funding, dedicated African American supporters and administrators established in 1912 the state's first public segregated college for black students, creating in time a historic campus of Classical Revival buildings that was listed in the National Register of Historic Places in 1996.

Near the college, African Americans established a middle-class suburb around Hadley Park, which was just one of many new neighborhoods created in Nashville during the early twentieth century. The largest was along the Cumberland River, east of downtown, where the DuPont chemical corporation built the planned industrial village of Jacksonville—now known as Old Hickory— during World War I. At its peak, this enormous industrial complex employed 50,000 workers and the company town

itself housed 30,000 residents. The most prestigious new suburb was west of Peabody and Vanderbilt on the land of the old Belle Meade plantation of the Harding family. The Belle Meade suburb, observes Don Doyle, symbolized the new financial and business class that transformed the old antebellum plantation "into its own suburban showcase of the wealth and power generated in the city since the Civil War."[4] Near the country club was the Tudor Revival-styled Belle Meade Apartments, a first for a Nashville suburb. The single-family residences, however, really distinguished this neighborhood. Set on spacious, landscaped lots, the mansions of Belle Meade were eclectic in style; there were somber Gothic towers, classical columns, and other elements reflective of the revivalist trend in American domestic architecture of the 1920s. No matter the combination of architectural elements, all of the properties—together with the wide boulevard leading west to Percy Warner Park—spoke to the confidence and success of the business class of Nashville in the early twentieth century.

Other grand estates were scattered south and west of the major suburban enclaves. In 1920, the firm of Marr and Holman, in association with New York architects Thompson, Holmes, and Converse, designed for financier Rogers Caldwell a red brick interpretation of The Hermitage, which was called Brentwood Hall. Leslie Cheek in 1929 chose New York landscape architect Bryant Fleming to design his massive "Cheekwood" estate—now home to Cheekwood Botanical Garden and Museum of Art. Two years later, W. Ridley Wills commissioned Hart Freeland Roberts to design a Colonial Revival mansion near Franklin Road; in 1947,

City Market, c. 1940, Library of Congress, Prints and Photographs Division.

the state purchased the estate known as Far Hills to be the official Governor's Mansion.

THE DEPRESSION DECADE, 1930-1940

The swagger of Nashville's business elite lost a step, or two, during the Great Depression, especially after the fall of the Nashville financial firm of Caldwell and Company in 1930. (Caldwell's own Brentwood Hall eventually came into state control and is now

the Ellington Agricultural Center of the Tennessee Department of Agriculture.) Only major projects already under construction, such as the Art Deco-styled Sudekum Building (1932, not extant), were completed during the initial Depression years.

When the administration of President Franklin D. Roosevelt stepped forward in 1933 to offer its "New Deal" solutions to the depression, federal officials found an attentive audience among Nashville businessmen and politicians. New Deal agencies such as the Public Works Administration (PWA) and the Works Progress Administration (WPA) cut entirely new swaths across the cityscape. Around Capitol Hill, the PWA tore down remaining nineteenth century mansions and commissioned Marr and Holman to design a new Tennessee Supreme Court Building. It selected Emmons Woolwine and Frederic Hirons to design the Tennessee (now John Sevier) State Office Building, which included lobby murals about Tennessee history by artist Dean Cornwell. The Treasury Department commissioned Marr and Holman to design an Art Deco-styled U.S. Post Office, built with PWA support, on Broadway next to Union Station. Funds from the Public Works Administration, as well as assistance from the Works Progress Administration, went to the construction and/or expansion of many public schools. The new buildings included Pearl High School (1939, McKissack and McKissack, architects), West End High School (1936–37, Donald Southgate, architect), and Eakin School (1936, Tisdale and Pinson, architects) near Hillsboro Village.

Perhaps the most drastic transformation in the city came at the town square, where PWA officials replaced historic buildings with a new Davidson County Courthouse and Public Building and a new City Market. The proposed demolition of the late antebellum Greek Revival courthouse, which had been designed by Francis Strickland (the son of William Strickland), sparked howls of protest from historical societies and civic groups. The criticism was somewhat muted by Woolwine and Hirons' design, which blended Doric colonnades in a rectangular, modernist design that was highlighted by Cornwell's murals and Art Deco interior elements. This blending of classicism and modernism is sometimes called "PWA Modern" style and is found in many public buildings of the New Deal era.

New Deal programs, however, constructed more than grand public buildings. In Nashville, the agencies updated the city's infrastructure by improving and paving many streets and building new bridges. Parks were enlarged and improved, as at Percy Warner Park and Shelby Park. Historic sites received attention; Fort Negley was partially restored as a Civil War historic site. Berry Field was established as the city's first modern airport; American Airlines landed the first plane there in 1937. The New Deal also cleared slums and built new public housing. Across from the Werthan Bag Company factory in north Nashville, a group of local architects banded together as Nashville Allied Architects and designed Cheatham Place (1936–38) as a model public housing complex for white workers. About a year earlier, federal officials had broken ground for a more controversial African American public housing project, called Andrew Jackson Courts (1935–38), located near Fisk University. In the last years of the New Deal, a

second major public housing project for African Americans, the J. C. Napier Homes (1941–42), opened in south Nashville.

In the mid-1930s, the local economy rebounded to the level where private companies and individuals were willing to fund new construction projects. Nashvillians embraced modern architectural styles—the Art Deco, Art Moderne, and International styles–to a limited degree. Keeble's International/Art Moderne design for Deepwood (1936) and Marr and Holman's Art Moderne-styled Belle Meade Theater (1935–36) represent two extant examples.

The scarcity of building materials and labor during World War II placed most new construction in Nashville on hold until the conflict was over. An exception was a neighborhood of minimally styled tract homes built for workers and managers at the adjacent Vultee Aircraft factory along present-day Briley Parkway.

CREATION OF MODERN NASHVILLE, 1945–1990

The evolution of modern Nashville during the post-war decades has mixed the new with the old. Rivers and railroads declined as passenger transportation systems, but kept their importance for moving freight by barge or boxcars. Their routes through the city remain, but activity along the tracks or riverbanks has changed. In the 1970s and 1980s, the once proud urban corridor of the railroad tracks had been largely abandoned and was in the process of rusting away, but restorations at Union Station and Cummins Station, and new construction in the Gulch, gave new vibrancy to the old industrial corridor of the city. The same is true for the Cumberland River where the renewal of Second Avenue, the Shelby Street pedestrian bridge, the construction of the Greenway, and the LP Field give an entirely new meaning to the pace of life and business along the Cumberland. Nashville's rivers also are much more of a recreational mecca than before, due to the U.S. Army Corps of Engineer's construction of Old Hickory Dam and Reservoir (late 1940s) on the Cumberland River and Percy Priest Dam and Reservoir (mid 1960s) on the Stones River.

Immigration also represents continuity between the nineteenth and twentieth centuries. To the earlier neighborhoods for African Americans, Irish, German Jews, and German Catholics have been added new neighborhoods from a broader mix of peoples and cultures, including immigrants from Asia, Central and South America, Africa, Eastern Europe, and the Middle East. Nashville is a more cosmopolitan city than ever before.

Yet the last fifty years have introduced new forces shaping the cityscape. First and foremost has been the impact of the automobile and its associated infrastructure of highways, interstates, fast-food restaurants, gas stations, shopping centers, and commuter suburbs. Clearly, the automobile was already making its mark on downtown Nashville before World War II, attested by surviving landmarks like the old Firestone Building (1931) at the junction of Elliston Place and West End Avenue.

The automobile, and the demand of its commuting drivers for better roads, more parking, and easy-to-park shopping, reoriented Nashville's appearance from the late 1940s to the present. Its major shopping malls and centers, located in the northern, southern, and western ends of the county, use interstate highway locations to attract consumers from Cheatham, Dickson, Robertson, Rutherford, Sumner, Wilson, and Williamson counties.

The automobile impact also had an aesthetic side. New flashy advertising signs popped up around town to catch the attention of motorists. Memorable signs are those for Ernest Tubb Record Shop and Beaman Pontiac on Broadway; Nashville Sporting Goods downtown; and Purity Dairy on Murfreesboro Road. Then, new buildings with wholly new functions and purposes were designed specifically to serve the culture of the automobile. Drive-ins and fast-food restaurants appeared everywhere; a few early ones, like the Krispy Kreme Doughnut Shop (1958, demolished and rebuilt in 2001) on Thompson Lane, remained until recent years.

Other times, the impact was destructive, as the seemingly insatiable appetite for additional parking resulted in the demolition of more and more historic buildings downtown, a process that accelerated in the mid-1990s. Church Street was once the city's commercial emporium, home to the large department stores of Cain-Sloan's, Castner-Knott's, and Harvey's. With the closure of Castner-Knott in 1996, not one large downtown department store remains open. The sites of Cain-Sloan and Harvey's are now parking lots. In the late 1980s, Church Street Centre was developed as a downtown mall, but it closed in 1998 and then was demolished (except for the parking garage) to make way for the new Public Library of Nashville and Davidson County (1999–2001), designed by Robert A. M. Stern.

The demand for better downtown access for automobile traffic combined with federal initiatives in urban renewal to accelerate downtown changes from the 1950s to the 1970s. The first major federal program was the Capitol Hill Redevelopment Project, which was designed to remove substandard housing near the capitol and replace it with new landscaped vistas, state office buildings, parking, and the James Robertson Parkway to improve traffic flow. "An economic and aesthetic success in its own right," concluded historian Don Doyle, the Capitol Hill project "turned a seedy slum into an inner-city greenbelt of lawn and trees, a convenient parkway, and new buildings."[5] It also displaced numerous African American residents and community institutions, particularly African American performance venues, that had stood on or near Capitol Hill since the Civil War and Reconstruction era.

Urban renewal also encouraged the construction of the Capitol Tower Apartments in 1961 and the decision by the Nashville insurance giant, the National Life and Accident Insurance Company, to commission the nationally recognized firm of Skidmore, Owings, and Merrill, with Bruce Graham as principal architect, to design the National Life Center (1966–70), now the William R. Snodgrass Tower and commonly known as the Tennessee Tower.

The fate of this modernist skyscraper over the next twenty years symbolized the rapid changes then occurring in Nashville's economy. American General Life Insurance Company took control of National Life in the merger mania of the early 1980s, but within fifteen years, the office tower passed to the state government, which eagerly used the skyscraper for its ever-increasing demands for office space. A similar fate befell the skyscraper that housed National Life's major competitor for most of the century.

The Life and Casualty Tower, designed in a regional adaptation of International style by Edwin Keeble in 1956, was the headquarters of the Life and Casualty Insurance Company. The first major skyscraper built in Nashville after World War II, the building became the city's primary landmark for travelers driving into Nashville for the next generation. Today, office space is shared by local businesses, banks, professionals, and government.

The year 1962 proved to be a benchmark year when Nashvillians and county residents voted to establish the Metropolitan Government of Nashville and Davidson County. This merger combined formerly separate city and county functions into a single governmental entity, which officially began on April 1, 1963. The push for more and better government services largely came from new middle-class residents who lived in suburbs of tract homes and ranch houses that multiplied across the county in the 1950s and early 1960s, neighborhoods like Hillwood, Donelson, Antioch, and Forest Hills.

The 1960s and 1970s witnessed new trends in the built environment. Downtown was no longer the only location for office buildings. On Murfreesboro Road, adjacent to the airport, John C. Wheeler designed the New Formalist-styled Genesco World Headquarters (1965). Music industry corporations congregated their offices along Sixteenth Avenue South, known as Music Row, where by 1967 stood the Country Music Hall of Fame and Museum by W. S. Cambron (demolished c. 2000). An instant tourist mecca, the Hall of Fame also reflected the significant impact of the music industry on the local economy. In 1974, when the Grand Ole Opry left the downtown Ryman Auditorium for its new Opryland theme park, hotel, and modern theater, another area in Nashville was opened to development. Due to real estate values, changing consumer demands, the suburban explosion, and the construction of new roads, especially the interstate highways in the 1960s, commercial, retail, and business activity dispersed across the county during the 1970s. The health care industry, for one, became a strong presence in west Nashville, near major hospitals like Baptist, St. Thomas, Vanderbilt Medical Center, and Centennial Medical Center.

As suburban Nashville prospered, downtown Nashville suffered. The early 1960s had witnessed, finally, the racial integration of downtown stores and restaurants. African American residents no longer had to endure the indignities of Jim Crow segregation where they worked and shopped. But integration happened at the same time that retail businesses were shifting to new suburban locations. To keep retail alive downtown, government stepped forward with plans to build a more attractive urban setting. In 1974 state officials commissioned Steinbaugh, Harwood, and Rogers to design Legislative Plaza. The public plaza visually linked the State Capitol, the War Memorial Building, and new state office skyscrapers like the Andrew Jackson Building (1970) and the James K. Polk Building (1976–80), while creating needed legislative office space. The Polk Building was also home to the Tennessee Performing Arts Center, which included a new State Museum and three different performing arts auditoriums for local theater, ballet, opera, and symphony companies.

NEW TRENDS FOR A NEW CENTURY

If the 1990s were any indication of new urban trends, the latest is one of downtown renewal. The designation of Second Avenue, Lower Broadway, and Fifth Avenue as National Register historic districts in the late 1970s and 1980s helped save these valuable buildings for adaptive reuse. Continuing revitalization along Second Avenue and Broadway has met with success, preserving portions of Nashville's historic downtown architecture as part of the modern cityscape. The rebound of business and new construction of such institutions as the Public Library, the Greenway, and the Schermerhorn Symphony Center, link both the past and present. The Country Museum Hall of Fame and Museum moved from Music Row to a new downtown location south of Broadway. The old waterfront along the Cumberland River became Riverfront Park and the Shelby Street Bridge was reopened for pedestrian use, linking downtown with Cumberland Park.

Corporate officials renewed a commitment to downtown. The Fifth Third Center (1983–86) and the AT&T Building (1993–95, known locally as the Batman Building) are important corporate anchors. Other public investments have brought new life to downtown. The city dollars behind the sparkling Music City Center, the Public Library, the Bridgestone Arena, the LP Field, and the restoration of the Courthouse and Public Square demonstrate a public commitment to a viable downtown. The State of Tennessee has played a major role with the construction of the Bicentennial Capitol Mall State Park north of the capitol. Private dollars have

At&T Building, Carol M. Highsmith's America, Library of Congress, Prints and Photographs Division.

continued to pour into renovation projects such as that at the Ryman Auditorium, and new condominium developments, some as sleek new modern towers, others in sensitive adaptive reuses of historic buildings. This blending of past and present has created new anchors for Nashville's urban future.

In the last overview of the city's architecture, published almost fifty years ago in 1974, one of the contributors concluded: "The passage of time makes all fine or typical buildings a part of architectural history. It is therefore the responsibility of the present leaders and others to be custodians of the best that remains for the sake of future generations."[6] This guidebook marks those buildings and sites that enhance our sense of place and identity, as Nashvillians and as Tennesseans of the twenty-first century. We leave it to this new century to nurture this legacy for the future.

NEW TRENDS FOR A NEW CENTURY

If the 1990s were any indication of new urban trends, the latest is one of downtown renewal and expansion. The designation of Second Avenue, Lower Broadway, and Fifth Avenue as National Register historic districts in the late 1970s and 1980s helped save these valuable buildings for adaptive reuse. Continuing revitalization along Second Avenue and Broadway has met with success, preserving portions of Nashville's historic downtown architecture as part of the modern cityscape. At the same time success created new pressure on the existing historic fabric of downtown; Nashvillians of the twenty-first century have the feeling that change has been too intense, too fast. They worry that the loss of historic

Cumberland Park, Carroll Van West, photographer.

businesses and buildings mean a loss of identity and place, that Nashville is just another Charlotte or Atlanta in the making.

Downtown Nashville in the second decade of the twenty-first century certainly has a new look. The process began in the late 1990s when the construction of the Bridgestone Arena, LP Stadium, and the Country Music Hall of Fame and Museum shifted tourist traffic and business interests to south and east of the traditional downtown core. The transformation of the Shelby Street Bridge into a pedestrian connection between downtown and East Nashville helped to spark development on both sides of the Cumberland River.

Those changes proved to be just the beginning. In the five years after the May 2010 flood the push for new and bigger intensified; the riverfront, for instance, has added Cumberland Park on the east side and the Ascend Amphitheater on the west side. Then came the significant city commitment to replace its 1980s convention center with the mammoth Music City Center south of Broadway. It is difficult to convey the impact the new convention center has on the city. Approved by Metro Council in 2010, construction began soon thereafter, based upon designs from TVA Design of Atlanta and Tuck Hinton Architects and Moody-Nolan Architects of Nashville. The architects wanted to create a technologically sophisticated place but also one that spoke to older traditions, using native stone to highlight entrances and street-level elevations of the building. Dozens of new commissions for public art enlivened the cavernous interiors while music heritage even received its nod through a small museum installation about Nashville songwriters. But the look of the building remained decidedly twenty-first century, best expressed through its curving roof line, which not only broke up the monotony of the exterior appearance but it also conveyed the sense of the curves on the body of an acoustic guitar or fiddle. The designers achieved LEED Gold certification for new construction, largely through the installation of over 800 solar panels and four-acres of green roof.

Construction of the Music City Center carved up sixteen acres of what had once been part of a mid-nineteenth century African American neighborhood known as "Black Bottom." One landmark of the historic neighborhood—the St. Paul AME Church building—remains across the street from the southeast corner of the Music City Center. The center opened in May 2013 to wide professional acclaim, wining awards from the Urban Land Institute (Excellence in Development Award) and the American Council of Engineering Companies (the Grand Iris Award). In its wake came not only downtown's first roundabout intersection but a rush for new hotel construction that has, in turn, signaled the end for the modernist-styled United Methodist Publishing House, designed by the prominent Nashville firm of Warfield and Keeble in 1957. In its place will be one of the city's tallest hotels—35 stories in height—with a scheduled opening in 2017.

Indeed, the push of the Music City Center to the south and west means more change is coming to the Demonbreun Street corridor as older warehouses and functional but architecturally underwhelming buildings give way to such new projects as the Bridgestone Americas headquarters, a thirty-story office building

Music City Center,
Carroll Van West,
photographer.

for some estimated 1,700 employees scheduled to open in the second half of 2017. Demonbreun Street's Cummins Station at the beginning of the new century was somewhat isolated within downtown; that is no longer the case as the Gulch pushes outward from the railroad tracks and development associated with the convention center moves westward. The modern yet iconic AT&T Tower will no longer be the dominant element of the city's skyline as more high-rises in SoBro and the Gulch compete for downtown prominence.

Change also marks recent history to Midtown Nashville west of Interstate I-40. New construction, and the promise of even more to come, has galvanized residents and property owners to partner for the preservation of Music Row. The last minute save of the RCA Victor Studios Building on Seventeenth Avenue North in December 2014 merely preserves one nationally significant building. What is to be the future of the neighborhood where Music City, U.S.A. became a reality? In his recent entry on "Music Row" in the *Encyclopedia of Country Music*, John Lomax III remarked: "Music Row retains much of the charm of a small town or a college campus. And despite its low-rise glass-and-steel office structures, most built during the 1970s and 1980s, this area still has a neighborhood flavor, thanks to its tree-lined streets and the many older two-story houses that remain, most restored and refurbished into small, homey offices."[7] But if more hotels, condos, and high-rise office buildings populate this area, how much

charm will be left—that is the issue troubling Nashvillians here and across the city.

East Nashville is a final example. When the National Trust for Historic Preservation held its annual meeting in Nashville in 2009, East Nashville was an afterthought as far as planned tours and sessions. But the growth here is extensive and seemingly never-ending, and the best, or worst, place to see the impact of gentrification on the city. What had long been racially and ethnically mixed neighborhoods of working-class and working middle-class residents has now become the "it" place to be. Adaptive reuse and historic preservation are valuable tools for urban revitalization: examples abound in this neighborhood as corner markets become trendy restaurants and laundromats become music clubs. But if used as sledgehammers to further divide the haves and the have-nots, they also can become tools of destruction, tearing apart the sinews of connectivity between communities and neighborhoods.

In the last overview of the city's architecture, published over fifty years ago in 1974, one of the contributors concluded: "The passage of time makes all fine or typical buildings a part of architectural history. It is therefore the responsibility of the present leaders and others to be custodians of the best that remains for the sake of future generations."[8] This guidebook marks those buildings and sites that enhance our sense of place and identity, as Nashvillians and as Tennesseans of the twenty-first century. We leave it to this new century to nurture this legacy for the future.

Nashville Architecture

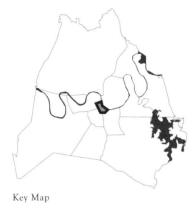

Key Map

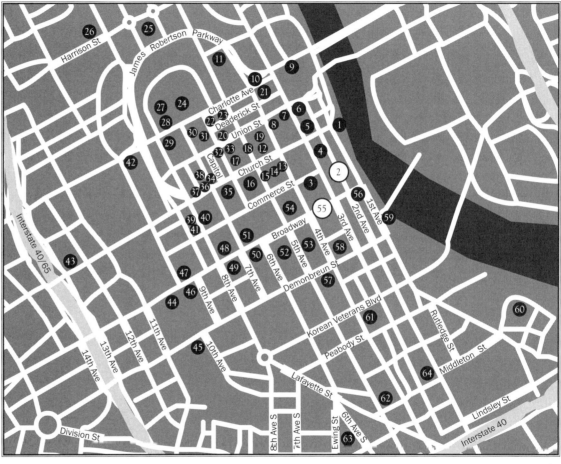

Downtown Nashville

Central Business District, Capitol Hill, Railroad Gulch, and Rutledge Hill

Architectural monuments abound in downtown Nashville; here is the city's most concentrated collection of significant historic buildings. Within this dense urban fabric of stores, offices, schools, hotels, skyscrapers, churches, sculpture, sidewalks, bars, parks, restaurants, and auditoriums is a story of change and urban growth over the last two hundred years.

In 1780 the city began along the banks of the Cumberland River at Fort Nashborough. As steamboats multiplied on the river, entrepreneurs established blocks of historic warehouses and businesses between First and Second Avenue, North, extending north to the original public square, where the Davidson County Public Building and Courthouse and Public Square Park now stand. In the decades after the Civil War, financial, retail, and entertainment districts would develop west of the Public Square, between Charlotte Avenue and Broadway.

The financial district lies in the eastern downtown blocks of Church and Union streets, between and along Fifth and Third Avenues, North. Here distinctive post-modern skyscrapers stand next to the city's first tall buildings from the early twentieth century. The western blocks of Church Street were once downtown's commercial heart, but at the beginning of the twenty-first century, a new, more civic focus has emerged from the recent creation of residential space, small urban parks, and the Public Library of Nashville and Davidson County. The downtown blocks west of Seventh Avenue, North, were used more for institutional purposes: beautiful historic churches and massive, imposing public buildings characterize this downtown zone.

Capitol Hill documents the impact of state government on Nashville since the city became the permanent Tennessee capital in 1843. Surrounding William Strickland's monumental Tennessee

Fort Nashborough, First Avenue and Church Street
Nashville, Tennessee

Fort Nashborough (postcard), Collection of Carroll Van West.

State Capitol is a virtual landscape of statehood, comprised of monuments to heroes, public parks, and public buildings constructed during different periods of governmental expansion in the twentieth century. The newest addition to this landscape is the Bicentennial Capitol Mall State Park, which is both a celebration of and memorial to two hundred years of statehood.

Recent change marks the history of Lower Broadway and Second Avenue, North. A world-famous entertainment district has emerged, anchored by the Bridgestone Arena, the Music City Center (2013), and the Ryman Auditorium on the west and Riverfront Park on the east, with popular tourist shops and theme restaurants in between. The old industrial corridor known as The Gulch has been a center of new residential and commercial development.

The new residential initiatives help to replace older neighborhoods that once surrounded downtown Nashville. Most vestiges of these disappeared in the twentieth century. To the south of Broadway, however, is the Rutledge Hill Historic District, where churches, schools, a fire station, and a few scattered residences mark these earlier residential patterns. St. Paul's African Methodist Episcopal Church, also south of Broadway, marks an early Civil War-era African American neighborhood in downtown Nashville.

1.

Riverfront Park (1981–86, 2014–15) and Fort Nashborough (1930, 1962, 2015–17) (NR)
170 First Avenue North

Riverfront Park is an early 1980s urban renewal project that transformed the old wharves on the Cumberland River into a public park and amphitheater. Riverfront Park is also home to the destination station for the Music City Star commuter rail, which links downtown to communities to the east along the old Tennessee Central rail line. North of the park is Fort Nashborough, which was reconstructed in 1930, and then rebuilt in 1962, on a smaller scale than the initial two-acre enclosure. The National

Register-listed fort recreates the construction techniques and plain look of the early settlement landscape of Davidson County. The puncheon log floors of the blockhouses, the rectangular single-pen log cabins, the combination limestone and wood chimneys, and the saddle notching of the logs were common elements of early homes.

The local chapter of the Daughters of the American Revolution (DAR), led by Lizzie Elliott, funded the fort's reconstruction as part of the organization's national effort to identify and preserve historic places in the early twentieth century. Joseph Hart was the consulting architect. Like The Ladies Hermitage Association, the DAR played a pivotal role in the early years of the state's historic preservation movement. During the first half of the twentieth century, reconstruction and restoration of log buildings were especially popular projects, creating what may be termed a "Frontier Revival" movement for historic preservation and decorative arts in Tennessee. The success of Fort Nashborough played an important role in creating new interest in the city's formative years. The fort will be demolished and rebuilt in 2016–17.

To the north of the fort is the Timothy Demonbreun statue, sculpted by Alan LeQuire, and erected in 1996. It honors the early French Canadian fur trader and Nashville resident, known historically as Jacques-Timothe De Montbrun. A few steps farther north is Puryear Mims' sculpture of town founders James Robertson and John Donelson shaking hands in 1780, representing the beginning of Nashville's history. Mims taught at Vanderbilt University. At the opposite end of the park is the Ascend Ampitheater, which opened in 2015.

Second Avenue Historic District (1869–1998)
(NR, HZD)

These blocks of warehouses and businesses represent the city's most concentrated collection of Victorian and early twentieth century commercial facades. Exuberant cornices, Italianate-styled arched windows, and delicate cast-iron ornamentation on the first floors enliven many buildings. The buildings generally are of uniform scale, from thirty to fifty feet in width, mostly two hundred feet in depth, and rising from three to five stories in height. The warehouses used every available inch of their lots; the First Avenue side was for unloading goods from the river wharves while the Second Avenue side was for distribution and sales. Front and rear doors open directly to the sidewalks. The buildings largely served the steamboat trade, which docked at nearby river wharves.

On the east side of Second Avenue are such outstanding Italianate commercial facades as the Washington Square (c. 1860–1875), the Spring Brook Building (1869), Watkins Block (1875), DeMoss & Sons (1879), Rhea Building (1887), Nelson & Co. (c. 1890), and the exuberant Romanesque commercial style of the Silver Dollar Saloon (c. 1893). On the west side is another set of architecturally significant buildings, such as the Art Deco-style facade at 131 Second Avenue North. These west side facades between Church Street and Broadway date to the late 1920s, a result of a fifteen to twenty-foot street widening project.

The 1971 nomination of Second Avenue to the National Register of Historic Places noted that the street "was one of the most remarkable groupings of Victorian commercial structures in the United States outside of the East Coast." Over the next twenty years, owners largely ignored or abandoned the buildings before undertaking a modest effort at renovation and adaptive reuse in the mid-1970s to early 1980s. Not until a decade later did Second Avenue once again hum with vitality, this time as an entertainment district, with theme restaurants and other tourist-oriented businesses. But the economic rebirth of Second Avenue also threatened the future survival of the historic commercial architecture that made the street such a distinctive place. Some renovations, like Butler's Run (1994–95, Tuck Hinton Architects), removed significant amounts of historic material. Other projects, such as the Wildhorse Saloon (1993–94, Earl Swensson Associates, architects), demolished historic buildings in favor of newly constructed Victorian revival designs. A 1985 fire destroyed an entire block. Serious consideration was given to removing Second Avenue from the National Register. A historic zoning overlay was placed on the district to retain Second Avenue's remaining architectural character as its place within the local economy enters a new era.

An unexpected chapter in that new era came in May 2010 when torrential rains caused the Cumberland River to reach record levels and to flood the basements and the first floors of the Second Avenue district. Now few residents can look at this part of town and not think of the 2010 weekend that challenged the entire city.

3.

AT&T Building (1992–94)
333 Commerce Street
Earl Swensson Associates, architects

Designed by Earl Swennson Associates for South Central Bell, the AT&T Building is a monumental skyscraper that has become a signature building in the Nashville skyline. Ronald M. Lustig was senior designer, and the structural engineer was Stanley D. Lindsey & Associates. ESA's design respected nearby historic buildings but also conveyed the modernity of the telecommunications industry by combining different materials and design elements. For instance, the red granite of the base gestures to the red brick of the Ryman Auditorium and Lower Broadway while the glass shaft of the skyscraper represents the fiber optics that are the lifeblood of modern telecommunications. Topping the 31-story skyscraper were the lighted letters of BellSouth, replaced in 2007 by the AT&T logo, framed by an arched opening and tall spires that house working communication towers, creating a total height of 632 feet.

At the base of the tower is the Winter Garden, an interior landscaped garden public space protected by a 12,000 square-foot steel and glass skylight. The Winter Garden connects the tower to the Tennessee Economic Development Center.

The skyscraper's distinctive crown and height made it an instant landmark in the city skyline; indeed, with its local nickname of "the Batman Building," the building became the most

AT&T Building, AIA Middle Tennessee.

Federal Reserve Bank of Atlanta, Gary Layda, photographer, Courtesy of Metro Nashville Historical Commission.

recognized downtown corporate building since the construction of the Life and Casualty Tower. And like the L&C Tower, the skyscraper is a statement of both corporate pride and urban self-image during an important decade of change in the city's history.

4.

Bush-Herbert Building (c. 1910) (NR)
174 Third Avenue, North

Now a restaurant and nightclub, the Bush-Herbert Building was originally constructed as offices and showrooms for Bush Brick Company and T.L. Herbert and Sons, two related firms that specialized in brick masonry and other construction materials. Behind the understated facade was an elegant office section, featuring Corinthian columns and a coffered ceiling. The most spectacular section, however, is the rear wall of the showroom, where the company displayed its brick products. The Bush Brick Company supplied bricks for many Nashville landmarks, including the Ryman Auditorium and the Tulip Street Methodist Church.

5.

Federal Reserve Bank of Atlanta Building (1922) (NR)
226 Third Avenue, North
A. Ten Eyck Brown, Atlanta, in association
with Marr and Holman, architects

Perpetuating the dominant classical motif of Nashville's "Wall Street," the Federal Reserve Bank Building signaled a federal recognition of Nashville as a regional banking center. Its Ionic columns supporting a massive classical pediment updated the Classical Revival tradition of the Stahlman Building and influenced later Nashville banks to construct similarly styled headquarters in the financial district.

6.

Stahlman Building (1906–1907) (NR)
Third Avenue North at Union Street
J. E. R. Carpenter and Walter D. Blair, architects
Everton Oglesby Architects, rehabilitation architects

This twelve-story Classical Revival building reflected the general three-part formula for turn-of-the-century American tall buildings, as expounded in the work of master architect Louis Sullivan. A three-story Doric colonnade distinguishes the base of the Stahlman Building while the shaft is represented by seven identical floors, which is then topped by a two-story classical cornice. The building formerly housed the Fourth National Bank on its ground floor while space in upper floors was leased to attorneys. From 1971 until 2005, Metro Government owned the building, using it for offices. The building was renovated in 2004–2005, with an eye to its historic detailing, and converted to residential use.

The architects, Carpenter and Blair, were a New York City partnership between Tennessee native J. E. R. Carpenter and Virginia-native Walter D. Blair, who had trained at the University of Pennsylvania School of Architecture. The firm operated from 1903–1908 and other notable designs include a bank in Pensacola, Florida, and Birmingham's Empire Building.

American Trust, Carroll Van West, photographer.

American Trust Building (1926) (NR)

235 Third Avenue North
Henry C. Hibbs, architect

Compared to the Stahlman Building of a generation earlier, the American Trust Building made an even more impressive Classical Revival statement in its intricate detailing, four-story Ionic colonnade, and fifteen-story height. Designed originally as a four-story building by an unknown architect, Hibbs's eleven-story addition rivaled the neighboring Nashville Trust Building.

Nashville Trust Building (1925–26) (NR)

315 Union Street
Asmus and Clark, architects
Hastings Architecture Associates, 1995 renovation

Originally opened as the Central National Bank and later known as the Nashville City Bank and Trust, this tall building also contributes to the tradition of colossal classicism for the city's major financial institutions. Compared to the Doric order used at the Stahlman Building and the Ionic order for the Federal Reserve Bank and the American Trust skyscraper, Asmus and Clark designed the base of their fourteen-story skyscraper in the Corinthian order and incorporated more ornate exterior details than their competitors. The result was a skyscraper of Beaux-Arts sensibilities, with graceful elevations and an opulent interior. In

1995, Hastings Architecture Associates renovated the building as the Nashville headquarters of Regions Bank. The architects uncovered and restored the rich architectural details of the original lobby, including arched mezzanine windows, marble wainscoting, original plaster moldings and cornices, and egg and dart detailing in the ceiling coffers. In the next decade, developers took this building and its once very competitive bank neighbor at 235 Third Avenue North, and converted both into a residential center.

9.
Davidson County Public Building and Courthouse (1936–37) (NR)
Davidson County Public Square
Woolwine and Hirons, architects

Barge Waggoner Sumner & Cannon, Inc. 2002–2007 rehabilitation

Hawkins Partners, Inc. and Tuck Hinton Architects, 2005–2006 Public Square reinterpretation

The pre-eminent example of PWA Modern style in Middle Tennessee, the Davidson County Public Building and Courthouse was a project of the New Deal's Public Works Administration. Designed by Emmons H. Woolwine of Nashville and Frederic C. Hirons of New York, it was one of the few PWA projects for which the architect was chosen through a juried competition. J. A. Jones Construction Company completed this steel, concrete, Indiana limestone, and granite building in March 1938 for a total project cost of $2,167,911; the project architect was John Clark.

Commanding the south facade are twelve giant Doric fluted columns, which support a cornice that features carved animal heads by sculptor Rene Chambellan. Murals with history-laden interpretations of Industry, Agriculture, Commerce, and Statesmanship by nationally recognized artist Dean Cornwell flank the lobby entrance. Art Deco-influenced details abound throughout the building, from the lobby's glass and bronze chandelier to the multicolored terrazzo floor. Befitting the primary public building of both the city and county, and like the New Deal itself, the Davidson County Public Building and Courthouse represented a blending of the old and new to create a building that evokes the past in its classicism and symbolism but that also is decidedly modern in appearance and infrastructure (the city's first central air-conditioned building).

Two events within three years in the early 1960s symbolize the courthouse's importance in the modern history of Nashville. On April 19, 1960, hundreds of African Americans and some white demonstrators marched to the courthouse to ask for an end to the segregation of city lunch counters. Nashville Mayor Ben West met the peaceful demonstrators and agreed that lunch counter segregation should end. It was a pivotal moment in the city's Civil Rights Movement. On May 10, 1960, Nashville became the first major southern city to begin desegregating its public facilities. The second event came three years later, on April 1, 1963, when the Metropolitan Government of Nashville and Davidson County officially began. Nashville and Davidson County were the first governmental entities to create a metropolitan government in

Davidson County Courthouse and Public Building, Carroll Van West, photographer.

Tennessee and President John F. Kennedy came to the city to join in the various celebrations that took place that day.

The rehabilitation of the Courthouse building included extensive interior restoration of the original murals, stenciling, woodwork finishes and light fixtures; exterior work included restoration of the limestone, steel frame windows, and large bronze doors. The Founders' Building was built on the grounds of the Public Square Park directly southeast of the Courthouse, on the site of an original planned structure that had never been built. The Founders' Building houses the elevator structure for the underground parking garage, and the upper floor provides an overlook with interpretive panels on the history of Nashville's public square. The site of the original public square was reclaimed from its use as a surface parking lot and returned to an inviting public greenspace, including the restoration of the two original fountains on the site.

Immediately north of the courthouse is the City Market (1936–37), an Adamesque Revival design, complete with domed central entrance, by Nashville architect Henry Hibbs. It was a Public Works Administration project, completed for a project cost of $494,640. It now is the Ben West Municipal Building.

10.

Morris Memorial Building (1924–25) (NR)

330 Charlotte Avenue

McKissack and McKissack, architects

Built by the National Baptist Convention, USA, Inc., the Morris Memorial Building was designed by the African American firm

Morris Memorial Building, Metro Nashville Historical Commission.

of McKissack and McKissack. Morris Memorial housed several key financial and professional African American institutions. Its proximity to, yet lack of inclusion in, the city's historic financial district speaks to the separation of black and white institutions in Jim Crow Nashville.

This four-story steel and masonry building is a restrained interpretation of Classical Revival style, defined by the Doric pilasters and cornice with modillion blocks used to define the entrance and by the dentilled cornice and balustrade of its roofline.

Municipal Auditorium, Gary Layda, photographer, Courtesy of Metro Nashville Historical Commission.

In 1922 brothers Calvin and Moses McKissack, III, formed the architectural firm of McKissack and McKissack and located offices in Morris Memorial. McKissack and McKissack built many important churches, schools, medical facilities, and other buildings in the city. The firm continues today though its main office is located in Washington, D.C. It is one of the nation's oldest continuously black-owned and operated architectural firms, with over 3,000 projects to its credit.

11.

Municipal Auditorium (1962)
417 Fourth Avenue North
Marr and Holman, architects

The Municipal Auditorium was the public centerpiece of the James Robertson Parkway urban renewal project of the late 1950s. The distinctive domed concrete and steel building was Nashville's last

major public building design from the firm of Marr and Holman. It hosted Nashville's first professional ice hockey team (the minor league Dixie Flyers) as well as many concert events and conventions. It seats 9,654, has a 63,000-square-foot exhibition floor, and contains a large public parking garage. In 2011 planning was underway to locate the Musicians Hall of Fame and Museum at the facility, due to its history as one of the city's premier concert venues. Concerts are still a mainstay of the auditorium's events. The museum opened in 2013 to wide acclaim. Inductees include Billly Cox, Charlie Daniels, and Duane Eddy.

12.

Men's Quarter and Printers' Alley (1874–1938) (NR)
Third and Fourth Avenues North at Church Street

One hundred years ago, this area was called the Men's Quarter, because its concentration of bars, restaurants, cigar stores, and hotels created an undeniably male space within the urban environment. Places like the Climax Saloon (1887), the Romanesque-styled Utopia Hotel (1891, Hugh C. Thompson, architect), and the Queen Anne-styled Southern Turf Saloon (1895), all in the 200 block of Fourth Avenue, catered to men, who wanted to drink, gamble, and smoke any time of the day. The flashy Victorian facades, especially the Queen Anne turret of the Southern Turf, added to its distinctive culture. Indeed, the adjacent Maxwell

Printers' Alley, AIA Middle Tennessee.

L&C Tower, Carroll Van West, photographer.

House Hotel (burned in 1969) had its main entrance on Fourth Avenue, but the owners opened a separate "ladies entrance" on Church Street so reputable women would not have to endure the sights, sounds, and smells of the Men's Quarter.

The name of Printers' Alley comes from the large number of newspapers and printers once in business here. From 1833 to 1922, the *Nashville Banner* operated at 313 Church; the *Tennessean* occupied the old Southern Turf building from 1916 to 1937. After the passage of statewide prohibition, speakeasies opened in the alley between the shops and offices, establishing a tradition of nightly entertainment. In 2014–15, new renovation of the alley began.

13.

The Life and Casualty Tower (1954–57)
401 Church Street
Edwin A. Keeble, architect

The Life and Casualty Tower, known locally as the L&C Tower, was Nashville's first post-World War II skyscraper and remains its best example of a regional interpretation of International style. Two days before the grand opening, in an April 28, 1957 story in the *Tennessean*, architect Edwin A. Keeble explained that function largely accounted for the building's orientation, materials, and unique design features:

> Every line in the Life and Casualty tower has a reason. Its tall, narrow shape provides light and a view. The [aluminum] fins protect it from the sun. The penthouse floors of boilers and air conditioning equipment were placed high to avoid extra rock excavation and the

expense and bad appearance of a 400-foot smoke stack. The ramp on the second floor eliminates the hill climb to the upper and main level of Church Street, splits lobby traffic and increases rentable street frontage.

Function certainly drove Keeble's masterpiece, but within this seven million-dollar, 409-foot high, thirty-one-story skyscraper, Keeble added many details to delight the eye, some with their inspiration grounded in the 1930s while others reflected the International style of the 1950s. The dark marble, Art Moderne-like look of its entrance, its four-story lobby, and neon L&C letters that adorn its top gave the skyscraper a human face and appeal. At one time, Keeble's neon L&C letters changed colors to tell Nashvillians the local weather forecast: red meant rain or snow, blue was for clear and sunny, and pink signaled a cloudy day. Little wonder that the L&C Tower dominated the skyline not only as a corporate symbol, but as a citywide symbol of rebirth and business progressivism in 1950s Nashville. Few corporate architects, then or since, have matched Keeble's feel for site, materials, and human scale. The Life and Casualty Tower is one of Nashville's great buildings of twentieth century architecture.

14.

Cohen Building (1890) (NR)
421 Church Street

Shopkeepers living and working in the same building were common in the nineteenth century, but few of these dual-purpose commercial buildings survive in major downtown locations. The Cohen Building, a Renaissance Revival-style three-story building

Cohen Building, Carroll Van West, photographer.

Downtown Presbyterian Church,
Carroll Van West, photographer.

Obscured from view for a quarter century by a store awning
and boarded-up windows, the recently uncovered facade features
two white glazed-brick arches that rise from the sidewalk to the
top of the second floor. Within the arches are two balustrated
loggia with bay windows projecting from the second floor.

15.

Downtown Presbyterian Church
(1849–51, 1880–82, 1917–19) (NHL)
427 Church Street
William Strickland, architect
Henry Hibbs, architect, 1919 expansion

The Downtown Presbyterian Church is the best surviving example
of Egyptian Revival ecclesiastical architecture in the country. It
was home to the First Presbyterian Church until 1955, when that
congregation moved to a new suburban location and remaining
members, committed to keeping a downtown church, renamed
the building Downtown Presbyterian Church. As a monumental
structure in late antebellum Nashville, the church witnessed major
religious and secular events and served as a Union hospital during
the Civil War.

Several alterations have marked the church since its construction almost 150 years ago. Three are especially important to the
building's current appearance. From 1880–82, the congregation
employed decorative artists Theo Knoch and John Schleicher, who
had worked with Strickland at the State Capitol during the 1850s, to
paint the interior in an Egyptian manner. At the same time, builders

constructed in 1890, is a rare Nashville exception. Meyer Cohen,
a successful pawnbroker and jeweler, ran his shop in the street
level floor while the upper two floors served as a residence for
Cohen and his wife George-Etta Brinkley Cohen, whom he
married in 1897. George-Etta Cohen decorated and furnished the
two-story townhouse with carved oak mantelpieces, stained-glass
windows, and fine furnishings. After Cohen's death, she deeded the
building and its contents to George Peabody College for Teachers
in 1925, and she lived and entertained here until her death in 1930.

added the reeded columns of the portico and the winged disc of the pediment to the exterior; they altered the sanctuary and added new rooms to the interior. In 1917–19, the church constructed a $100,000 Sunday school building, which contained a domed chapel by Nashville architect Henry Hibbs. Finally, in 1937, the congregation modernized the interior and undertook exterior repair of the distinctive towers. A more recent project occurred in 2001 when the sanctuary ceiling was restored to its 1880s color scheme.

The north facade exhibits such Egyptian Revival characteristics as the reeded columns with lotus blossom capitals, the cavetto cornice, and the winged sun disk. The interior is reminiscent of the ancient Egyptian temple at Karnak. Compared to the dominant classicism of antebellum Tennessee, the Egyptian Revival style of the Downtown Presbyterian Church was exotic, distinctive, and cosmopolitan. This National Historic Landmark remains a unique architectural statement today.

16.

McKendree United Methodist Church (1910)
523 Church Street
Wilson and Odum, architects, 1966–67 renovation

The surviving Classical Revival-styled McKendree United Methodist Church and the nearby Downtown Presbyterian Church are reminders of the residential character of this part of downtown in the latter half of the nineteenth century, when gracious late Victorian homes meshed with established churches to create one of the city's elite neighborhoods.

The 1910 building is the fourth to be built for the congregation at this same Church Street location. Named for Methodist bishop William McKendree, who visited Nashville on several occasions during the early 1800s, McKendree is recognized as a "mother" church for the Methodist faith in Middle Tennessee. Since 1833, the church site and congregation have hosted several noteworthy services, including the funeral of President James K. Polk and the inaugurations of Tennessee governors Andrew Johnson, Neill S. Brown, Aaron V. Brown, and William B. Campbell.

The Classical Revival sanctuary of 1910 received its first addition in 1932, when a $30,000 Sunday School Building was constructed on the south elevation. In 1945, the interior was altered as the balcony was squared and a central aisle was placed in the middle of the sanctuary; fifteen years later, new pews, pulpit, communion table, organ screens, carpeting, and a chapel were installed. In 1966–67, the firm of Wilson and Odum designed a new front for the church, which extended the building 50 feet closer to Church Street. The addition contained several rooms, including a fellowship hall and kitchen, which were located in the basement. The last major addition, the Christian Life Center that faces Commerce Street, dates to 1990.

17.

Fifth Third Center (1983–86)
450 Church Street
Kohn Pederson Fox, architects

Strickland's interpretation of Egyptian architecture is mirrored, modernized, and glamorized in the postmodern style of the Fifth

Fifth Third Center, Gary Layda, photographer, Courtesy of Metro Nashville Historical Commission.

Third Center, which stands directly across from the Downtown Presbyterian Church on Church Street. The original owner was the Third National Bank, which commissioned the firm of Kohn Pederson Fox, a nationally significant architect of modern corporate skyscrapers, to design the city's first important expression of post-modern style. According to architectural historian Alan Gowans, postmodern style is "a contemporary image, drawing textures and color combinations from that older material culture to create something new and of the 1980s."[1] In the case of the Fifth Third Center, the architects were influenced by Strickland's earlier Egyptian motifs—clearly seen in their use of ashlar granite, protruding shelves, and battered columns at the base. The city's classical traditions, represented by the classical-inspired pediment at the roofline, also inspired the designers. They wanted to produce an instant corporate stamp on the city skyline, one that in its majesty and size overshadowed the 1950s and 1960s skyscrapers of Nashville's insurance industry. Their dramatic design succeeded in meeting both goals, producing a classic 1980s expression of the postmodern style.

18.

Fifth Avenue Historic District (c. 1868 to 1935) (NR)

Facing the 500 block of Church Street, 400 block of Union Street, and the 200 blocks of Fourth, Fifth, and Sixth Avenues North, this historic district documents a fashionable retail and office district from one hundred years ago. In its many elegant shops, this section of downtown appealed to women of the early twentieth century just as the adjacent Men's Quarter created a largely male domain within the city.

Fifth Avenue Historic District,
Carroll Van West, photographer.

The Arcade, 1970, Jack E. Boucher, photographer, Historic American Building Survey, Library of Congress.

St. Cloud Corner, a 1979–80 renovation of two nineteenth century buildings, anchors the district at the corner of Church Street and Fifth Avenue North. The district features a mixture of commercial architecture, ranging from Italianate and Romanesque styles to Art Deco. Several examples also exist of the Chicago commercial style, characterized by a three-part facade composed of rectangular sash windows, glazed brick, and restrained ornamentation. The former Tynes Building at 227 Fifth Avenue North is a good example of this style. Art Deco is well represented by the former Kress Building at 237–39 Fifth Avenue North; modernist styling was the Kress Company's corporate signature for almost all of its downtown stores built across the country in the 1920s and 1930s. In February 1960 the Kress store also was the setting for one of Nashville's initial sit-in demonstrations, where African American youth peacefully protested the segregation of the city's lunch counters and stores. The former Field, French, and Company Building at 240–42 Fifth Avenue North, also known as the French Piano Company Building, is an outstanding Late Victorian-styled commercial building constructed in 1889. Its ornate sheet metal facade contains human faces, scallops, and garlands in its upper story along with a sunburst design at the roofline.

19.

The Arcade (1902–1903) (NR)
Between Fourth and Fifth Avenues, North
Thompson, Gibel, and Asmus, architects

At the north end of the Fifth Avenue Historic District, at the former site of Overton Alley, is the splendid Nashville Arcade, which was the city's first enclosed shopping area and the turn-of-the-century forerunner of the omnipresent shopping mall of today. Local capitalist Daniel C. Buntin and several partners commissioned the local firm of Thompson, Gibel, and Asmus to design the two-story structure with an iron and glass roof. The Nashville Bridge Company installed the rolled steel bracing system; the contractor was the Edgefield and Nashville Manufacturing Company.

The Arcade has two distinct areas. The street level promenade is the primary retail area; the second story mezzanine is primarily for shops and offices. For seventy years, the Arcade was popular and profitable. In 1969, one shopkeeper claimed: "if you stand in the Arcade long enough, you'll see everybody you know."[2] Although recent business, outside of the still-busy lunchtime restaurants and snack bars, has declined, the Arcade actively recruits tenants. One hundred years ago, arcades were popular solutions to the increased demand for retail space in rapidly expanding American cities. As one of the few to survive into the twenty-first century, the Arcade is among Nashville's most treasured architectural spaces.

20.

James K. Polk Building (1976–1980, 2003)
505 Deaderick Street
Taylor & Crabtree, architects

At the southeast corner of Legislative Plaza, across from the War Memorial Building, is another multi-purpose state office building, the James K. Polk Building. A joint effort between state government and the Tennessee Performing Arts Foundation, the Polk

Building contains two different functions within one building: its cantilevered concrete base houses the Tennessee State Museum and the Tennessee Performing Arts Center while its glass tower holds state government offices. The Polk Building's distinctive glass curtain walls are suspended from the exposed structural members and concrete central core visible at its top. To allow for the open spaces necessary in the museum and theaters, the central concrete core serves as the single support system for the building's cantilevered trusses and contains the mechanical and elevator systems of the building. Andrew Jackson Hall was renovated and a modern marquee added in 2003. The Polk Building has proven to be an ingenious design solution to two pressing needs in state government in the late 1970s: more office space and the need for improved museum and theater facilities.

21.

St. Mary's Catholic Church (1844–47, 1926) (NR)
328 Fifth Avenue, North
Adolphus Heiman, architect
Asmus & Clark, 1926 renovations

Two fluted Ionic columns supporting a classical pediment dominate the west gable end of this Greek temple form building. The research of architectural historian James Patrick points to German immigrant Adolphus Heiman as the architect. St. Mary's was one of the first permanent Catholic Church buildings constructed in Tennessee and served as the Nashville cathedral almost 70 years; it is downtown's oldest extant church building. During the 1890s, the interior

James K. Polk Building, AIA Middle Tennessee.

St. Mary's Catholic Church, 1970,
Jack E. Boucher, photographer,
Historic American Building
Survey, Library of Congress.

was remodeled with new stained glass windows and electricity. In 1926, major renovations occurred under the direction of the Nashville firm of Asmus and Clark. The north and south elevations received a brick veneer while the west facade was finished in locally available limestone. Fluted stone Ionic columns replaced the original brick or stucco columns; new windows in the nave, new white-oak doors, and iron gates were also installed. The original octagonal belfry of Corinthian columns was altered as well. The result was a building that combines an early twentieth century understanding of classicism with Heiman's original Greek Revival design.

John Sevier State Office Building, (postcard), Collection of Carroll Van West.

John Sevier State Office Building (1937-40) (NR)
400 Sixth Avenue North
Woolwine and Hirons, architects

With its corner siting at Charlotte and Sixth Avenue North facing towards the recent War Memorial Building, the John Sevier State Office Building was another major Public Works Administration project on Capitol Hill. Its combination of fluted pilasters, limestone veneer walls, and classical entablature, with scattered Art Deco details, creates an impressive PWA Modern style similar to Woolwine and Hirons' design for the Davidson County Public Building and Courthouse.

Its original name was the Tennessee State Office Building. The later substitution of John Sevier not only memorializes the state's first governor, but also recognizes the two lobby murals by important early twentieth century artist Dean Cornwell. The *Discovery of Tennessee* portrays important individuals from the settlement era, centering on the commanding figure of John Sevier. The *Development of Tennessee* highlights the next generation of leaders, with Andrew Jackson given center stage. The common theme of both murals—the common folk and great heroes working together to build a community, a state, or the nation—was often found in New Deal-sponsored art.

23.

Cordell Hull Building (1952-53)

425 Fifth Avenue North

Hart and McBryde, architects

The Cordell Hull Building was constructed to meet the needs of a rapidly expanding state government and executive bureaucracy during the post-war years. Its rather austere exterior, punctuated by uniform rows of small windows and lacking a commanding, eye-catching entrance, suggests the conformity and uniformity characteristic of early 1950s American culture. Compared to its neighbors, the Hull Building is monumental in size, but not in spirit. The only human touches are provided by Puryear Mims' sculptures of Tennesseans *at Home*, *on the Farm*, *in Industry*, and *at War*. The building is named for Cordell Hull, a Tennessean who was U.S. Secretary of State during the administration of Franklin D. Roosevelt. Hull was awarded the Nobel Peace Prize for his effort in establishing the United Nations. The 1950s partnership of Joseph W. Hart and James B. McBryde also designed the Nashville Mental Hospital of 1952 and the Wherry public housing project in nearby Smyrna.

24.

Tennessee State Capitol (1845-1859) (NHL)

William Strickland, architect

The Tennessee State Capitol, designed by acclaimed Greek Revival architect William Strickland, has been described as "definitely original, definitely the work of a man thinking in terms of a problem and a site."[3] Placed on what was then called Cedar Knob, the Capitol has struck a dramatic pose in the Nashville skyline for decades. Its commanding hilltop location, its bright masonry of Tennessee limestone, and its temple form met three of the four basic traits of the Greek Revival in America. Strickland's skillful rendering of Greek ornamental design met the fourth trait. He used all three Greek orders: a Doric basement, Ionic porticoes on the four elevations, and a Corinthian cupola, with the Greek details both on the exterior and interior reflecting careful craftsmanship and artistry. His inspiration for the dominant Ionic porticoes came from the Erectheum in Athens while the cupola design was inspired by the Choragic Monument of Lysicrates, another Athens landmark.

The east facade facing the public square and Cumberland River originally was the primary entrance to the building; consequently, the Tennessee Historical Society placed Clark Mills' heroic equestrian statue of General Andrew Jackson there in 1880. With the construction of the War Memorial Building in the mid-1920s, the south elevation emerged as a new focal point of the building. The construction of the Bicentennial Mall to the north of the Capitol may again change the way Tennesseans orient themselves to their Capitol in the twenty-first century.

Strickland's classical design for the Capitol took fourteen years to complete, outlasting Strickland himself. He died in 1854 and, in respect to his wishes, was buried in a tomb within the building. Two architects–William's son Francis Strickland (1854–1857) and then Harvey M. Akeroyd (1858–1859)—finished the building and

Tennessee State Capitol,
Carroll Van West,
photographer.

may be credited, in part, with the Victorian influence found in several interior spaces. Another prominent antebellum Nashville architect, Adolphus Heiman, served in an advisory role during the building's construction.

The work of these later architects may help to explain, in part, the various Victorian interior schemes found in the Capitol. Two German immigrant artists, Theo Knoch and John Schleicher, painted frescoes on the ceiling in the main hallway; *Westward Expansion* was their primary subject, surrounded by symbolic depictions of the Muses of Literature, Sculpture, Music, and Painting. The State Library, with its delicately detailed cast-iron staircase by Wood and Perot of Philadelphia, was the most Victorian room in the building. Its original gasolier was made by Cornelius and Baker of Philadelphia. In the State Library, Knoch and Schleicher painted ceiling portraits of such notable Tennesseans as Dr. Gerard Troost, the first state geologist, and educator Dr. Phillip Lindsley, President of the University of Nashville.

Murals in the Governor's Reception Room, designed by George Davidson and painted by Jirayr H. Zorthian in 1938, depict the early settlement history of Nashville. Several interior renovations took place during the New Deal after the Tennessee Supreme Court left for its new building on Seventh Avenue North to the west side of Capitol Hill. The Governor's Office, for example, received a new Colonial Revival-styled interior.

A second round of modern renovations occurred during the mid-1950s, when another Capitol tenant, the State Library, moved into its new building adjacent to that of the Supreme Court. The old library became a legislative reception room and the capitol basement was renovated into offices, accessed by the Motlow Tunnel, which led from the Capitol's south elevation to Charlotte Avenue. In the late 1980s, the rooms occupied by the State Library and the old Supreme Court Chambers were restored to their circa 1859 appearance.

Slaves and convict labor, under the supervision of stone masons, had carved and carried limestone from a local quarry to the original construction site. In 1953–55, Indiana limestone was used to replace large sections of the exterior; some of the original limestone capitals and columns now comprise the Stonecarver's Memorial, designed by Charles Warterfield, Jr., on the northern slope of Capitol Hill. Other original remnants still in Davidson County have been used in the Bicentennial Mall and are in the gardens at Cheekwood.

Also surrounding the Capitol are more formal monuments to people important in Tennessee history. Clark Mills' equestrian statue of a heroic General Andrew Jackson came as part of Nashville's centennial celebration in 1880. After the purchase and planned demolition of the Greek Revival home of James K. Polk, the former president's tomb, designed in an Egyptian Revival style by William Strickland, was moved from the grounds of the home to the northeast corner of the Capitol grounds in 1893. In 1909 George J. Zolnay's statue of Sam Davis, a Confederate war hero from nearby Smyrna, was placed at the southwest corner. Sixteen years later, with the completion of the War Memorial Building, Nancy Cox McCormack's well-known statue of Edward

Bicentennial Mall State Park, Tuck Hinton Architects.

Ward Carmack, a former U.S. Senator, journalist, and prohibitionist was installed near the south elevation. Felix de Weldon's statue of Alvin C. York, a hero of World War I, was placed at the southeast corner in 1968. Twenty-seven years later, Jim Gray memorialized the third Tennessee President, Andrew Johnson, in a bronze statue a few yards south of the Jackson Garden.

25.

Bicentennial Capitol Mall State Park (1994–96)

900 James Robertson Parkway
Tuck Hinton Architects
Ross/Fowler Landscape Architects

The newest and largest monument in the Capitol Hill complex honors two hundred years of statehood. The Bicentennial Mall stands near the location of the old French Lick and creates a new vista of the Capitol's north facade, rescuing that distinguished landmark from the shadows of the city's modern skyscrapers. The mall memorializes traditional state history with a granite map of Tennessee at its James Robertson Parkway entrance, a Court of Three Stars in honor of the state's three grand divisions, a Pathway of History, and a Walk of the Counties, where time capsules from all ninety-five counties have been buried. An outdoor amphitheater, as well as landscaped gardens and an impressive monument to World War II veterans, are included within this unique urban park. A huge ninety-five-bell carillon honors Tennesseans important in music.

The architects patterned the new Bicentennial Mall after the famous Capitol Mall in Washington, D.C., that highlights the Lincoln Memorial, Washington Monument, and U.S. Capitol. In time, new state government buildings will line the mall, creating a grand urban space and possibly re-directing downtown growth in a new northern direction.

Part of that new tradition is already in place at the new Farmers Market (1994–96), also designed by Tuck Hinton Architects. The new 40,000 square-foot building replaced a market that had served local nurseries and farmers for many years. Recalling a large shed barn and silos, executed in concrete and decorated by brightly painted nine and a half foot high concrete cornstalks, the Farmers Market is a modern interpretation of the historic relationship between rural life and the urban beat of Nashville.

26.

U.S. Tobacco Manufacturing Company, Inc. (1910s, 1930s, 1979)

905 Harrison Street

In 1888, taking advantage of the state's expanding tobacco market and the city's excellent rail line, Henry Bruton and two partners formed Bruton Snuff and located a factory here. In 1900 the American Tobacco Company purchased Bruton, but in 1911, the federal government broke up this national monopoloy, and the former Nashville branch became known as the Weyman and Bruton Company. It became the U.S. Tobacco Company in 1922. The multiple buildings of this large industrial complex date from the 1910s to 1979; several buildings date from the 1930s. The company continues to produce, finish, store, and package snuff from this location.

Tennessee State Library and Archives, Carroll Van West, photographer.

which directly faces the building. Its projecting central block of six Ionic columns makes it one of the last Neoclassical-styled public buildings constructed in Nashville until the city's revival in classical design at the close of the twentieth century. Classicism was the preferred style for libraries, both large and small, in Nashville during the first half of the twentieth century. It conveyed the building's function as a temple of knowledge and enhanced the city's preferred public image as the "Athens of the South."

Henry Clinton Parrent, Jr., had trained in engineering at Vanderbilt and took a degree in fine arts at the University of Pennsylvania before joining the architecture firm of Henry C. Hibbs as a draftsman in the 1920s. Parrent established his own firm in 1949 and had completed his design for the Nashville Electric Service headquarters just before taking the commission to design the new state library and archives.

27.

Tennessee State Library and Archives (1952–53) (NR)
403 Seventh Avenue North
H. Clinton Parrent, Jr., architect

Parrent's design for the State Library and Archives reflects both the horizontal massing of the nearby War Memorial Building and the Ionic portico of the west elevation of the State Capitol,

28.

Tennessee State Supreme Court Building (1936–37)
401 Seventh Avenue North
Marr and Holman, architects

The Tennessee State Supreme Court Building is another excellent example of PWA Modern style. Funded by the Public Works Administration at a cost of $650,000, this four-story 140 by 87 foot Tennessee marble building rests on a granite base. Its horizontal massing, classically inspired pilasters, and Art Deco detailing served as a model for Marr and Holman's later PWA-funded courthouses in Madison, Obion, Sumner, and Franklin counties.

Tennessee State Supreme Court Building, Gary Layda, photographer, Courtesy of Metro Nashville Historical Commission.

Snodgrass Tennessee Tower, Gary Layda, photographer, Courtesy of Metro Nashville Historical Commission.

Thomas S. Marr and Joseph W. Holman organized their architectural firm in 1913. Over the next three decades, it was one of the region's most prolific, with industrial, commercial, institutional, and domestic designs in many Middle Tennessee towns, especially in Nashville.

29.

Snodgrass Tennessee Tower (1966–1970, 1978)
Union Street at Seventh Avenue North
Skidmore, Owings, and Merrill, New York, architects

Upon its completion in 1970, the thirty-one-story National Life Center, headquarters of the National Life and Accident Insurance Company, was the city's tallest building. The internationally known New York City firm of Skidmore, Owings, and Merrill (SOM), which had already made its mark with a series of skyscrapers for the Prudential insurance corporation, was the architect, with Bruce Graham as primary designer. After the purchase of National Life by American General Insurance in 1982, the skyscraper's name changed to the American General Center. In 1994, state government purchased the building and renamed it Tennessee Tower. Five years later, state officials again renamed the tower as the William R. Snodgrass Tennessee Tower, in honor of the long-time Comptroller of the Tennessee Treasury.

The skyscraper is similar to other SOM projects of the 1960s in its impressive height, bright Italian Travertine marble, and conspicuous setting. It rivaled the Life and Casualty Tower for dominance of the Nashville skyline, overshadowing the adjacent State Capitol and War Memorial Building, and placing an unmistakable corporate stamp on the cityscape. Its concentric tube construction—where two rectangular load-bearing concrete tubes are placed one inside the other in order to create as much open office space as possible—was an important contribution. Yet today, the skyscraper's monumentality and daring blend of modern styling and cutting-edge engineering, while acknowledged, are not particularly valued. The "less is more" credo of the 1950s and 1960s, represented here in the building's strict geometry and lack of surface ornamentation, appealed to many modernist architects of that time but found few converts among the general public.

War Memorial Building (postcard), Collection of Carroll Van West.

30.

War Memorial Building (1924-25)

Seventh Avenue North between Union Street and Charlotte Avenue

Dougherty and Gardner, Nashville, architects, in association with McKim, Mead, and White, New York City, architects

Built in honor of those who died in World War I, the War Memorial Building was the first major state government building constructed after the State Capitol. Its Neoclassical style is best conveyed by the massive fluted Doric columns of the open atrium, in which stands the heroic bronze statue of *Victory*, sculpted by Belle Kinney of Nashville and her husband Leopold Scholz. Well received by the public and critics alike, the War Memorial received an AIA Gold Medal for its blending of modern technology in a building of majestic classicism.

The building was the city's first multi-purpose public structure, including offices and a large auditorium of 2,200 seats that later became home to the Grand Ole Opry and the Nashville Symphony. The auditorium still hosts concerts and various public gatherings. In the basement was the Tennessee State Museum; the Military Branch of the State Museum still occupies basement rooms. The atrium and auditorium largely retain their historic appearance, but most of the offices and exhibit spaces were renovated and modernized in the late twentieth century.

The architectural partnership of Edward E. Dougherty and Thomas A. Gardner received several local commissions during the late 1910s and 1920s. Dougherty had studied at the Ecole des Beaux Arts in Paris, and practiced in Atlanta, before moving to Nashville in 1916. Here he established a firm with Thomas Gardner, a native of Winchester, Tennessee. Gardner lacked formal training in architecture, but from 1900 to 1912, he quickly rose through the ranks in the engineering department of Cumberland Telephone and Telegraph Company, serving as both Chief Draftsman and Chief Engineer. Other southern landmark designs by the firm include the Central Presbyterian Church in Atlanta, the First Baptist Church in Knoxville, and the Central Baptist Church in Miami.

31.

Legislative Plaza (1971–74)

Sixth Avenue North between Union Street and Charlotte Avenue
Steinbaugh, Harwood, and Rogers, architects

The innovative Legislative Plaza was finished at a cost of $8.5 million in 1974. It connects to the War Memorial Building, both above and below ground; at the north end of the Plaza, a tunnel links it to the State Capitol. On its surface, the plaza of granite squares creates a modernist public space for festivals, demonstrations, and special events. Underneath the plaza are offices, committee rooms, a cafeteria, and underground parking for the Tennessee General Assembly. This maze of subterranean passageways, offices, and escalators creates a fascinating labyrinth of governmental activity, as legislators, staff members, lobbyists, and the general public move from the Capitol to the plaza to the War Memorial Building virtually undetected by those traveling the city streets and sidewalks above.

As befitting any grand open urban space, the Legislative Plaza has impressive monuments and fountains. Belle Kinney's 1926 memorial to the sacrifice made by Tennessee Confederate Women during the Civil War stands at the southwest corner. Nearby is Vietnam Veterans Park (1986), with a memorial statue by Alan LeQuire. Facing the building is the Korean War Memorial, created by Russ Faxon (1992).

32.

Hermitage Hotel (1908–10) (NR)

231 Sixth Avenue North
J. Edwin Carpenter, architect
Gresham, Smith and Partners, architects, 1980 restoration
Gobbell Hays Partners, architects, 2002–03 restoration

The Hermitage Hotel still conveys the elegance and opulence of its original classical Beaux Arts style. Restored into hotel suites using historic preservation tax credits in 1980, with later restorations in 1994–95 and 2002–03, the Hermitage Hotel once again serves as a favorite gathering place for business and political leaders in downtown Nashville.

The Hermitage Hotel's most famous event happened in 1920, when both supporters and opponents of woman suffrage used the hotel as a headquarters in their campaigns before the state legislature. The suffragists won; Tennessee was the thirty-sixth and final state needed for the ratification of the women's suffrage amendment, the nineteenth amendment to the U.S. Constitution, and women received the right to vote. The Hermitage

Hermitage Hotel, Carroll
Van West, photographer.

Hotel was also a very important musical venue. The first broadcast of WSM radio, for example, featured a performance here. Popular orchestra leader Francis Craig regularly played at the hotel.

J. Edwin Carpenter, a native of Mt. Pleasant, Tennessee, was the architect. Trained at Massachusetts Institute of Technology and the Ecole des Beaux Arts in Paris, Carpenter produced a rich classical design, typical of the Beaux Arts' tradition in the east facade's coupled Ionic columns, polychrome terra-cotta detailing, and enriched entablature. The hotel's spectacular lobby and mezzanine features a cut stained-glass ceiling.

33.

Nashville City Center (1986–88)
Union Avenue at Sixth Avenue North
Stubbings Associates, Cambridge, Massachusetts, architects
Gresham, Smith and Partners, Nashville, architects

This modernist 27-story skyscraper of white quartz, pre-cast concrete, and bands of blue glass contains 492,000 square feet of office space. Its impressive two-story lobby features four free standing Ionic columns, which serve as an architectural link between the building's modern styling and the city's architectural roots. It is the headquarters for First Tennessee Bank in Nashville.

Nashville City Center, AIA Middle Tennessee.

34.

Castner-Knott Building (1906, 1911, 1958, 1998–1999) (NR)
616–618 Church Street
Marr and Holman, architects, 1958–59 renovation
Manuel Zeitlin Architects, 1998–99 renovation

Of the three major mid-twentieth century department stores—Castner-Knott's, Cain-Sloan's, and Harvey's—that defined many Nashvillians' memories of downtown shopping, only the Castner-Knott building remains intact in the twenty-first century. In 1898, Charles Castner and William Knott established their business in the trendy Fifth Avenue retail area. Eight years later, they unveiled their new five-story department store at the corner of Seventh Avenue North and Church Street, beginning a westward commercial expansion into formerly residential property.

The huge, architecturally ornate department store had become a fixture in eastern cities a generation earlier. The new Castner-Knott's certainly spared little expense in becoming Nashville's first consumer palace. The Classical Revival-style building lured shoppers with ten-by- twelve-foot plate glass windows, a covered carriage entrance, and coffered ceilings. In 1911, Castner-Knott expanded the store to incorporate the Italianate-styled Armstrong building, which fronted on Church Street and Capitol Boulevard.

To compete better with its downtown rivals, Harvey's and Cain-Sloan's, as well as the emerging suburban shopping center, Castner-Knott undertook major renovations in 1958–59, under the supervision of architects Marr and Holman. All levels of the two buildings were connected, the storefront windows were covered in polished granite panels, a corner entry was added at Church Street and Capitol Boulevard, and the first floor interiors were redesigned with Art Moderne details. The very next year, due to its long-standing policy of segregation of services—a policy followed by all of the major downtown stores—Castner-Knott became one of the targeted spots for the Nashville Sit-In demonstrators.

In the late 1970s, the building's exterior changed dramatically when steel panels were added to the entire facade. However, business at Caster-Knott's downtown store continued to suffer. Even the 1989 construction of a catwalk connecting the store to the new downtown mall named Church Street Centre failed to reverse sagging sales.

In 1996, officials closed the downtown store. In 1998–99, a renovation sensitive to the building's historical and architectural significance took place, unveiling once again the consumer palace of the early twentieth century, now converted to office space, in its original brick and limestone detailing and its wide expanses of windows.

Nashville Public Library, AIA Middle Tennessee and Hart Freeland Roberts.

Public Library of Nashville and Davidson County
(1999–2001)
615 Church Street
Robert A. M. Stern Architects, New York
Hart Freeland Roberts, Nashville, architects

The neoclassical styling of the Public Library reflects the city's architectural and cultural roots as the "Athens of the South" as well as its confident assertion of future prospects for downtown public life. As a comfortable place for intellectual discussion and reflection—as well as a venue for cultural events and conferences—the new library has significantly enhanced downtown life. Stern's design blends the necessary infrastructure for a modern library in the computer age together with older design elements from earlier urban libraries, such as the central outdoor courtyard, reminiscent of the one at the Boston Public Library. The courtyard's Carnegie Porch contains various architectural elements from an earlier downtown Nashville Public Library. Various works of public art and sculpture adorn the building while history exhibits are highlighted in the Nashville Room and in the central lobby.

The three-story, 300,000 plus-square-foot library replaced Church Street Centre, a downtown shopping mall built in the late 1980s, the Watkins Institute building, and Grant's Department Store.

Bennie-Dillon Building (1925–1927) (NR)
700 Church Street
Asmus and Clark, architects
Gobbell Hays Partners, architects, 1998–99 renovation

An early Nashville skyscraper, this twelve-story steel and masonry building embodies the three-part "tall building" design scheme of Louis Sullivan in its well defined sections of base, shaft, and cornice. Reflecting the Renaissance Revival style of its neighbor, the Doctor's Building, the Bennie-Dillon features elaborate terra cotta decoration, topped by an expressive Gothic arch theme at its roofline. Constructed by Foster and Creighton as an office building, the property was closed and seemingly slated for the wrecking ball. Thanks to a resurgence of downtown prosperity, new investors discovered the building's potential and converted it to apartments in 1998–99.

Doctors' Building (1916, 1921) (NR)
710 Church Street
Dougherty and Gardner, architects
Tuck Hinton Everton Architects, 1984-86 renovation

The Doctors' Building replaced the last remaining nineteenth century mansion on Church Street—the home of railroad executive E. W. Cole—when it was constructed in 1916. Dr. Matthew

In 1921, three floors were added to the building. By 1924, seventy-three doctors and dentists listed offices in the building while the sixth floor housed offices for the Methodist Episcopal Church, South, which had acquired the property three years earlier. As the medical profession moved closer to the major West End hospitals during the 1960s and 1970s, the Doctors' Building gradually lost its tenants. From 1984 to 1986, with the use of preservation tax credits, new owners renovated the building into modern offices. In 2007, the building was renovated as a hotel.

YWCA Building, Gary Layda, photographer, Courtesy of Metro Nashville Historical Commission.

38.

YWCA Building (1911) (NR)
209 Seventh Avenue North

The six-story Young Women's Christian Association Building provided a proper urban home and gathering place for the increasing number of young women seeking a career in the offices, shops, and other businesses of downtown Nashville in the early twentieth century. The Nashville YWCA was organized in 1906 and four years later private donors raised $90,000 to construct the present building. What happened in Nashville occurred throughout the South during these years, as the YWCA built large, modern multi-purpose facilities for working women. The organization wanted to establish a gendered space for women in urban built environments dominated by men and male institutions. The Nashville YWCA provided lodging—at first the rate was one dollar per night—eating facilities, a reading room, parlor,

McGannon, a Vanderbilt professor and officer of the Tennessee-Hermitage Bank, commissioned Dougherty and Gardner to build a modern functional building to serve the city's rapidly expanding medical profession. Dougherty and Gardner produced a refined, even complex commercial interpretation of Renaissance Revival style, covered entirely by ornate glazed terra-cotta tiles. Wreaths, swags, urns, garlands, projecting lion heads, and enriched cornices made the Doctors' Building one of the most elegant new offices on Church Street.

gymnasium, and pool. YWCA instructors also offered classes in spelling, arithmetic, and public health.

The Nashville YWCA is a distinguished example of Georgian Revival style in its red brick laid in Flemish bond, pedimented entrance, prominent first story limestone belt course, and limestone keystones that highlight the windows on the east facade. The local YWCA used the building until 1978 when the YWCA moved to new quarters on Woodmont Boulevard. Four years later, new owners took advantage of historic preservation tax credits to renovate the building into offices, during which the building's original auditorium was demolished to make way for a modern office tower.

39.
Gleaves-Claiborne-Savage House (1857) (NR)
167 Eighth Avenue North

The earliest records of this address date to 1857 when William Gleaves built this Italianate-styled townhouse; two years later, Mary Claiborne acquired it for use as an up-scale boarding house. The dwelling is one of two remaining downtown buildings that are clearly pre-1860 residences. With cast-iron window hoods and paired bracketed cornice, this three-story dark red brick townhouse also served as offices for physicians Dr. Giles Savage and his daughter Dr. Kate Savage Zerfoss and as a Jewish social club (the Standard Club). The Smith family purchased the building in 2005, and an extensive renovation occurred in 2006, restoring the building's grand interior spaces. The building now houses a private residence and a restaurant.

40.
Berger Building (1926) (NR)
162 Eighth Avenue North
O. J. Billis, architect

Nashville merchant Samuel Berger commissioned residential architect O. J. Billis to design this impressive two-story brick and masonry Classical Revival-influenced commercial building. It delights the eye, with such details as green- and white-glazed terra cotta, lion's heads, the floral cartouche of the elliptical cornice, and black carrara glass of the first floor. The result is one of downtown's most intact commercial facades from the Jazz Age.

41.
Frost Building (1913) (NR)
161 Eighth Avenue North
Gardner and Seal, architects
Hart Freeland Roberts, architects, 1993 renovation

The Frost Building is named for Dr. J. M. Frost, who was the first executive director of the Southern Baptist Convention's Sunday School Board (now Lifeway Christian Resources). That institution's name is chiseled across the entablature of the commanding east facade. Known until 1955 as the Executive Building, it is among the city's best examples of Classical Revival commercial architecture. Two colossal fluted Corinthian columns, flanked by Corinthian pilasters, dominate the east facade and define the building's entrance. A balustraded parapet graces the roofline.

Frost Building, Gary Layda, photographer, Courtesy of Metro Nashville Historical Commission.

In 1993, the Baptist Sunday School Board commissioned the Nashville firm of Hart Freeland Roberts to renovate the interior while restoring the office of J. M. Frost to its original appearance.

42.

Tennessee State University, Avon N. Williams, Jr., Campus (1967–1971)
Tenth Avenue North at Charlotte Avenue
Earl Swensson Associates, Architects

TSU's Avon N. Williams, Jr., Campus was initially designed as a Nashville branch of the University of Tennessee in the late 1960s. Its architecture exhibits not only modernist principles, but also the new building technology of exposed aggregate concrete. Earl Swensson Associates's architect Alan Cooper, who had learned much about the elasticity of concrete during his years with J. L. Sert in Boston, composed an entire campus of classrooms, offices, student center, and cafeteria into one expressive building. This open, inviting structure may be classified in the modernist style of Brutalism. It was the first major downtown building for Earl Swennson Associates, which was originally established as a small Nashville firm in 1961. By 1991, the firm had completed 1,500 projects in thirty-six states.

The campus is named in honor of Avon N. Williams, Jr., a civil rights activist, attorney, and state legislator, who fought for the integration of Tennessee State University and Nashville public schools during the 1960s and 1970s. The campus became part of TSU due to a successful federal court case that led to the merging of UT Nashville into the Tennessee State University system.

TSU Avon Williams Campus,
Gary Layda, photographer,
Courtesy of Metro Nashville
Historical Commission.

43.

Nashville Electric Service Building (1952)

1214 Church Street
Hibbs, Parrent, and Hall, architects

The construction of I-40 during the 1960s, and the accompanying demolition of surrounding buildings, gave this monumental concrete office complex, built for $2.3 million, greater prominence within the cityscape. Its neoclassical style was a popular national movement of the 1920s and 1930s that produced buildings of colossal proportions but of little classical enrichment except for huge columns and domes, and in this case, an undersized cupola.

The Nashville city council established Nashville Electric Service (NES) during the mid-1930s. Once the Tennessee Valley Authority arrived in Nashville in 1939, the utility became a powerful force in the local economy. In 1939, for instance, NES's initial 52,000 customers used 257.5 million kilowatts of electricity. Within ten years, demand for power had boomed and the utility

Union Station, 1970, Jack E. Boucher, photographer, Historic American Building Survey, Library of Congress.

served 200,000 customers. By the end of the twentieth century, NES served 300,000 customers in Middle Tennessee as one of the largest public electric utilities in the nation.

44.

Union Station (1898–1900) (NR, LL)

1001 Broadway
Richard Montfort, architect
Edwards and Hotchkiss, architects, 1986 renovation

This grand Richardsonian Romanesque railway terminal symbolizes the importance of rail traffic to Nashville's growth and prosperity at the beginning of the twentieth century. On opening day, October 9, 1900, Union Station's opulence left Nashvillians in awe. A reporter for the *Nashville American* on that day described Union Station's interior as "altogether the most magnificent and artistic—in color, configuration, and furnishing   first floor of any station in America." The barrel-vaulted ceiling, with its amazing stained glass skylight, dominates the main waiting room. The multi-colored decorative scheme, complete with depictions of agriculture, industry, commerce, and transportation in Tennessee, came from designer M. J. Doner of Chicago.

As a massive urban gateway to the "metropolitan corridor" of the Louisville and Nashville railroad empire, Union Station served Nashville proudly for the next five decades. With its 220-foot clock tower topped by a 19-foot high bronze statue of Mercury, taken from the Commerce Building of the Tennessee

Centennial Exposition, the terminal was a downtown beacon to travelers, servicemen, and businessmen alike. It was a massive stone landmark that rivaled Strickland's Capitol for prominence in the Nashville skyline.

People entered through the forceful Richardsonian arch of the north facade; they next traversed through the magnificent lobby before descending picturesque wrought iron staircases to the great steel spans of the shed. What an impressive way to enter what was then the modern marvel of train travel!

Passenger trains suffered a significant decline after World War II. Then in 1952, high winds blew down the statue of Mercury from its lofty perch, a signal, as it turned out, that the grand days of railroad travel in Nashville were nearing an end. In 1975, the station was condemned and closed; Amtrak continued to use the shed for passenger traffic for four more years. With its condemnation, the building was allowed to deteriorate, but determined citizens kept it from the wrecking ball. To save the building, Metropolitan Government acquired it in 1985 and leased it to developers who renovated it in 1986 by converting the station into a hotel and restaurants.

The magnificent train shed was one of the country's historic engineering marvels, a 250 by 500 foot structure with a clear span of 200 feet. At the time of its construction in 1900, the shed was the longest single-span, gable roof structure in the country. Fire damaged part of the shed in June 1996, and it was demolished in 2001.

45.

Cummins Station (1906–1907) (NR)
209 Tenth Avenue South
Oliver Contracting Company, builder

Cummins Station was initially a huge modern warehouse, built adjacent to the new Union Station complex by William J. Cummins and other investors of the Wholesale Merchants Warehouse Company. At 132 by 500 feet, with five floors and 480,000 square feet, and built of reinforced concrete with a red brick veneer, the warehouse was the first reinforced concrete building in Nashville and touted as the largest such building in the world. Soon many large Nashville companies, including such familiar names as H. G. Hill and Cheek-Neal Coffee Company (Maxwell House Coffee), were doing business there.

In 1993, renovations by several different Nashville architectural firms began to transform the warehouse into modern office and retail space. The renovations kept the industrial character of the warehouse intact, yet created new and exciting spaces and designs within the rock-steady steel beams and concrete floors.

The eclectic offices, restaurants, and shops found in Cummins Station have helped shape the transformation of the nearby area known locally as The Gulch. This area of town, dominated by the railroad tracks that both separate it from and link it to downtown, was the site of additional railroad related structures. As this mode of transportation was gradually replaced by automobile, trucking, and air transportation, the Gulch suffered a decline. Following

successful rehabilitations at Union Station and Cummins Station, and due to the area's proximity to downtown, the Gulch is experiencing a renaissance as an urban neighborhood center. It has two parallel dominant uses: high-rise residential structures primarily for young, urban professionals, and entertainment/restaurant venues, often in rehabilitated buildings, presumably for the enjoyment of those same young professionals. Music institutions the Station Inn and 12th and Porter are located in the Gulch, along with newer additions to the live entertainment scene.

46.

Frist Center for Visual Arts (1933–34, 1999–2001) (NR)
901 Broadway
Marr and Holman, architects
Tuck Hinton Architects, 1999–2001 renovation

Nashville's new downtown arts center, the Frist Center for Visual Arts, was once the city's major post office facility. When the federal government in the early 1930s chose to build a new U.S. Post Office as its third major downtown building, it turned to Marr and Holman, who had contributed to the design of the Federal Reserve Building a few years earlier. Although initially planned before the beginning of President Franklin D. Roosevelt's New Deal, construction in 1933–34 involved several New Deal agencies, with $1.6 million coming from the Public Works Administration.

With the colossal fluted pilasters of the north facade, Marr and Holman's design mixed classical references within the context of a modernist Art Deco–styled interior and exterior. The north facade

contains fret banding, vertical casement windows, aluminum grillwork, and huge stone eagles at either entrance, announcing the building's symbolic tie to the federal government. The lobby contains such Art Deco elements as polished terrazzo and marble floors, polychromatic marble walls, Art Deco-styled light fixtures, black marble stairs with aluminum handrails, and brightly colored abstract designs on the plaster ceiling. As found in other New Deal-era post offices, stainless steel images of a ship, truck, and train represent the transportation system that brought mail to the building. The architects created a well-executed and expressive statement of "stripped classicism" architecture, considered to be their best extant design.

The conversion of the Post Office into the Frist Center for Visual Arts kept most of the building's signature architectural elements, incorporating the design aesthetics of the New Deal era into a thoroughly modern and functional center for exhibits and art education. The U.S. Post Office continues to operate a facility downstairs, with an entrance on Tenth Avenue South.

Christ Church Cathedral (1887–1894, 1947) (NR)
900 Broadway
Francis H. Kimball, New York City, architect

Christ Church Cathedral, an Episcopal church, is a significant downtown interpretation of Late Victorian Gothic style. Church architect Francis H. Kimball used cut Sewanee sandstone, a gift from the University of the South, to produce a modern interpretation of an English medieval church placed in an urban residential setting. Its polychromatic facade and robust architectural detailing, including stone gargoyles of animals and birds, places the church among the best examples of late nineteenth century Gothic ecclesiastical architecture in Tennessee.

The richly appointed sanctuary features two sets of Tiffany windows that honor the children of Mr. and Mrs. Leslie Warner and Elizabeth Childress Brown, a native of Murfreesboro and wife of Tennessee governor, Civil War general, and railroad executive John C. Brown. The delicately carved pews are original as are the marble Baptismal font, the carved altarpiece and pulpit by Melchior Thoni of the Edgefield & Nashville Manufacturing Company, and the great rose window of the south facade, given in honor of tobacco heiress Jane Washington in 1894. In 1947,

Christ Church Cathedral, Courtesy of
Metro Nashville Historical Commission.

Russell Hart of Nashville designed the Gothic tower, completing the building as it had been initially envisioned. A classroom addition was constructed at the northwest corner in 1959.

Christ Church was the first Episcopal congregation in Nashville. As a leading church for the Episcopal faith in the state, it has served as a training ground for eight ordained bishops. It is now the Cathedral for the Diocese in Tennessee.

48.

Hume-Fogg High School (1911–17) (NR)

700 Broadway

William B. Ittner, St. Louis, with Robert S. Sharp, Nashville, architects

Hume-Fogg High School stands on the site of the city's first public school and is named in honor of the two schools that preceded it. These two schools, Hume and Fogg, were named for early Nashville educators, Alfred E. Hume and Francis B. Fogg. This block-long four-story stone building reflects Collegiate Gothic styling, a turn-of-the-century architectural movement that began with massive new campuses at Princeton, Yale, and Duke universities and then became all the rage for school buildings, large or small, across the nation. Over the main Broadway entrance is a set of cut stone figures symbolizing the classical curriculum taught at the school. The figures represent literature, composition, science, mathematics, domestic arts, instrumental drawing, and fine arts.

School board members, the Mayor, and the City Council selected William B. Ittner as the architect after visiting his recently

Hume-Fogg, Gary Layda, photographer, Courtesy of Metro Nashville Historical Commission.

completed Soldan High School, which was similar in style and size, in St. Louis. George Moore and Sons was the general contractor while Oman Stone Company executed the stonework. Nashville architect Robert S. Sharp supervised and finished the school.

U.S. Customs House, Gary Layda, photographer, Courtesy of Metro Nashville Historical Commission.

The drama and music programs had many prominent graduates, including radio and television star Dinah Shore, Hollywood director Delbert Mann, poet and author Randall Jarrell, artist Red Grooms, and 1950s cult model Betty Page.

49.

U.S. Customs House (1877–82, 1903, 1916) (NR, LL)

701 Broadway
William A. Potter, James Knox Taylor, James A. Wetmore, Washington, D.C., architects
Gresham, Smith and Partners, architects, 1978 renovation
Everton Oglesby Askew Architects, 1994 renovation

The grand Victorian Gothic-styled U.S. Customs House marked the end of Southern reconstruction and the beginnings of Nashville's recovery from the Civil War when President Rutherford B. Hayes laid its cornerstone in 1877. Approval for a federal building in Nashville dated to 1856. Construction delays, then the Civil War, intervened and the city had to wait for more than twenty years to have adequate facilities for federal courts, customs, and a large enough post office to handle the ever-increasing amount of local mail.

Treasury architect William A. Potter designed an ornate stone Gothic block, with a soaring central clock tower, out of Kentucky limestone with red Missouri granite columns. Gothic lancet windows and a Gothic triple-arch entrance grace the elevations. The post office was on the first floor; customs activities operated from the second floor; and federal courtrooms occupied the third floor.

This building was adequate until Nashville's explosive growth in the early twentieth century demanded more room. In 1903 came a new similarly styled Victorian Gothic rear addition, designed by Treasury architect James Knox Taylor. Thirteen years later, flanking wings at the southeast and southwest corners, designed by James A. Wetmore, were added, giving the building its present exterior appearance.

With the construction of the Estes Kefauver Federal Building in 1974, the federal government declared the Customs House surplus property and deeded it to the Metropolitan Government. The building was leased to private developers who renovated it into office space. Its recent tenants include federal bankruptcy and appeals courts.

50.

First Baptist Church Tower (1886)

Broadway at Seventh Avenue, South
Thompson and Zwicker, architects

In 1970, the congregation of First Baptist Church opened a new downtown church, designed by Edwin A. Keeble & Associates, replacing a Victorian Gothic building from 1886. Since the original three-staged brick tower, with its lancet windows and molded pointed arch entrances, had been such a city landmark, the congregation retained the tower, thus linking the past to the future at this significant Nashville Baptist congregation.

51.

Masonic Grand Lodge (1925)

100 Seventh Avenue North
Asmus and Clark, 1925

The Classical Revival that reshaped Nashville's urban environment during the 1920s is boldly expressed in this four-story concrete building. Greek Ionic engaged columns distinguish the west facade, while matching Ionic pilasters wrap around the south elevation that faces Broadway.

Asmus and Clark were the architects of several major buildings in Nashville during the early twentieth century. Christian A. Asmus, a native of Germany, began his Nashville practice in 1896; his first major commission came the following year in the design and construction of many of the buildings at the Tennessee Centennial Celebration. In 1919, Asmus became an AIA member and the following year he formed a partnership with Richard R. Clark, a native of Scotland.

52.

Bridgestone Arena (1994–96)

501 Broadway
Hart Freeland Roberts, Nashville, and Hellmuth,
Obata & Kassabaum, Kansas City, architects

The Bridgestone Arena is the city's major indoor entertainment facility, home to the Nashville Predators of the National Hockey League. The center anchors future downtown development and expansion south of Broadway, including the new city convention center recently opened. Designing the massive saucer-shaped multi-purpose structure was a joint enterprise. Hart Freeland Roberts brought an appreciation of local needs, city history, and local architectural tradition to the project. Experience in building similar downtown facilities came from the Kansas City firm of Hellmuth, Obata & Kassabaum. The contractors were Perini Building Company of Massachusetts and the Nashville firm of R. C. Mathews Contractors.

The arena's architecture is a tribute to the city's role as "Music City U.S.A." The main entrance at the corner of Broadway and Fifth Avenue is positioned to face the Ryman Auditorium in order to pay homage to that landmark of popular culture and entertainment.

Within the arena is the Tennessee Sports Hall of Fame and Museum. A 250-foot tower houses radio and television transmission facilities while the Visitor's Center of the Nashville Convention and Visitors Bureau occupies its base.

53.

Nineteenth Century Residences (circa 1820, 1880)

104 and 106 Fifth Avenue South

The oldest residential building in downtown Nashville is 104 Fifth Avenue South. Built circa 1820 by the McCann family, this two-story symmetrical three-bay Federal style house was a typical middle-class urban residence of the time. About sixty years later, 106 Fifth Avenue South was constructed and both buildings served commercial businesses on the first floor while the second floor was used for residences. A 1994 restoration adapted the interiors into retail and restaurant space.

54.

Ryman Auditorium (1888–1892) (NHL)

116 Fifth Avenue, North
Hugh Thompson, architect
Hart Freeland Roberts, architects, 1993–94 renovation

Built originally as the Union Gospel Tabernacle, Ryman Auditorium gained its greatest fame from 1943 to 1974, when it served as home to the Grand Ole Opry, the premier live program of country music on WSM Radio. Funding for the construction of the estimated $100,000 tabernacle came largely from the efforts

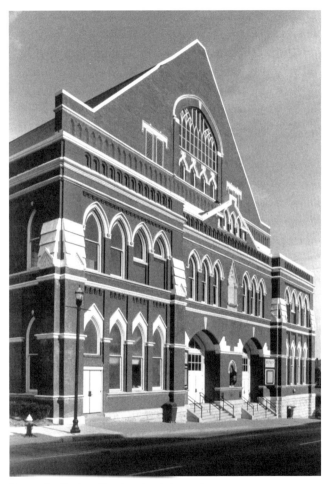

Ryman Auditorium, Gary Layda, photographer,
Courtesy of Metro Nashville Historical Commission.

of Reverend Sam Jones and Tom Ryman, who was a wealthy steamboat captain in Nashville. After Ryman's death in 1904, Jones proposed that the building's name be changed to Ryman Auditorium in his honor. The new name also reflected how the building served both secular and religious audiences in Nashville. Here local residents could see a range of speakers, actors, musicians, and preachers, such as William Jennings Bryan, Booker T. Washington, Enrico Caruso, Bob Hope, Billy Sunday, and Helen Hayes.

Nashville architect Hugh Thompson created a restrained Victorian Gothic design for the auditorium. Its steep gabled roof, gable-front main facade, Gothic lancet windows, and red brick combine to make a stately architectural statement. The real architectural delights are inside, the result of original design as well as changes from the turn of the century. In 1897, the Confederate Veterans Association donated funds to pay for a newly-constructed balcony, known since as the Confederate Gallery. Another group of citizens raised money in 1901 and 1904 so a large stage could be constructed for the traveling companies of the Metropolitan Opera of New York City and the French Grand Opera Company of New Orleans. Two years later, dressing rooms were added to accommodate a stage production of *Camille*, starring actress Sarah Bernhardt.

Over the next sixty years, little additional modernization took place and by the early 1970s, the owners of the Grand Ole Opry decided to leave the Ryman for the Opryland complex east of downtown. Once threatened with demolition, the building was saved, but it slowly deteriorated as it was used only for tours and for occasional television programs, videos, and movies. In 1988–90, a modest restoration stabilized it. Three years later, Gaylord Entertainment commissioned Hart Freeland Roberts and R. C. Mathews Contractors to restore the Ryman to its former glory as a grand public assembly hall. With about 2,200 seats available, music and stage performances are scheduled throughout the year.

55.

Broadway Historic District (c. 1880 to 1950s) (NR, HZD)

The economic redevelopment shaping downtown in the mid-1990s directly impacted the Broadway Historic District, which has served as a main thoroughfare entrance to downtown since the late nineteenth century. The district includes historic multi-story brick and masonry buildings in an eclectic range of commercial architectural styles. Broadway has always been a place that shaped its appearance to match the business that took place there. In its decades as a warehouse and furniture center, from the Civil War era to 1930, its buildings were typical of urban commercial architecture: three to five stories in height, largely unadorned except for impressive cast-iron or stone cornices. In their different treatments of Classical Revival style, two banks stood out in what was otherwise a rather uniform urban streetscape.

During the mid-twentieth century, commercial activity along Broadway went in new directions. First came the impact of the country music industry, especially between Fourth and Fifth Avenues, where places like Tootsie's Orchid Lounge and the Queen

Country Music Hall of Fame and Museum, Tuck Hinton Architects.

Anne-styled Merchants' Hotel catered to those who came to the Grand Ole Opry at the Ryman Auditorium. Then there was the influence of the automobile culture; once sedate furniture stores and shops traded in their old facades for flashy combinations of glass, metal, and brightly lit signs. The Heilig-Myers storefront of turquoise blue metal siding and large plate glass is an outstanding example of 1950s commercial architecture while Art Deco styling

distinguishes the facade of the former Harley-Holt Furniture. The sign for Ernest Tubb Records is among the most famous in the city.

After the Grand Ole Opry left the Ryman in 1974 came years of neglect, abuse, and abandonment. The district's National Register nomination of 1980 admitted that several buildings needed new uses and renovation. Little rehabilitation occurred, until recent times, when the revival of Second Avenue combined with the Ryman's restoration and the construction of the Music City Center, Bridgestone Arena, and the AT&T Tower to create a new business climate. Increased development pressures brought some inappropriate changes and renovations of these fragile buildings. Lower Broadway shed its old looks for a new clientele, often for the best with sensitive renovations but sometimes for the worst as layers of bright paint and garish signs were heaped upon historic exteriors. In 2007, a historic zoning overlay was placed on Lower Broadway, with the intention of better managing change. Clearly, preservation of the district's historic structures remains vital to the city.

Then came the disastrous flood of May 2010, which hit the blocks nearest the river the hardest. No buildings were lost, but the flood waters marked a new chapter in this district's long history.

56.

Acme Farm Supply Building (circa 1890) (NR)
101 Broadway

The three-story brick warehouse, with limestone foundation, is a rare extant remnant of the wholesale trade that once dominated the Nashville riverfront. Built circa 1890 by entrepreneur J. R. Whitemore, the building housed flour, buggy, and drug companies before it became a feed and seed store, which operated from 1943 to the late 1990s. It was converted to a restaurant in 2014.

57.

Country Music Hall of Fame and Museum (1999-2001)
205 Fourth Avenue South
Tuck Hinton Architects

This distinctive architectural profile of the Country Music Hall of Fame and Museum, which incorporates the themes of a piano keyboard and a radio tower within a 300-foot-long facade, adds immeasurably to the surrounding urban environment. The modern facility includes a huge lobby highlighted by the use of native stone and expansive high-tech exhibit spaces. In 2013, the museum expanded as part of the project for Music City Center, a huge convention complex designed by TVS Design of Atlanta, Tuck Hinton Architects of Nashville, and Moody-Nolan Architects.

58.

Schermerhorn Symphony Center (2003-2006)
1 Symphony Place
David N. Schwarz, Earl Swensson Associates,
and Hastings Architecture, architects
Hawkins Partners, Inc., landscape architects

The modern take on classicism found at the Schermerhorn Symphony Center reflects not only the high cultural ambitions of the

Shelby Street Bridge c. 1995,
Carroll Van West, photographer.

Nashville Symphony, it also re-asserts the city's identity as the Athens of the South for the twenty-first century. Named for the one of the symphony's most prominent and influential maestros, Kenneth Schermerhorn, the center's neo-classical style masks a technologically advanced performance hall, with state-of-the-art acoustics and a convertible seating system, which allows tailoring the seating needs to the performance. The magnificence of the center also mirrors the rising national reputation of the Nashville Symphony, and creates yet another impressive venue for the great diversity of music regularly performed in the city.

59.

Shelby Street Bridge (1907–1909) (NR)
Howard M. Jones, engineer

Built as a connection between downtown and East Nashville, the 3150-foot long Shelby Street Bridge, also known as the Sparkman Street Bridge, created a residential and business boom in East Nashville. The bridge is an outstanding example of early twentieth century engineering and technology and contains the first reinforced concrete trusses built in the United States. The designer was Howard M. Jones, a native of Murfreesboro, Tennessee, who studied engineering at Vanderbilt before finishing his degree in 1895 at Union College, in New York State. Jones worked with contractor Foster-Creighton Company, which, in turn, sold one-third of the construction contract to the Gould Contracting Company of Louisville. Jones' Parker-truss bridge had several unique features, including six bridge trusses of reinforced concrete, which were designed to handle heavy streetcar and automobile traffic at the same time. Jones later designed Nashville's Jefferson Street Bridge and the White Bridge (neither is extant). Closed to automobile traffic in 1998, the Shelby Street Bridge has been adapted to pedestrian use, providing outstanding views of the on-going river traffic on the Cumberland, and access to Cumberland Park on the river's east bank.

60.

Rolling Mill Hill (1890s-1940)

Peabody, Hermitage, and Middleton Streets

Once a large hospital complex operated as Nashville's General Hospital, the remaining buildings are remnants of the former public hospital. The oldest extant portion is a 1890s addition to the original hospital building; most of the later 1931–32 hospital building remains, as well as the boiler building and smokestack. This area is being redeveloped into a mixed-use project that will include apartments, offices, recreational space, retail establishments, and open green spaces. The district also includes a National Register-listed municipal garage, constructed in the late 1930s with support from both the Public Works Administration and the Works Projects Administration.

61.

St. Paul's AME Church (1874, 1914)

400 Fourth Avenue South
Everton Oglesby Askew Architects, 1996–97 renovation

In 1863 Bishop Daniel Payne organized St. Paul's, Nashville's first African Methodist Episcopal church, as part of the early effort to establish communities of newly freed African Americans in the war-torn capital city. The congregation soon prospered and in 1874 constructed a large brick church to serve its expanding membership. Because of its size and prominent downtown location, St. Paul's served as the gathering place for important community, political, and religious events in the African American community.

In 1914, the primary facade received an eclectic Victorian update, including flanking square towers and incorporating decorative elements from Gothic, Romanesque, Neoclassical, and twentieth century commercial styles. The congregation moved to a new building in 1953. The church building was a warehouse in 1996 when Everton Oglesby Askew Architects restored it as the firm's offices.

62.

Elm Street Methodist Church (1871) (NR)

614 Fifth Avenue South
Tuck Hinton Architects, 1995 renovation

The Elm Street Methodist Church formed in 1867 and built this impressive sanctuary four years later. The church is the only extant Italianate-styled sanctuary in Nashville. Although losing its original tower to a fire in 1925, the church retains its hooded, arched windows and doors and classical-influenced cornice. The congregation once numbered 1,200 members, but by 1971 the number of members had decreased to such an extent that the congregation disbanded. Tuck Hinton Architects moved into the building in 1995 and adapted it for the firm's offices.

63.

Holy Trinity Episcopal Church (1852–53, 1887) (NR)
615 Sixth Avenue, South
Wills and Dudley, New York, architects

Surrounded by modern commercial buildings and warehouses, and facing the busy Lafayette Street, is one of Tennessee's most distinguished examples of antebellum Gothic Revival architecture, Holy Trinity Episcopal Church. Its relatively small scale, limestone construction, battlemented tower, stained glass lancet windows, and limestone buttresses are reminiscent of a medieval English parish church. Designed by noted Anglican church architects Frank Wills and Henry Dudley of New York, the building is of Tennessee blue limestone, with a lovely exposed hammer-beam cedar roof covering the seventy by thirty-five-foot nave; the slender stone tower at the northeast corner was added in 1887.

The Civil War was not kind to Holy Trinity. Federal troops used it as a stable and powder magazine, destroying many interior features. What remains today largely dates after 1870, including

a pipe organ (1872), new pews (1893), and new pulpit (1935). The interior was generally repaired and redecorated in 1952.

After being downgraded from a parish to a mission in 1895, church officials turned the building over to its African American members, who organized their own congregation by 1902. The next decades found the congregation and the church significantly involved in the city's Civil Rights Movement. Not until 1961 was its standing as a parish re-established.

64.

Rutledge Hill Historic District (1853–1940) (NR)
Second Avenue South at Middleton Street

The Rutledge Hill Historic District contains the few surviving dwellings, schools, and public buildings of an elite nineteenth century neighborhood. Here is where Nashville's first colleges were located, beginning with Davidson Academy in 1785 and the University of Nashville in 1826. Adolphus Heiman's Gothic Revival-styled Literary Building (1853–54) of the University of Nashville marks the neighborhood's antebellum roots. After the Civil War, Vanderbilt University, George Peabody College, and Montgomery Bell Academy all located campus buildings here. The Litterer Laboratory of 1909, once home to the prominent University of Nashville Medical School and then the Vanderbilt Medical College, is the only extant college building from the turn-of-the-century. On the west side of Second Avenue South, the surviving Geddes Engine Company No. 6 (c. 1886), a Victorian-style firehouse, is a reminder of the many residences

Holy Trinity Episcopal Church,
1970, Jack E. Boucher,
photographer, Historic
American Building Survey,
Library of Congress.

and buildings that once comprised the neighborhood. On the east side of Second Avenue South is Howard School (c. 1940), a New Deal-era building in PWA Modern style constructed by the Public Works Administration.

Middleton and Rutledge streets contain the district's surviving domestic architecture, which covers a surprisingly broad spectrum of eclectic Victorian styles, including Italianate, Second Empire, Queen Anne, and Romanesque Revival. The Culbert House (c. 1880) at 40 Rutledge was the three-story Queen Anne residence of Irish iron maker William Culbert. Across the street at 37 Rutledge was the Italianate cottage of Dr. John B. Stephens.

With its square, pyramidal roof entrance tower and mansard roof, the Buchanan House (c. 1880) at 28 Middleton Street is an excellent example of Second Empire style. At the corner of Lindsley Avenue and Second Avenue South is the Lindsley Avenue Church of Christ, which was first built as a Cumberland Presbyterian sanctuary in 1894–96. Designed by Robert Sharp in a Victorian Gothic style, as interpreted in that decade by the Arts and Crafts movement, the church is an exuberant display of stone, brick, and terra cotta details in the context of an asymmetrical red brick building. It was sold to the Lindsley Avenue Church of Christ in 1924.

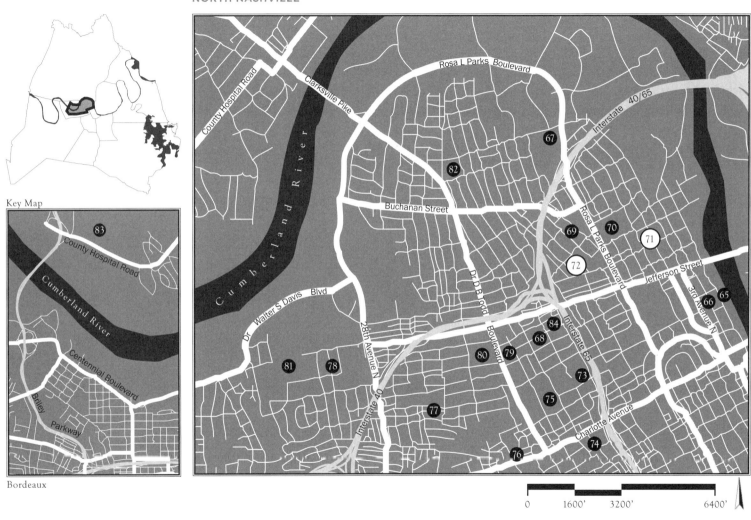

NORTH NASHVILLE

Key Map

Bordeaux

N

Ge *...d Tennessee State University*

Na... ity are
bes... eigh-
bo... h of
the... wly ar-
riv... erman-
to... l into
Na... ividuals
de... wn as
M... vock—
ur... erthan
Bag Company, the U.S. Tobacco ... Motor
Works were among the important industries in North Nashville.

New North Nashville was the name initially given the area
from Sixteenth to Nineteenth Avenue North, but it is better recog-

nized today as the Fisk-Meharry neighborhood, the historic center
of the city's African American community. The Civil War and
emancipation gave thousands of African Americans fresh opportunities, and challenges, in the years of Reconstruction. Flocking
to Nashville, they established vibrant residential and commercial neighborhoods around Fisk University, which was joined
in the early twentieth century by the Meharry Medical College,
when school officials moved the campus from its original South
Nashville location. Various congregations, such as the Hopewell
Missionary Baptist Church, the Nashville Christian Institute, the
Fifteenth Avenue Baptist Church, and the Capers Memorial CME
Church, created other important community landmarks.

Jim Crow segregation, from 1890 to the early 1960s, helped
to solidify these blocks as an African American educational,

cultural, and commercial center. Jefferson Street became a primary commercial artery for Nashville's blacks. The street was full of businesses until the mid-1960s, when the end of segregation combined with urban renewal and interstate highway construction to reshape the community. For instance, the interstate closed the historic Ritz Theater and adversely affected hundreds of homes and businesses. The interstate also cut off streets from major arteries, creating literal roads to nowhere.

New forces are shaping North Nashville today. More than twenty neighborhood associations, the Jefferson Street United Merchants Partnership (JUMP), and the North Nashville and the Fifteenth Avenue Baptist community development corporations are among the citizens groups that are reshaping business and community. In 2011 the city announced plans to build a new 28th Avenue bridge connector between North and West Nashville to end the area's isolation. As Nashville Mayor Karl Dean observed, "We are literally reconnecting two parts of our city that were divided over 40 years ago when the interstate was built."[1]

65.

Riverfront Apartments (1986)
726 First Avenue North
Tuck Hinton Everton Architects, 1986 renovation

During the first half of the twentieth century, Kerrigan Iron Works was an important Nashville designer and producer of decorative and industrial iron work. Philip Kerrigan led the state's twentieth-century revival in ornamental ironwork. His best known work came at architect Bryant Fleming's Nashville masterpiece, Cheekwood, where Kerrigan's work provides an important visual link between the gardens and house, with the single most important feature being the Wisteria Arbor that links the house's primary public rooms to the south gardens and the imposing landscaped vista of the Harpeth Hills. Kerrigan's ability to conceptualize his commission in this manner was a major reason why Fleming so respected the young craftsman and would use him in future estate designs. During World War II, Kerrigan Iron Works completed many military commissions.

In 1986, Brookside Properties commissioned Tuck Hinton Everton Architects to design a 145-unit apartment complex using land from Kerrigan's original works and its historic nine hundred-foot long metal shed. Facing the river, the main three-story apartment block actually tucks into the historic shed, leaving the rest of the covered space for parking. The architects incorporated industrial artifacts as sculptural features throughout the complex while using an industrial aesthetic in the building's materials, including metal siding, window frames, and roofing. With its respect for the past, and understanding of the needs of the present, Riverfront Apartments is an impressive achievement of 1980s adaptive design.

66.

Nashville Union Stockyards Building (1921)
901 Second Avenue North

This two-story Classical Revival brick building is the most significant architectural remnant of the once extensive stockyards of

Union Stockyards
Building, Carroll Van West,
photographer.

Nashville. Utilizing its corner siting to good effect, the building's triple entrance, with each door defined by a pediment and separated by a brick Doric pilaster, curves around the street corner, providing equal access to the building when approached by either Whiteside Street or Second Avenue, North. Flanking the central entrance are long two-story wings of alternating symmetrically placed windows and brick Doric pilasters. The concrete insets of a cattle's head, located between the entrance pediments and the cornice that wraps around the primary elevations, add charm and clearly identify the building's purpose. Due to Nashville's excellent highway and rail connections, the stockyards served a large Mid-South region since many farmers turned increasingly to cattle and swine production in the first half of the twentieth century. The year before the new office building was constructed, in 1920, the stockyards sold over 614,000 hogs. By 1980, however, the livestock market had significantly decreased and the office building was renovated into the popular Stockyard Restaurant.

67.
St. Cecilia Motherhouse (1860–62, 1880, 1888–89, 1903; 2006) (NR)
801 Dominican Drive
H. M. Akeroyd, J. L. Smith, Brown and Brown, architects

St. Cecilia Motherhouse has experienced four distinct phases in its construction. The projecting central entrance, bracketed cornice, and arched window hoods of the original 1860–62 building are Italianate. The architect was the English-born H. M. Akeroyd, who had been an associate of William Strickland. The west wing, added in 1880, expanded the convent; its style, by architect J. L. Smith, was a more refined Italianate design. Nine years later, another expansion added a Romanesque-styled chapel and new living quarters. The chapel contains lovely stained glass windows by Munich craftsman F. X. Zettler. The east wing of 1903, designed by the Nashville firm of Brown and Brown, was for the academy. It blended well with the Italianate style and brick and stone material of the earlier late nineteenth century sections.

Located at the site of the first Roman Catholic school in Tennessee, the St. Cecilia Motherhouse is the permanent home of the Dominican Sisters congregation in Nashville and one of the most important North Nashville architectural landmarks. Its restoration

in 2006 again brought the building's architectural achievement to the community's attention.

68.
Andrew Jackson Courts (1935–1938)
1457 Jackson Street
Nashville Allied Architects, architects

The New Deal's Public Works Administration funded Nashville's first public housing projects as part of its national demonstration program in creating affordable public housing. The announcement that the government would construct Andrew Jackson Courts near Fisk University (segregated, black only housing) was first met by applause. The eminent Fisk University sociologist Charles S. Johnson called the proposed project "a rare opportunity to introduce enlightened social planning and guidance" into a neighborhood long handicapped by "poor physical surroundings." But soon many residents, and landlords, raised their voices in protest. They worried about the loss of treasured homes and churches, as well as the possibility of lower property values for those who lived in a middle-class neighborhood near the project. They asserted that community needed federal money for sewers, streetlights, paved streets, and other improvements more than the housing project.[2]

Federal and city officials investigated and then ignored their complaints; construction took place between 1935 and 1938. The WPA's 1939 *Guide to Tennessee* described Jackson Courts as follows: "the houses are simple in design, carefully planned, and well

Cheatham Place Administration Building, Carroll Van West, photographer.

built. There are individual yards and garden plots. The homes cover only about 20 percent of the entire site, the remainder of the land being used for yards, gardens, and play space."[3] The sparse landscaping, the row-house appearance of the apartments, and the generally clustered nature of the buildings mark Andrew Jackson Courts as architecturally inferior to the open spaces, low density, and diversity of size and architectural treatments found at the PWA's Cheatham Place, which was a segregated white-only housing project.

69.

Cheatham Place (1936–38)

1564 Ninth Avenue North
Nashville Allied Architects, architects

The second PWA housing demonstration project was the white-only Cheatham Place, which developed in the Kalb Hollow district between the Buena Vista School and the mammoth Werthan Bag Company factory. Nashville Allied Architects designed both Cheatham

Werthen Bag, 1970, Jack E. Boucher, photographer, Historic American Building Survey, Library of Congress.

Place and Jackson Courts. Richard R. Clark headed the architectural team, which included notable Nashville architects Henry Hibbs, Emmons Woolwine, Francis B. Warfield, and Eli M. Tisdale.

Cheatham Place had 352 apartments in two-, three-, and four-room units on twenty-one landscaped acres. According to the description in the 1939 WPA Guide, "kitchens are designed to provide efficiency in working space and are supplied with modern appliances. A community building provides social rooms, clinic rooms, and office."[4] With its restrained Colonial Revival buildings and landscaped site, observed the Nashville *Tennessean* on January 24, 1937, Cheatham Place would be a "new and clean little town within Nashville" that would "resemble a cozy English village . . . with green lawns, flower and vegetable gardens, parks, paved sidewalks, and an air of freshness and healthfulness." The newspaper writer predicted that Cheatham Place would be an uplifting model environment, thus reducing "crime, vice, immorality, disease, and all social evils." Today one would be hard-pressed to find a "cozy English village" at Cheatham Place, but many of its original features remain, speaking to the dreams of human and cultural transformation held by New Deal housing reformers.[5]

70.

Werthan Bag Company (1870–late 1880s; 2003–2009) (NR)

1400 Eighth Avenue North
Polifilo; Gobbell Hays Partners; Lamb & Associates, architects

Most nineteenth century factories were purely functional in their architectural design: long, typically brick, rectangular buildings of two to three stories, punctuated by repetitive rows of windows and topped with flat or gable roofs. A few had architectural embellishments, perhaps to distinguish themselves from their competitors or perhaps to better fit into the residential neighborhoods where they were located. The Werthan Bag Company factory, a series of buildings that began as the Tennessee Manufacturing Company in 1870, shows traces of Second Empire style in its corner towers and handsome brick corbelling of its Eighth Avenue North facade.

Nineteenth century mills employed mostly women and children and thus established unique gendered work spaces within the urban landscape. When the factory opened in 1871, for example, it had 202 female and 66 male employees. Werthan Bag Company bought the mill complex in 1928. The company sold the textile mill and bag plant for development in 1998. Over the next decade, an award-winning rehabilitation with five different phases has converted the complex into loft condominiums known as the Werthan Mills Lofts.

71.

Germantown Historic District (c. 1850–1920) (NR)

Located between Jefferson Street, Third Avenue North, Van Buren Street, Taylor Street, and Eighth Avenue North is the Germantown historic district. After its incorporation into Nashville in 1865, Germantown expanded steadily for the next four decades. Religious institutions such as the Catholic Church of the Assumption (1859, 1880s), North High Street Methodist Church (1869) and the Monroe Street Methodist Church (1906) joined

Germantown Historic District, Carroll Van West, photographer.

with cottage industries like butchery to maintain the district's ethnic character. Two important Nashville architects—Adolphus Heiman and Henry Gibel—lived in Germantown.

Industrial growth during the early 1900s combined with hostile public attitudes about German culture during World War I to convince many original owners to leave. By the Great Depression, the neighborhood was littered with abandoned property and ill-kept yards, while single-family houses had been turned into multi-family apartments. The construction of the Cheatham Place public housing project by the New Deal's Public Works Administration in 1937–38 signified the working class quality of the neighborhood.

Urban pioneers in the 1970s and 1980s turned to historic preservation as a tool to revitalize Germantown. New businesses and restaurants were opened. Once elegant Victorian houses were restored as single-family homes. Less ornate cottages were repaired and repainted. The impressive architectural diversity of the neighborhood is apparent once again at such properties as Ratterman Row. Every fall, the Church of the Assumption, Monroe Street United Methodist Church, and Germantown residents host an Oktoberfest that celebrates the ethnic roots of the neighborhood.

The Church of the Assumption (1859), at 1225 Seventh Avenue North, is the cultural heart of Germantown, just as it was over one hundred years ago. German immigrant Jacob Geiger planned the original Gothic Revival sanctuary, which was expanded to meet the needs of a larger congregation in the 1880s. Across the street, at 1226 Seventh Avenue North, merchant John Buddeke built a two-story brick townhouse (late 1850s), with massive cast-iron Italianate-styled window hoods and cornice. The Ratterman House, 1215 Fifth Avenue North, is another late antebellum two-story brick Italianate dwelling, again with cast-iron window hoods and a heavy denticulated and bracketed cornice.

Most buildings in the historic district date from 1870 to 1920. Vernacular houses are common. The "shotgun" was an African American building form that became generally popular as working class housing during the post-Civil War decades. The house at 1326 Seventh Avenue North is a 1870s version of a shotgun. Also on this street is what architectural historians have called a "C-shape" cottage, where the rooms of the house wrap around the side porch in the shape of a "C"; the one at 1222 Seventh Avenue North has an Eastlake-style entrance porch.

The Queen Anne style is represented by the two-story brick store at 624 Jefferson Street (c. 1880), with its decorative second story brickwork and projecting tower, and the Odd Fellows Hall, 1210 Seventh Avenue North, with terra cotta details and lion's head medallions flanking the double window above an Eastlake porch.

Classicism became part of the district in the early 1900s. The Neuhoff House (1904) at 1237 Sixth Avenue North has such Classical Revival features as a denticulated cornice and the Tuscan columns of the veranda.

The Geist Blacksmith Shop on Jefferson Street dates to the 1880s, when John Geist, Sr., a German immigrant, opened his blacksmith shop. The family replaced the original frame building c.1900 with the existing brick building, where the family operated the shop and iron forge, creating ornamental ironwork for local buildings, including the Church of the Assumption, until third-generation craftsman George Geist retired in 2006. At that time, the shop was considered the city's oldest family owned and operated business.

72.

Buena Vista Historic District (c. 1890–1930) (NR)

Once known as the town of McGavock, the development of the Buena Vista neighborhood is associated with the rise of streetcar suburbs in Nashville at the turn-of-the-century. "Buena Vista" has been associated with the area since 1812 when Nashville attorney John E. Beck, Jr., built a home here. His wife Lavinia Robertson Beck, daughter of Nashville founder James Robertson, named the house "Buena Vista." In the early twentieth century, the neighborhood's working class and middle class residents lived in a diversity of domestic architecture, from Italiante-styled cottages to shotgun houses to larger Classical Revival dwellings.

Important landmark buildings also shaped the character of the neighborhood. The Christ Temple Apostolic Church at 1600 Tenth Avenue North was once home to the Polk Avenue Day Home for Working Women's Children. The Tudor Revival styled Buena Vista school at 1531 Ninth Avenue North dates to 1931.

The first branch library in Nashville, the Carnegie Library, North Branch, was built at 1001 Monroe Street in 1915. Initially it was built to be a segregated black-only facility. Nashville architect C. K. Colley designed the one-story brick library in Classical Revival style. A projecting entrance, with a pediment supported by two Ionic columns, centers the five bay facade. A denticulated cornice and stone belt courses ties Colley's composition together. During the mid-1980s, the Monroe-Buena Vista Neighborhood Strategy Area allocated some of its funds to ensure the

CARNEGIE · LIBRARY ·

NORTH · BRANCH
1001

1001

Carnegie Branch Library

Public Library

Buena Vista Historic District,
North Library, Carroll Van West,
photographer.

preservation and continued use of the building. In 1987–88, Hart Freeland Roberts restored the building, maintaining the architectural integrity of this historic library as an impressive civic landmark.

Churches also contribute to the cultural vitality of the neighborhood. The Mt. Zion Baptist Church (1905) at 1112 Jefferson Street is an impressive Romanesque Revival building that houses one of the city's oldest African American congregations. The First Street Missionary Baptist Church (1891, 1952) at 1212 Ninth Avenue North, once housed a Swiss Reformed congregation. Nashville architect Henry Gibel designed the Hopewell Missionary Baptist Church (1903–1906) at 908 Monroe Street in an eclectic Victorian style. Originally known as Third Baptist Church, the building was sold to the Hopewell Missionary Baptist congregation in 1959.

73.

Marathon Motor Works (1881–1914) (NR)
1200-1310 and 1305 Clinton Street

Today's Marathon Village, an adaptive reuse project that began in the early 1990s, combines important North Nashville factories from the late nineteenth and early twentieth centuries. The first was the Nashville Cotton Mills, constructed in 1881, with later expansions in 1885 and 1887. Its original four-story Italianate-styled tower entrance, with window architraves, bracketed cornice, and quoins, created an instant industrial landmark. The mill's production increased quickly and soon the factory

Marathon Motors, Carroll Van West, photographer.

had six hundred employees, many of whom lived in no longer extant worker cottages and duplexes. In the aftermath of the 1893 depression, Nashville investors reorganized the company into the Phoenix Cotton Mills, which continued production until 1908.

In 1910, Nashville businessman A. H. Robinson purchased the Marathon automobile division of the Southern Engine and Boiler Works in Jackson, Tennessee, and moved the car company to the empty Phoenix mill buildings. Over the next three years, Marathon Motor Works produced approximately five thousand cars. In 1912, the company built an impressive $40,000 office and showroom, while making a 40,000 square foot addition to the mill complex, all in a restrained Classical Revival industrial style. Production of the automobile in Nashville, however, ceased in 1914 and the next year the car company resumed production in Indianapolis.

Marathon Village returned to being a cotton mill, when the Washington Hosiery Mills took over after World War I. Werthan Bag Company also bought parts of the complex for use as a secondary mill and warehouse for its products until 1984. Both the Craig Morris Glass Company and Hemphill Press have used the old Marathon office and showroom.

Renovation of the complex into a mixed-use retail, artistic, cultural, and office space began in the 1990s. The office portion of the old complex is enjoying a new life after adaptive reuse and the cotton mill part of the complex is experiencing renovation too. Antique Archaeology (2011) has become a tourist mecca.

Capers Memorial CME Church (1925) (NR)
319 Fifteenth Avenue, North
McKissack and McKissack, architects

This church houses one of Nashville's oldest African American congregations, dating to 1832 and the establishment of the African Mission of McKendree Methodist Episcopal Church. In 1867, several members of the congregation joined the newly formed Colored (now Christian) Methodist Episcopal Church and took the name of Capers Memorial. The church continued to grow in members and prosperity for the next fifty years. In 1924, city officials condemned the Gothic-styled church that stood at Twelve Avenue and Church Street, forcing the congregation to move. In 1925, Capers acquired the present location and hired the noted African American architectural firm of McKissack and McKissack to design a new brick sanctuary in Classical Revival style.

Martin Luther King Magnet School at Pearl High School (1936-39) (NR)
613 Seventeenth Avenue North
McKissack and McKissack, architects

Another major Public Works Administration landmark in North Nashville is the historic Pearl High School (1939–1983), which re-opened as the Martin Luther King Magnet School in 1986 and was renamed as the Martin Luther King Magnet School at Pearl High

MLK Magnet at Pearl High School, Carroll Van West, photographer.

decades of the twentieth century. The school produced many local, state, and national leaders, and was respected throughout the region for its music, drama, and sports programs. Pearl alumni have established a school archives documenting these significant contributions to Nashville's history and culture.

Architects McKissack and McKissack designed the most modernist of the city's New Deal schools, with the facade's stripped classicism highlighted by creative, abstract grillwork in an Art Deco fashion above the entrance doors. The new school contained up-to-date laboratories and facilities, together with a large auditorium, which was suitable for school functions and public events. In 1945–46, a compatible two-story vocational education building was added to the high school; in 1964 came a new gymnasium, a belated recognition of the school's excellent basketball teams. Later additions were made to the school's north wing in the 1980s.

76.

Spruce Street Baptist Church (1954–55)
504 Spruce Street (Twentieth Avenue North)
McKissack and McKissack, architects

In 1841, African American members of Nashville's First Baptist Church began to hold separate meetings. By the winter of 1847–48, the church's leadership agreed to sanction a black mission church, which first met at the City School House. Within five years, in 1853, Nelson Merry, a free black, became the officially ordained pastor of the mission. Out of this very early history of the African American Baptist church in Nashville would emerge

School in 2002, the same year that the school was listed in the National Register of Historic Places. As a segregated black-only school until the late 1960s, Pearl was a source of racial identity, pride, and opportunity for local African Americans in the middle

Spruce Street Baptist Church,
Metro Nashville Historical
Commission.

Spruce Street Baptist, the recognized "mother" church for African American Baptist congregations in Nashville. Initially located on Eighth Avenue North (historically Spruce Street), a 1950s urban renewal plan forced the congregation to move. The current building's forceful red brick Colonial Revival-styled symmetrical facade emphasizes stability and permanence. Its architecture mirrors the church's historical and cultural significance. The church was a frequent meeting place during the Civil Rights Movement and has always been a major social and cultural contributor to the city's African American community.

77.

Nashville Christian Institute Gymnasium (1954) (NR)
2420 Batavia Street

The Nashville Christian Institute, affiliated with the Church of Christ, was established in 1940 by renowned African American minister Marshall Keeble (1878–1968), a native of nearby Rutherford County. In May 2000 *The Christian Chronicle* named Keeble as its person for the decade 1940 to 1950 in recognition of his contribution to the Churches of Christ and the Restoration Movement of the twentieth century.

The institute's primary objectives were to provide African American boys and girls with a Christian education, and to train young men for the ministry. When the school opened in a former public school building in 1940, it was the nation's only Church of Christ school for African American children. Keeble served on the Board of Directors and was named President in 1942. NCI's enrollment grew through the 1940s, and through donations from members of the Church of Christ, Keeble refurbished the former Ashcraft School and built a dormitory and gymnasium in the mid-1950s. Keeble resigned as president in 1958, although he remained involved with NCI. Chronically plagued with financial difficulties, the school closed in 1967, shortly after the desegregation of Nashville's public schools. Keeble delivered the final commencement address.

The brick gymnasium is the institute's only remaining building and is used as a neighborhood recreation center.

78.

La Siesta (c. 1930)
1025 Thirty-first Avenue North

The name "La Siesta" suggests a home of Spanish Revival style, which enjoyed a degree of popularity in Nashville suburbs during the 1920s. Instead, La Siesta is an exquisite, and for Nashville a rare, example of steamlined International/Art Moderne style. While these homes were typically built of steel and concrete, creating a white exterior color, this Hadley Park residence is a brick building. The glass block wall adjacent to the entrance door, the curved porch, the flat roof terrace, and the metal frame corner windows of the second floor mark the dwelling as an interesting regional interpretation of modern domestic architecture.

79.

Fisk University (1867–1950) (NR)
Jubilee Hall (1873–76) (NHL)
1000 Seventeenth Avenue North

Fisk University dates to the Reconstruction era immediately after the Civil War when various reform and religious groups helped newly freed African Americans to build their own institutions. Fisk Free Colored School, named for General Clinton B. Fisk, who headed the Freedmen's Bureau in Tennessee, began in 1866; the next year, Fisk University was created. By 1871 the success of the building combined with the decay of the original buildings (former

Fisk University, Jubilee Hall, Carroll Van West, photographer.

U.S. Army barracks) and uncertain federal funding led school officials to look for a new campus. Administrators began their own fund-raising and, in 1871, they created the Fisk Jubilee singers. After a slow start on a Northern concert tour, the Jubilee Singers soon attracted enthusiastic audiences and brought back $20,000 to the university. After a European tour raised $50,000 in 1873, Fisk had sufficient funds to begin building its permanent campus.

The magnificent Victorian Gothic-styled Jubilee Hall (1873–76) became the center, and symbolic heart, of the Fisk campus. Designed by New York architect Stephen D. Hatch, Jubilee Hall is a six-story brick building, highlighted by a Gothic tower. Its mix of red brick with light stone lintels and belt courses achieves a polychromatic effect, reflecting the design principles of English critic and artist John Ruskin. It was dedicated on January 1, 1876, as part of a grand celebration of the anniversary of the Emancipation Proclamation. The building's interior includes a large floor-to-ceiling painting of the Jubilee Singers, which has become a recognized symbol of the university. Jubilee Hall is listed as a National Historic Landmark.

About a generation later came Fisk's second Gothic landmark, the Memorial Chapel (1892), which reflects an Arts and Crafts interpretation of Gothic Revival, by architect William B. Bigelow of New York. Almost one hundred years later, the chapel was restored to its former architectural elegance with the guidance of the Nashville firm of Barge, Waggoner, Sumner, and Cannon.

Twentieth century buildings at Fisk moved away from the Gothic traditions associated with the university's beginnings.

In 1908, the library building program of Pittsburgh capitalist Andrew Carnegie added the Craftsman-styled Library, now Academic Building, by Nashville African American architect Moses McKissack. Like other historic Fisk buildings, it was renovated with special funding from the U.S. Department of Interior during the early 1990s.

Another Nashville architect, Henry Hibbs, designed a much larger library, Cravath Hall, in 1930. Placed in the center of the historic campus, the library was later renovated into the university's Administration Building. Its restrained Art Deco style massing and exterior details, along with striking historical-themed interior murals by Fisk faculty member Aaron Douglass, introduced modernism to the Fisk campus. University officials began a project to clean and restore the Douglass murals in the early twenty-first century. An outstanding collection of modern art, based on the collection of photographer Alfred Stieglitz, is housed at the old university gymnasium (1888), a Romanesque-style building that was the first gymnasium in the country built on a historic African American college campus. In 1949, the gym was initially transformed into the Carl Van Vechten Art Gallery; a second renovation in 1988 gave the museum more modern and refurbished exhibit spaces.

The campus also has several historic residences associated with significant faculty members. The James Weldon Johnson House (1931), for instance, is an excellent example of Dutch Colonial Revival style. Johnson was one of the pre-eminent figures of the Harlem Renaissance, a NAACP field secretary, and a Fisk faculty member during the Depression decade. Arna Bontemps, who lived next door in a Colonial Revival styled dwelling, was a noted writer, poet, and playwright, who headed the Fisk University Library in the mid-twentieth century.

Fisk also has a unique New Deal era building. The Little Theatre is a mid-1930s WPA rehabilitation project that converted Nashville's last Union hospital barracks from the Civil War into the university's new theatre building.

80.

Meharry Medical College (1930–1931, 1973) (NR)
1005 Dr. D. B. Todd Jr. Boulevard

Meharry Medical College was the first medical school for African Americans in the United States. It began as the medical department of Central Tennessee College in 1876, with a campus on First Avenue South. The Hubbard House in South Nashville is the only extant building from the original college campus.

In 1930–31, a new six-acre campus was located adjacent to Fisk University. Funding came from the General Education Board, a Rockefeller philanthrophy; George Eastman of the Kodak corporation; the Carnegie Foundation, and the Julius Rosenwald Fund. Nashville citizens and Meharry alumni raised an additional $50,000. The architects were Gordon and Kaebler, a Rochester, New York, firm that had earlier participated in the design of the Eastman Theatre in Rochester. They designed the original four buildings composed of red-brick with limestone trim in an understated Collegiate Gothic manner. The Hulda Margaret Lyttle Hall (1930, 1948) was the original Nursing School and Nurses' Home.

It is named in honor of one of the first three graduates of the Hubbard School for Nurses and a life-long hospital administrator and teacher. In 2010, the building underwent a successful historic preservation rehabilitation.

Meharry continued to grow as the college expanded its programs for its students and its services to the surrounding neighborhoods. Dr. Harold D. West became the college's first African American president in 1952. The historic campus of the 1930s remains extant, but is now surrounded by modern facilities and buildings built in the late twentieth century. The Kresge Learning Resources Center (1972–73), by architect Louis Stevenson, expresses Brutalist style in a dominant fashion, almost overwhelming the original campus.

81.

Tennessee State University (1909–1950) (NR)
3500 John Merritt Boulevard

The historic campus of Tennessee State University dates to the college's beginnings in 1912 as Tennessee Agricultural and Industrial State Normal School, the first state public African American institution of higher education. Three buildings—the administration building, a male dormitory, and a female dormitory—were constructed in a restrained Collegiate Gothic style. None of these are extant. In the late 1920s, a distinguished campus of Classical Revival architecture began to emerge. Hale Hall, the original library, and the Harned Science Hall were under construction by 1927. D. A. Williston, a landscape gardener, improved the campus

Meharry Medical College, Lyttle Hall, Carroll Van West, photographer.

Tennessee State University Library, Carroll Van West, photographer.

landscape, installing sidewalks, asphalt roads, new trees, and ornamental plantings.

In 1932–34, the college constructed its three most formally designed historic buildings and expanded the campus to the south side of Centennial Boulevard. A Corinthian column tetrastyle portico distinguishes the Jane E. Elliott Women's Building, which was designed by the Nashville firm of Marr and Holman. The Administration and Health Building, by the Nashville firm of Tisdale and Pinson, has a fifteen-bay facade, with a projecting central entrance of a pediment with hexastyle portico; a Colonial Revival-styled cupola tops the hipped roof. Inscribed over the entrance are the words "Think, Work, Serve," which was the college motto. To the immediate east is the Industrial Arts Building, a classical design attributed to McKissack and McKissack.

Additional changes came during the New Deal. The Works Progress Administration expanded Williston's landscaping plan and built stone fences as well as a new football stadium. Then during World War II, the state approved the expansion of the library and the construction of a new engineering building; these were constructed between 1943 and 1949. McKissack and McKissack gave the library a new Classical Modern facade, which faced the Administration Building. The firm gave a similar Classical Modern look to the Engineering Building, especially in its projecting five-bay limestone entrance with plain Doric pilasters. In 1996, the historic core of the TSU campus was listed in the National Register of Historic Places.

Of the university's recent buildings, the Floyd-Payne Campus Center (1993–94), by the Nashville firm of Tuck Hinton Architects in association with Yearwood Johnson Stanton & Crabtree of Nashville, reflects the classicism of the adjacent historic buildings, like the WPA constructed gymnasium of 1940, as it establishes its own distinctive profile within the campus landscape.

82.

Temple Cemetery (NR)
2001 Fifteenth Avenue North

In 1851, when the Hebrew Benevolent Burial Association purchased part of the land that is now the cemetery, it represented the earliest collective action by Nashville's Jewish community and established one of the city's oldest organized cemeteries. Three years later, the growing Jewish community chartered its first congregation in Nashville, and the first in Tennessee. Many of Nashville's most prominent early Jewish residents are buried here, including Dr. Jacob Mitchell, one of the earliest Nashville residents. In 2005, Congregation Ohobai Sholom committed to a preservation and restoration project, including cleaning and leveling of stones and markers and restoration of the historic stone walls surrounding the cemetery.

83.

Tennessee State Penitentiary (1895-97)
Centennial Boulevard
Samuel M. Patton, Chattanooga, architect

Now closed as a correctional facility, the Tennessee State Penitentiary originally was a state-of-the-art prison. Chattanooga architect Samuel M. Patton designed the structure, which was built by H. H. Squair and Company of Rockwood, Tennessee. Patton chose a Romanesque design scheme, centered on the massive central block of the Administration Building. The nine-story central tower visually dominates the prison; turrets and towers enliven the roof life and are repeated in the corner towers of the complex.

Most of the prison's primary buildings—the prison cell blocks, hospital, dining hall, classrooms, and utility structures—were finished by 1900. The result was a building of enormous frontage—700 feet—with the cell wings creating impenetrable walls fifty feet high. The complex would eventually include some fifty different buildings, enclosed in twenty-foot high stone and concrete walls. The red brick Women's Prison stood in one corner of the Main Prison compound; before its construction, male and female prisoners were housed in the same facility.

Tennessee State Penitentiary, 1971, Jack E. Boucher, photographer, Historic American Building Survey, Library of Congress.

Inmates made the brick for the prison at the State Farm while all of the masonry came from quarries in East and Middle Tennessee. Vitrified brick, used in prison cells, came from a company at Robbins in Scott County; foundries in Nashville and Chattanooga produced the iron work.

Since closing as a correctional facility, the penitentiary has been used for the filming of several television productions and major motion pictures, including the award-winning *The Green Mile* (1999), *The Last Castle* (2001), and *Walk the Line* (2005).

84.

Clark Memorial United Methodist Church (1945)
1014 14th Avenue North

This mid-twentieth century understated interpretation of a Gothic church is home to one of the city's oldest African American congregations. It was established in South Nashville but moved to North Nashville in 1936 and used a property at Meharry Boulevard and 12th Avenue, North, loaned by the Seventh Day Adventist Church until the new building was finished. The congregation added an educational wing in 1956 and built a parsonage the following year.

But those developments paled in significance to what began to happen at the church two years later. In 1959 James Lawson, a Civil Rights activist and Vanderbilt divinity student, began conducting workshops in non-violent resistance and protest to a group of college students. Several students who attended the Clark Memorial workshops, such as Diane Nash, John Lewis, Bernard Lafayette, and Marion Barry, would emerge as national leaders in the Civil Rights Movement of the following decades.

Clark Memorial expanded its education building in 1981 and named it the Grady Sherrill-Matthew Walker Wing, after two dedicated members of the congregation.

EAST NASHVILLE

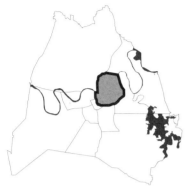

Key Map

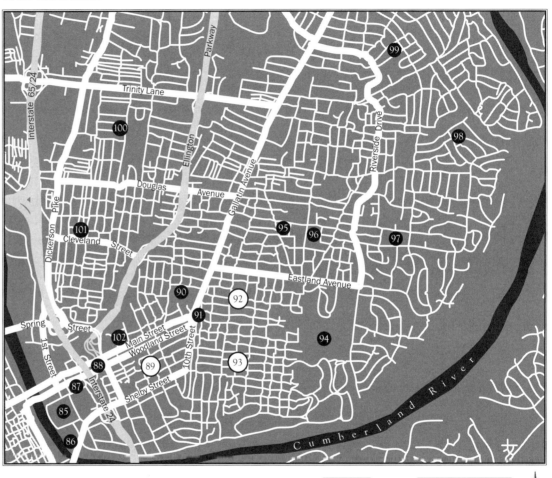

0   2400'   4800'   9600'

East Nashville

Edgefield, Lockeland Springs, East End, Eastwood, and Inglewood

An attitude of self-reliance and independence that is rooted in location and history is a basic characteristic of East Nashville. For the first sixty plus years of settlement, the river ensured its physical separation from the city. East of the river was a place of scattered plantations, farms, and the modest homes of Cumberland River boatmen and workers. By encouraging a wave of new construction and expansion, Nashville's first suspension bridge in 1853 changed all of that, temporarily that is, until it collapsed two years later. The bridge was quickly repaired and put into use; by 1857 a railroad bridge ran parallel to it. Then in 1862, Confederate troops destroyed the suspension bridge. The railroad bridge filled the gap until the Nashville city engineer Major W. F. Foster directed the suspension bridge's repair in 1866. Despite the bridge problems, most of those who had already moved to East Nash-

ville chose to stay. The most illustrious early resident was Neill S. Brown, a former U.S. minister to Russia and governor of Tennessee. A Metropolitan Historical Commission marker on Main Street identifies his homesite.

With the repair of the suspension bridge, and the end of Civil War occupation, suburbs east of the river developed at a faster pace. The first was Edgefield, which incorporated as a separate town in 1868, remaining independent from Nashville, in reality and in attitude, until annexation in 1880. The opening of a mule car line by the Nashville and Edgefield Street Railroad Company in 1872 was an additional spur to development as was an outbreak of cholera in the central city the following year.

For the rest of the century, different real estate developers transformed the rural landscape into new, fashionable neighborhoods for those who wanted to escape the increasingly industrial and polluted downtown area. They also established more modest neighborhoods for those struggling to gain a foothold in the city's New South economy.

The East End neighborhood traces its roots to 1875; the area known as Lockeland Springs dates to the 1880s. These commuter suburbs were served by easily accessible streetcars on either Woodland Street or Fatherland Street connecting East Nashville with downtown's businesses and industries.

Although their physical isolation from downtown was solved by a quick trolley ride, or a slower hike, over the bridge, East Nashvillians retained their sense of place and their pride in their neighborhood and in themselves. This rootedness in place helps to explain the resiliency of neighborhood residents as they experienced hard times in the twentieth century. On March 22, 1916, the worst fire in Nashville history left one person dead and 648 East Nashville buildings in ruins. In 1933, in the depths of the Great Depression, a tornado ravaged Woodland Street and swept on to Porter Road and Inglewood. By the mid-century upper middle-class merchants and professionals, who had not already left for the suburbs west of town, deserted a place that was looking abandoned and forgotten. Layers of small industrial and commercial concerns replaced homes and families with non-descript warehouses, businesses, and empty lots. Slumlords left the working class with dilapidated homes. Residents worried whether this pattern of deterioration could ever be reversed.

Modern times would prove that the flame of independence and self-reliance once characteristic of many East Nashvillians still flickered. Old and new residents stepped forward with their own solutions. They created three neighborhood associations—Historic Edgefield, Inc. (1976), Lockeland Springs Neighborhood Association (1979), and East End Neighborhood Association (1980), with several more to come in the following decades. With the help of local and state government preservation agencies, they established historic districts, which stabilized and then reversed the destruction of local housing by unchecked development. Newcomers were encouraged to invest in the rehabilitation of commercial and residential property; those who persevered through the hard times gained an enhanced sense of pride in a place that they treasured as special and unique.

Hard times returned at the end of the century, with a vengeance in April 1998, when a tornado again struck East Nashville, leaving hundreds of properties damaged and some community landmarks, such as St. Ann's Episcopal Church, virtually destroyed. The May 2010 flood damaged many historic properties, and reminded everyone in East Nashville of the neighborhood's historic relationship with the Cumberland River. Once again, East Nashville residents proved themselves able to withstand adverse conditions, and have largely repaired all traces of the natural disasters. With its historic neighborhoods in the lead, East Nashvillians remain resilient, and determined to move ahead.

85.

LP Field (1997–99)

One Titans Way

Hellmuth, Obata, and Kassabaum, Kansas City, architects

LP Field is home to the National Football League's Tennessee Titans and the home field for the Tennessee State University Tigers. The coliseum replaced a large part of the old industrial district of East Nashville and led to the relocation of such popular gathering places as the Gerst House restaurant. In cost and impact, this huge entertainment structure, constructed at an estimated cost of $300 million and able to hold almost 69,000 spectators, represents the largest single downtown improvement project in a generation. Flooded in May 2010, officials worked non-stop over the next month to have the coliseum ready for the annual CMA Fest, a summer country music festival that holds its night concerts at the stadium.

Nashville Bridge, AIA Middle Tennessee.

86.

Nashville Bridge Company Headquarters (c. 1909, 2011)

101 Shelby Avenue

Standing adjacent to the Shelby Street Bridge is the six-story former headquarters of the Nashville Bridge Company, which constructed bridges and other structures across Tennessee and the southeast as well as in many Central and South American countries in the early twentieth century. In 1915, the company shifted much of its work to its Marine Department and its barge business expanded. During World War II, the company constructed dozens of vessels for the U.S. Navy; after that conflict, the company continued to expand its barge-building facilities. By the 1980s, the Nashville Bridge Company was recognized as the largest builder of inland barges in the world. As construction of the Nashville Coliseum began in 1997, the company abandoned its Nashville works and headquarters and moved operations to Ashland City. In

Edgefield Historic District, Metro Nashville Historical Commission.

2011, the building was rehabilitated into offices for Metro Parks. Adjacent Cumberland Park opened in 2012.

87.

Juvenile Justice Center (1994)
100 Woodland Street
Hickerson Fowlkes Architects

The postmodern styled Juvenile Justice Center contains almost 90,000 square feet, constructed at a total project cost of $12.5 million. Nashville architects Hickerson Fowlkes placed all of the city's juvenile corrections needs—courts, short-term detention system, offices, recreation facilities, and public rooms—into a two and a half-story multi-color brick and concrete building. The two-level barrel vault atrium creates an impressive public space, which also separates the building's security functions from the areas of public access and movement. The architects designed the building to be as environmentally positive as possible, relying on natural lighting and using no formaldehyde, lead, pentachlorophenol, or chloroflourocarbons in its construction.

88.

St. Ann's Episcopal Church (1882–85, 1999–2000)
419 Woodland Street
Hunt Potter, architect (1882 building)
Shofner Evans, architect (2000 building)

St. Ann's has been an East Nashville landmark since the mid-1880s. The first church building was Victorian Gothic in style, with a striking gable front entrance, lancet French glass windows, brick buttresses, and rough-cut stone foundation. The 1998 tornado destroyed much of that building, but the congregation refused to move. The Reverend Lisa Hunt, parish rector, proclaimed: "This is not a demolition zone. This is a construction site. This is a Resurrection."[1] Two years later, Christmas Eve 2000, the new church opened for its first services in a new landmark building, a modern interpretation of Gothic style, which pays homage to the original building in its red brick exterior, gable roof, and Gothic arch entrance.

89.

Edgefield Historic District (c. 1850–1940) (NR, HZD)

Also suffering from serious tornado damage was one of Nashville's first successful suburbs, Edgefield. The neighborhood dates to 1853 and its greatest prosperity came in the decades following the Civil War. Despite a terrible 1916 fire, a 1933 tornado, and the 1998 tornado, the district contains the city's most concentrated area of Victorian domestic architecture, along Fatherland, Boscobel, and Russell streets between South Fifth and South Tenth streets. To protect its special qualities, the city created Nashville's first local historic preservation zoning district in 1978.

Fatherland, Russell, and Boscobel streets demonstrate well Edgefield's architectural diversity. Of these streets, Fatherland contains the more vernacular homes while more stylized academic interpretations of Victorian architecture are located along Russell Street.

The house at 711 Fatherland is a brick, two-story, three-bay unadorned dwelling; its six-over-six windows have flat jack arch lintels. It is probably the earliest house in the district, attributed to Oscar Boehm and dating circa 1858. According to some accounts, it is claimed as the last Tennessee residence of outlaw Jesse James and his family (it is documented that James lived in Nashville at one time). At 606 Fatherland is another mid-nineteenth century two-story brick house, with its symmetrical five-bay facade highlighted by a center gable with elaborate Gothic-styled denticulation.

The 800 and 900 blocks of Fatherland have several excellent examples of the frame, one-story, gable-front and wing vernacular dwelling, large numbers of which were built by local craftsmen after the Civil War. The builders varied these balloon-frame houses by placing the gable-front on different ends of the usually symmetrical wing. They created more diversity by decorating the basic form with Gothic, Eastlake or Queen Anne details, sometimes even combining the different elements to create a truly distinctive but eclectic Victorian cottage. The house at 821 Fatherland, for instance, has Eastlake details added to its front porch; while the dwelling at 933 Fatherland has Queen Anne-styled fish scale shingles and a projecting bay window in its front gable.

On Russell Street, the Edgefield district begins at the 500 block, with two one and one-half story bungalow-style apartments, marked by shed dormer windows on their steep gable roofs. This residential type was often built in the district after the terrible fire of 1916. The house at 504 Russell, however, survived that catastrophe and is one of the district's best and earliest examples of a one-story Italianate cottage, complete with a small projecting tower, a bay window, and prominent brackets on its facade. The Mizells-Britt House (c. 1890),

at 514 Russell, is an excellent brick and terra cotta example of Dutch Renaissance style, especially in the Dutch gable of the third floor.

Dual towers, a rusticated stone base, commanding arched entrance, and terra cotta details distinguish the Tulip Street Methodist Church (1891–92) at 522 Russell Street. Built for $58,000, this is one of the finest Richardsonian Romanesque designs, executed in red brick, found in the city's historic suburbs. T. L. Dismukes was the initial architect, but the church was finished by J. E. Woodard. The blending of details and materials reflect well the basic qualities of strength, permanence, and solidity that are characteristic of Richardsonian Romanesque style. Although damaged in the 1998 tornado, the church has been restored.

The Edgefield Baptist Church (c. 1890s) at 700 Russell is a brick Victorian Gothic-styled building. Unfortunately, the storm of 1998 damaged the beautiful stained-glass wheel window centered in the facade of the red brick Romanesque-style Russell Street Church of Christ (c. 1890s), at 819 Russell.

Between the two churches are stylistically diverse late nineteenth century homes. The Herbert-Hamilton House (c. 1890) at 714 Russell is in Dutch Renaissance style, noted for its double arched entrance and the stepped gable of its projecting facade. At 800 Russell is a one-story brick Queen Anne dwelling, the Horn House (c. 1890), with a distinct corner tower that has a metal domed roof. The Greene House at 809 Russell is a spectacular example of Queen Anne style (c. 1900), which also exhibits the influence of classicism in the columns and pediment of its porch and the lunette in its front gable end.

90.

East Nashville High and Junior High Schools
(1932, 1937) (NR)
110-112 Gallatin Pike
Marr and Holman and George D. Waller, architects

Two of Nashville's most prolific architectural firms of the
mid-twentieth century, those of Marr and Holman and of
George D. Waller, shaped the community landmark of East
High and Junior High Schools. Marr and Holman in 1932 designed
East High, at 110 Gallatin Pike, with a commanding classical-
influenced facade, best seen in the pair of urns along the roofline
above the entrance. After the school received substantial damage
in the 1933 tornado, crews funded by the Civil Works Administration, a short-lived New Deal agency of 1933–1934, carried out
repairs. Three years later, the New Deal's Public Works Administration funded the construction of the East Nashville Junior High
School at 112 Gallatin Pike as part of its ambitious plan to upgrade
the city's public schools with new buildings and additions. Architect George D. Waller designed a complementary brick building
to the earlier high school.

East Nashville High School has a significant association with the
Civil Rights Movement in Nashville. In 1955, African American
student Robert Kelley applied for admission to school, but officials
denied his request. His father, local barber A. Z. Kelley, filed suit,
beginning decades of litigation against the segregated school
system in the landmark case of *Kelley v. Board of Education*. The

East Nashville High and Junior High, Gary Layda, photographer,
Courtesy of Metro Nashville Historical Commission.

school also has a connection with twenty-first century developments in the national historic preservation program. In 2005 First Lady Laura Bush held a press conference at the school where she announced the creation of the Preserve America Community Neighborhood program.

91.

East Branch Library (1919, 1999–2000) (NR, LL)
206 Gallatin Road
Albert R. Ross, New York, architect
Woodson Gilchrist Architects, 1999–2000 renovation

East Branch Library, AIA Middle Tennessee.

In early twentieth century, new institutions, schools, and churches were constructed to serve East Nashville residents. The library program of Andrew Carnegie funded the ornate Classical Revival-styled East Branch Library (1919). The beautiful masonry building, designed by Carnegie architect Albert R. Ross of New York, features a symmetrical five-bay facade centered on a classical entrance with Doric pilasters supporting a projecting pediment. Carnegie libraries were generally Classical Revival in style, the better to emphasize Carnegie's belief that the libraries were temples of knowledge and opportunity for middle- and working-class Americans. To meet that reform agenda, the libraries typically contained, in addition to their general collections, special spaces and collections for women and children and provided meeting rooms for community groups.

92.

East Nashville Historic District (c. 1870–1940) (NR, CZD)

Dating from the 1870s to the 1940s, the historic houses of the East Nashville Historic District represent largely vernacular interpretations of domestic architectural styles from those years, including small-scale Italianate cottages, Queen Anne-influenced gable-front and wing homes, bungalows, and American Four-Squares. At 1201 Holly Street is the picturesque and colorful Queen Anne-Eastlake dwelling (1889) of architect Hugh C. Thompson, who designed the Ryman Auditorium. Thompson also designed the residence at 122 South 12th Street, known as the Ambrose House (1890).

East Nashville Historic District, Gary Layda, photographer, Courtesy of Metro Nashville Historical Commission.

The East End United Methodist Church (1907), at 1212 Holly Street, is a district focal point. This red brick interpretation of Richardsonian Romanesque architecture is home to the state's oldest Boy Scout troop, #3, which was chartered in 1910, the first year of the scout movement in this country. Another prominent church is the Classical Revival-styled Fatherland Baptist Church.

A striking Beaux-Arts landmark is the Woodland Presbyterian Church (1916), at 211 North Eleventh Street. As was typical of the grandiose compositions of Beaux-Arts classicism, Nashville architect C. K. Colley designed a truly imposing structure, dominated by its great dome and its four fluted Doric columns that support a massive pediment.

93.

Lockeland Springs Neighborhood (c. 1870–1940) (CZD)

Once Robert Weakley's antebellum plantation estate, which he named Lockeland Springs, the neighborhood of Lockeland Springs developed in the late nineteenth and early twentieth centuries. Throughout the neighborhood are asymmetrical hip-roofed frame cottages which combine Victorian and classical detailing. Particularly good examples are the dwellings at 1601, 1609, and 1619 Woodland. Nearby is the Lockeland School (1939), another of the New Deal-funded schools constructed by the Public Works Administration, this time designed in a restrained Tudor Revival style. The school stands at the site of the old Weakley estate.

Annexation of the Lockeland Springs neighborhood in the early 1900s led to the construction of the landmark Holly Street Firehall (1913) at 1600 Holly Street. James Yeaman designed this Classical Revival-styled building, complete with a two-story portico of fluted Corinthian columns. As the city's first motorized firehall, it is also the oldest operating firehall in Nashville.

The influence of the Classical Revival on the district's vernacular housing is evident in the Tuscan columns and classical cornice of the house at 1302 Woodland Street and the pediment and balustrade of the dwelling at 1111 South Thirteenth Street. The bungalow style is represented by the homes built at 1202 Calvin Avenue (1912) and at 1404 Ordway Place (c. 1930). The American Four-Square style is found at 1311 Ordway Place.

94.

Shelby Park (1905, 1909–12, 1923)

South Twentieth Street and Shelby Avenue
E. C. Lewis, Edwin Keeble, and others, architects

The 651-acre Shelby Park began at the turn of the century as a modest private park of 151 acres, complete with amusements and a roller coaster. In 1905, the Edgefield Land Company went into bankruptcy and offered the land to the city as a public park in order to meet some of its debt obligations to customers. In 1909, three years after the area's annexation, the city Park Board spent $40,000 to acquire the 151 acres for a public park; two years later, the Board added another 80-acre tract. Shelby Park opened as a segregated white-only public park on July 4, 1912, as Hadley Park in North Nashville opened as a segregated black-only public park, the first known type of its kind in Tennessee.

The landscape and buildings at Shelby Park were shaped by the designs of Major E. C. Lewis, who had earlier created the landscaped wonderland at Centennial Park. Lewis's original design and buildings—like the distinctive Craftsman-styled Mission House (not extant) and the Rustic-styled Sycamore Lodge (moved to the Boy Scout camp, Boxwell Reservation, in 1984)—created a rustic and naturalistic look to the park, in keeping with contemporary ideas of urban landscape design. Lewis and the Park Board, however, were out-of-touch with the tastes and needs of the surrounding middle-class neighborhoods. Residents wanted not a rural oasis but a recreational center.

In 1915, Dr. A. S. Keim of the Young Men's Christian Association organized Nashville's first city park baseball league, and new baseball diamonds were installed. In 1923, the Board purchased fifty acres for the city's first municipal golf course; four year later, sixty more acres were acquired to expand the course to eighteen holes. A swimming pool was constructed in 1932; also in that decade, the Works Progress Administration built a gazebo for band performances. During the 1940s, the U.S. Navy built a training center—a concrete building that looks like a ship prow—that remains on the riverfront. Listed in the National Register of Historic Places, this modernist style building was designed by important Nashville architect Edwin A. Keeble, who served in the Navy during World War II. Integration of the park came in the early 1960s. One immediate change was the closing of the swimming pool in 1961; it was demolished three years later.

Shelby Park today is a major recreational center, with baseball/softball diamonds, a community center, courts for basketball and tennis, playgrounds, shelters, and twenty-seven holes of golf in the Shelby Golf Course and the adjacent Riverview Golf Course. An adjoining 810 acres comprise Shelby Bottoms Greenway and Nature Park, offering five miles of paved multi-use trails and five miles of primitive hiking trails. The city's Greenway system, which has developed from the late twentieth century to the present, has become one of the defining features of the public landscape, linking communities and open spaces throughout the county.

95.

Hobson United Methodist Church (c. 1866 and 1926)
1107 Chapel Avenue
C. K. Colley and Charles Ferguson, architects

Dating to 1851, the congregation of Hobson United Methodist Church is the oldest in East Nashville. After the Civil War, the congregation purchased land at what is now known as Chapel Avenue and built a two-story red brick Gothic-styled church building, which is extant and still in use. In 1929, the congregation built a new brick Classical Revival-styled building, with a facade dominated by a classical pediment support by six two-story fluted Ionic columns.

96.

Bailey Junior High School (1929-30, 1933, 1939-40)
2000 Greenwood Avenue
Dougherty Clemmons and Scale, 1939-40 additions

A distinguished example of Classical Revival style in a public school building, Bailey Junior High School was rebuilt in 1933, following the tornado of that year. As part of the massive Public Works Administration project to improve Nashville's public schools in the late 1930s, the New Deal and local sources combined to fund an expansion for a new gymnasium and elementary classrooms, designed by Nashville architects Dougherty Clemmons and Scale. The school is named in honor of John E. Bailey, a long-time Supervisor of Music for the Nashville public schools.

Weakley-Truett-Clark House,
Metro Nashville Historical
Commission.

97.

Weakley-Truett-Clark House (c. 1820, 1870, 1936–39) (NR)
415 Rosebank

The Weakley-Truett-Clark House began as a two-story brick Federal house circa 1820. As was typical of homes from this period, the five-bay facade was symmetrical but unadorned in appearance. In about 1870, the Truett family installed the two-story classical portico and arched windows that now distinguish the building. The Truetts operated Rosebank Nursery, which was a successful Nashville nursery throughout the mid-1800s. Over the last 120 years, the dwelling has always retained a late vernacular interpretation of the Greek Revival style even as Sheffield Clark, Jr., in 1936–37, directed a Colonial Revival renovation, which added one-story brick wings at each end. The Clark family also gave a new colonial name, "Fairfax Hall," to the home. Another

Ivy Hall, Carroll Van West, photographer.

Colonial Revival remnant is the formal garden, created by Anna Lou Anderson Clark in 1937. To emphasize her colonial theme, she had an old log cabin moved from Inglewood School to the garden. Nearby a one-story board and batten tenant house was also constructed, by 1940, for the domestic servants.

98.

Riverwood (c. 1798, 1830s, 1850s, 1920s) (NR)
1833 Welcome Lane

Riverwood is an excellent example of how early Davidson County farmhouses evolved over time into fashionable twentieth century mansions. The present two-story symmetrical three-bay house began as a two-story dwelling, built circa 1798 by Irish immigrant Alexander J. Porter. A generation later, by the 1830s, a Federal style home was built about fifteen feet away from the original farmhouse; the older portion became a kitchen. The most significant changes, however, came during Davidson County's agricultural boom of the 1850s when the house was expanded to include additional rooms on the front and a full second story. At that time, a two-story portico, of six fluted Doric columns supporting an unadorned entablature, was added to the facade. The earlier vernacular farmhouse had evolved into a refined Greek Revival mansion.

In the early twentieth century, Riverwood experienced one last expansion when two modern bathrooms and a pantry were added in three small masonry wings on both sides of the dwelling. These last changes probably occurred after the death of Riverwood's owner, newspaperman Duncan B. Cooper, in 1922.

A former Confederate officer who served with Nathan Bedford Forrest, Cooper was found guilty of second-degree murder after a 1908 gunfight between himself, his son Robin Cooper, and politician and editor Edward Ward Carmack left Carmack dead. Governor Malcolm Patterson later pardoned Cooper, who retired to Riverwood.

99.

Ivy Hall (1934–36) (NR)
1431 Shelton Avenue
Edwin A. Keeble, architect

Ivy Hall, also known as the Dr. Cleo Miller House, is a Tudor Revival masterpiece, designed by Nashville architect Edwin A. Keeble, with decorative metal work from the Kerrigan Iron Company. The Tudor Revival was one of several revivalist styles popular in the American domestic architecture during the 1920s and 1930. Due to its stylistic allusions to English castles and manor houses, Tudor Revival style proved especially enticing to wealthy businessmen and professionals.

Ivy Hall is a home of gracious proportions, highlighted by multi-pane casement windows, decorative chimneys, entrance tower, and half-timbered wall surfaces. Keeble's interior was functional and modern. It contained such technological innovations as central steam heat, radio electric outlets wired to an external antenna, and internal conduit wiring as well as the decorative metal work of the drapery rods, heating grates, and light fixtures by Kerrigan Iron Company.

Sudekum House, Gary Layda, photographer, Courtesy of Metro Nashville Historical Commission.

The original owner was Dr. Cleo Miller, a prominent mid-twentieth century Nashville physician, who helped to establish Edgefield Hospital and several East Nashville clinics. The National Register listing of this Inglewood landmark in the mid-1990s helped to spur the preservation of other Inglewood dwellings in Inglewood in the twenty-first century. In 2011, the Inglewood Neighborhood Association launched plans to create National Register districts.

100.
Sudekum House (1890s) (NR)
1606 Lischey Avenue

This three-story frame Queen Anne house was home to Nashville developer and businessman Tony Sudekum. As is common with many Queen Anne homes in Nashville, the house has both Victorian details (the peaked, open tower) and elements of classicism (the porch columns and pediment). Sudekum is best known for his Sudekum Building (the old Tennessee Theater), which once stood on Church Street. Until its demolition in 1992, the Sudekum Building was the city's best example of an Art Deco skyscraper.

101.
McGavock-Gatewood-Webb House (c.1840, c.1870, c.1915) (NR)
908 Meridian Street

The evolving history of this historic residence mirrors the patterns of change that have shaped East Nashville for over 150 years. It was originally constructed by 1840 as a two-story brick, late Federal

McGavock-Gatewood-Webb House, Photo by MTSU Center for Historic Preservation, National Register Collections, Tennessee Historical Commission.

styled hall-and-parlor house for the family of James McGavock. His daughter Lucinda inherited the house and 94 acres in 1841; she married Jeremiah George Harris, editor of the *Nashville Union* and a long-time U.S. Navy paymaster, in 1842. Their daughter, Lucie, inherited the property in 1865; she married Dr. Van Lindsley in 1868.

During their years in residence, Lucie and Van Lindsley made several alterations to the house, adding the second-floor wooden wrap-around porch with balustrade, and shifting the primary

First Baptist East Nashville, Metro Nashville Historical Commission.

facade of the house from the north to the east facing Meridian Street; this new section featured Italianate details both on the exterior and interior.

After Dr. Lindsley's death in 1885, Lucie began to subdivide the surrounding acreage, and she relocated to New York in 1891, when she sold the property to Wesley Emmett Gatewood. Gatewood sold the property to Alonzo Webb in 1905, and the house was subdivided into apartments by 1915, about when a Craftsman-styled entrance was installed on the Meridian Street facade. The house was used primarily as a rental property throughout the remainder of the twentieth century.

102.

First Baptist East Nashville (1928–1931) (NR)
601 Main Street

The congregation of First Baptist Church East Nashville traces its roots to 1866, when former slave Randall Vandavall established a church for African Americans, worshipping first in his home, then later in abandoned Union Army barracks, and constructing a brick church in 1898. The church's present location is due to the leadership of the Rev. W. S. Ellington (pastor, 1915–1949), who led the congregation in constructing a new Main Street sanctuary from 1928 to 1931. The building's impressive four columned Ionic portico with pediment made a powerful statement of African American independence and achievement in the Jim Crow South of the Depression era. The new church combined its beautiful Classical Revival styled sanctuary with a Sunday School building that served many community needs. For example, the church often hosted meetings for the Nashville branch of the National Association for the Advancement of Colored People (NAACP) during the Civil Rights movement. In 1958, at the invitation of the church's Women's Day Committee, Little Rock, Arkansas, activist Daisy Bates told the congregation that support for the NAACP in its fight for civil rights was crucial.

The Classical Revival church features interior baptistery murals by Frances E. Thompson (c. 1900–1992), a Tennessee native who led the art department at Tennessee State University from the 1940s to her retirement in 1974.

Key Map

SOUTH NASHVILLE

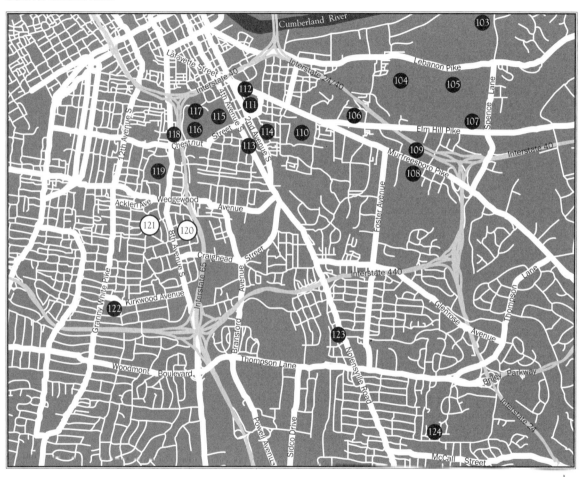

Cumberland River

103

Lafayette Street

Interstate 40

Interstate 24/40

Lebanon Pike

104

105

Spence Lane

112

111

117

115

4th Avenue S

106

Elm Hill Pike

107

118

116

2nd Avenue S

114

110

Chestnut Street

113

Murfreesboro Pike

109

12th Avenue S

119

108

Foster Avenue

Acklen Ave

Wedgewood

Avenue

121

120

8th Avenue S

Craighead

Avenue

Street

Interstate 440

Glenrose Avenue

Granny White Pike

Interstate 65

122

Kirkwood Avenue

Thompson Lane

Interstate 40

123

Branford Avenue

Woodmont

Boulevard

Thompson Lane

Nolensville Road

Brile Parkway

Powell Avenue

Sisco Drive

Interstate 24

124

McCall Street

0   ½ mi   1 mi   2 mi

South Nashville

Cameron-Trimble, Berry Hill, and Woodbine

South of the Cumberland River and Interstate Highway 40 is a large diverse area, with nineteenth century neighborhoods, twentieth century suburbs, industrial parks, and commercial strips.

From First to Tenth Avenue South, part of nineteenth century Nashville remains, although it has been seriously buffeted by railroad, then highway and interstate construction, not to mention well-intentioned but ineffective urban renewal. The Dixie Highway in 1920s first impacted Victorian residential neighborhoods and then after World War II, that two-lane road was expanded into the multi-lane Murfreesboro Road and served as a primary north-south commercial and industrial corridor. The interstate came next and split the southern halves of Second to Tenth Avenues away from the city's downtown core and then isolated the J. C. Napier Homes Public Housing Development between the never-ending flow of interstate traffic and the busy four-lane Murfreesboro Road. Highway impact contributed significantly to the inadequacies of the Napier development, which was once a model housing project, complete with landscaping, parks, and a community building.

The Cameron-Trimble neighborhood, the oldest African American neighborhood in the city, contains a range of landmarks like the Old City Cemetery (1822), Fort Negley (1862–64), and St. Patrick's Church (1890–91) from the nineteenth century and the Hubbard House (1920), Cameron School (1939–40), and other properties from the early twentieth century.

Farther to the south of the old downtown core are modern corporate offices, factories, and businesses located on the system of highways and parkways, such as Murfreesboro Road and Briley Parkway, that developed in post-World War II Nashville.

Omohundro Waterworks, Metro Nashville Historical Commission.

103.

Omohundro Waterworks (1888-89, 1926, 1929-30) (NR, LL)

Omohundro Drive

C. K. Colley (1888-89), Nashville and Chester Engineers, Pittsburgh (1926-29), architects
Foster and Creighton Company, engineers

An engineering marvel from the late nineteenth and early twentieth centuries, the Omohundro Waterworks began operation in 1889 as a part of an overall city plan to update its urban infrastructure. In the hundred years since, the waterworks have been constantly improved and expanded to the complex water filtration system of today. C. K. Colley designed the three-story brick and limestone George Reyer Pumping Station (1889) which was built by Nashville's Foster and Creighton Company. The building features a single huge interior space, measuring 80 by 120 feet and 60 feet in height, with three levels of arched clerestory windows in its hip roof providing natural light. Standing nearby is an original 200-foot smokestack for the boiler that once powered the machinery. The Lebanon Pike Stone Arch Bridge (1888), designed by City Engineer J. A. Jowett and built by Foster and Creighton Company, carries a three-foot wide water main across Brown's Creek to the Eighth Avenue Reservoir, located several miles to the southeast. Closed to vehicular traffic in 1925, the stone bridge parallels the modern bridge.

In the late 1920s, the city improved the works, constructing a new three-story brick boiler house along with the Robert L. Lawrence, Jr., Filtration Plant in 1929. The filtration plant was a modern engineering showplace, with an open hall of diamond patterned terrazzo tile flooring, flanked by brick arcades and covered by a polished hardwood ceiling. Still in use, this water treatment plant, along with the K. R. Harrington Water Treatment Plant in Donelson, provides the water for Davidson as well as parts of Rutherford and Williamson counties. On an average day, the two waterworks pump eighty-two million gallons of drinking water.

104.

Calvary Cemetery (1868)

1001 Lebanon Pike

Before the establishment of Calvary Cemetery, a five-acre section in the southwest corner of the City Cemetery was used as a Catholic burial ground. When the Nashville and Chattanooga Railroad came through in the 1850s, it cut off this section from the rest of the cemetery. After the Civil War, the Catholic Diocese opened Calvary Cemetery and moved the Catholic graves to this new cemetery on Lebanon Pike.

This historic Catholic cemetery is notable for its outstanding Victorian funerary art set within a stone wall-lined landscaped setting. The cemetery is further graced by its stone Victorian Gothic gateway entrance on Lebanon Pike. Like its neighbor, Mount

Olivet Cemetery, Calvary is a good Nashville example of the rural cemetery movement of the nineteenth century.

Mount Olivet Cemetery (1856) (NR)

1101 Lebanon Pike

Mount Olivet Cemetery, Carroll Van West, photographer.

Investors in 1856 established Mount Olivet Cemetery on 105 acres fronting Lebanon Pike. The design and monument types at this cemetery were part of the Victorian rural-cemetery movement, which reflected a desire to establish a virtual garden of graves that served as a restful urban oasis. This type of cemetery "was also a place of pride for town and family, whose monuments and statues reminded visitors of their success and their future. The cemetery offered a celebration of life and death, hope for the dead, and repose for the living."[1] Wealthy families acknowledged their prominence and success through large, ornate family crypts and monuments.

Mount Olivet's winding roads and paths take advantage of its hillside location. Gravestones reflect a wide range of Victorian architectural styles, such as Gothic, Romanesque, and Egyptian Revival. Classicism, and classical virtues, are alluded to in many gravestones. Pedestals decorated with ivy (symbolizing memory), oak (immortality), and acorns (life) were common.

Antebellum political leaders John Catron and John Bell were buried at Mount Olivet. After the Civil War, in 1869, a group of women organized the Confederate Circle as the final resting place for nearly 1500 soldiers who died in battle around Nashville. In 1887, the Confederate Monument Association, another group comprised mostly of women, raised money for a forty-five-foot-tall granite memorial to honor the dead Confederates. It was finished in 1889. Since 1900, the United Daughters of the Confederacy has owned Confederate Circle.

Most of Nashville's business leaders of the late nineteenth and early twentieth centuries are interred at Mount Olivet. A pyramid with sphinxes, for example, marks the grave of Major F. C. Lewis, who directed the Tennessee Centennial Exposition in 1897.

106.

Mount Ararat Cemetery (1869)

800 Elm Hill Pike

The newly freed people of Nashville, excluded from what were then segregated white cemeteries like Mount Olivet, created their own public cemetery during the Reconstruction era. Mount Ararat Cemetery (1869) was the first organized African American cemetery in Nashville and is situated between today's Elm Hill Pike, Fesslers Lane, and Interstate I-40. In 1914, cemetery trustees erected a stone and iron entrance gate, which marks the cemetery's location. Dr. Robert F. Boyd, an important physician and educator from the late nineteenth century, and early twentieth century sculptor and gravestone carver Will Edmondson are buried at Mount Ararat. Edmondson's gravestone art and sculpture may also be viewed at the Cheekwood Museum.

107.

Greenwood Cemetery (1888)

1428 Elm Hill Pike

By 1888, local blacks had need for a second cemetery. Minister, businessman, and undertaker Preston Taylor established the Greenwood Cemetery at the corner of Elm Hill Pike and Spence Lane. It has since served as a major city cemetery for local African Americans. Among the burials there are DeFord Bailey, the first

Greenwood Cemetery, Metro Nashville Historical Commission.

black Grand Ole Opry star, Tennessee State University coach John Merritt, and three original Fisk Jubilee Singers, including Georgia Gordon Taylor, Preston Taylor's first wife. The gravestones of both Mt. Ararat and Greenwood contain valuable examples of folk art traditions as well as Victorian tombstones, featuring allegorical figures in mourning, angels, cherubs, and such animals as lambs and doves. Both cemeteries are in need of restoration and preservation.

Aladdin Building, Carroll Van West, photographer.

108.

Aladdin Building (1948–49, demolished c. 2010)
703 Murfreesboro Road
Spencer J. Warwick Associates, Cincinnati, architects

The Aladdin Building was one of Nashville's great, yet unrecognized, pieces of modern industrial architecture. Constructed by R. C. Mathews of Nashville, the factory played an important role in the city's post-war boom and was located between the mainline of the Nashville, Chattanooga, and St. Louis Railway and the recently completed four-lane expansion of the Dixie Highway (Murfreesboro Road), a major north-south automobile route.

Even before the building was completed, newspapers were praising its virtues. "The brilliant, modernistic plant," announced the *Tennessean* of April 17, 1948, will be "smokeless, odorless and noiseless." The factory "strikes an unusual design which might well set the style for a new type of industrial architecture," added Chamber of Commerce president E. W. McGovern.[2]

This "new type of industrial architecture" was actually Nashville's introduction to the International style, but executed in a regional interpretation that utilized brick, glass block, steel, and horizontal lines to create its distinctive appearance. Long horizontal rows of windows characterized Aladdin's highway facade, but the monotony of typical factory facades was broken by that central clock tower, which marked the factory's formal entrance, highlighted by glass block windows. The interior offices continued the modernist theme of the exterior.

A year after its Nashville opening, Aladdin introduced its first school lunch box kit—featuring television cowboy Hopalong Cassidy—and lunchboxes became a staple of the company. Aladdin continued to experience growth through the 1980s at its Nashville facility, as Aladdin products including foam-insulated mugs were sold in grocery chains and drugstores nationwide. Unfortunately, during this time, Aladdin also suffered from mismanagement and high costs. In 2002, the company closed its Nashville plant, and later partially demolished the building.

109.

Lane Motor Museum (former Sunbeam Bakery) (1950–51, 2003)
702 Murfreesboro Road
Marr & Holman, architects

The American Bread Company also took a modernist approach to mid-century industrial design for its new Nashville bakery, just not as stylistically flamboyant as that of its neighbor across the highway, the Aladdin Building. The long symmetrical brown brick façade highlighted banks of windows, punctured by a slightly projecting central entrance. The best-known product from the technologically advanced factory was Sunbeam bread, which was a franchised brand started in 1942 by the Quality Bakers of America in Pennsylvania. The bakery stayed in business until 1994.

Its huge interior space, with wood floors and brick walls, proved ideal for the building's second use, as home to the Lane Motor Museum, which opened in 2003. As is fitting for its location

Adams Building, Trevecca Nazarene University, Steve Hoskins, photographer, Trevecca Nazerene University.

along one of the nation's historic highways, the Dixie Highway, the museum contains an international collection of automobiles manufactured throughout the twentieth century.

110.

Trevecca Nazarene University
333 Murfreesboro Road

Rev. J. B. McClurkan established the beginnings of today's Trevecca Nazarene University when he established the Literary and Bible Training School for Christian Workers in downtown Nash-

ville in 1901. Ten years later, the school evolved into Trevecca College and in 1914 it moved to East Nashville, where it became an official college of the Church of the Nazarene three years later. In 1935 Trevecca officials established Murfreesboro Road campus and graduated its first four-year class in 1942.

The Trevecca campus has an impressive group of limestone buildings in Colonial Revival or Classical Revival styles from the mid-twentieth century, including McClurkan Hall (1942, A. L. Snell, architect); the Adams Administration Building (1944); and Tidwell Hall (1948–50). The Nashville firm of Tisdale and Tisdale designed the Wakefield Fine Arts Building (1952) and the Mackey Building (1963). At the end of the century, Wendell D. Brown and Earl Swenssen Associates reflected the university's earlier classical designs in their Waggoner Library (1999–2000) as its classical rotunda not only commands the building's facade but also defines the central space of the university. The oldest building, Smith Hall (1939), has been moved twice on the campus; this Tudor Revival cottage was the first President's House.

111.

Hubbard House (1920) (NR)
1109 First Avenue South
Moses McKissack III, architect

The George W. Hubbard House in the Cameron-Trimble neighborhood is an excellent example of the early twentieth century blending of Colonial Revival and American Four-Square styles.

Hubbard House, Gary Layda, photographer, Courtesy of Metro Nashville Historical Commission.

Cameron Junior High School, Carroll Van West, photographer.

The single-story, paired Doric column porch is typical of Colonial Revival style, as practiced in Nashville at that time. Also common are the Craftsman-style details found in the shed dormer and the brackets of the eaves.

The house was built in 1920 as a gift to Dr. George W. Hubbard, upon his retirement as president of Meharry Medical College. It is the last remaining building of the original Meharry campus. Founded in 1876, Meharry was the first medical school in the country established for the education of African American physicians.

Across the street is the historic Seay-Hubbard Methodist Church, a red brick building of restrained Gothic styling. The church was constructed with bricks and timbers from old Meharry buildings and stands at the location of the Administration Building.

112.

Cameron Junior High School (1939–40) (NR)
1034 First Avenue South
Henry Hibbs, architect

Cameron Junior High School was built in the late 1930s as part of a joint effort of the city and the New Deal's Public Works Administration to build new schools. It replaced an earlier historic African American school, on 5th Avenue South, Cameron School, named for Henry Alvin Cameron, a Nashville teacher killed in World War I.

Nashville architect Henry Hibbs gave the new three-story brick school with a restrained Gothic Revival design, especially notable in the projecting Gothic bay centered over the front entrance. The real improvements came on the inside since the new Cameron had a gymnasium, auditorium, and well-equipped classrooms. The location of school was chosen, in part, to serve children who lived in the nearby J. C. Napier Homes Public Housing Development. In 1954, the school expanded to include a new senior high school, leading to a generation of academic, music, and athletic excellence. An active alumni group maintains a heritage room at the school. In 1978, Cameron was designated Nashville's pilot middle school, and continues to serve grades 5–8.

113.

St. Patrick's Catholic Church (1890) (NR)

1219 Second Avenue South

B.J. Hodge and M. Hodge, architects

A pyramidal spire topping a red brick octagonal tower highlights this late nineteenth century church, built to serve a growing Irish population in South Nashville. Its slate mansard roof, round-arched windows, and brick pilasters combine to make it Nashville's only extant ecclesiastical example of the Second Empire style. Fire damaged the building in 1998 but restoration efforts proved successful.

Since its opening, St. Patrick's has been a cultural and religious center for Nashville's Irish community, serving as host to a Catholic school, meetings of civic and social clubs, community picnics and events, and an annual St. Patrick's Day celebration. One of its most distinctive contributions came from 1892 to the 1960s when six itinerant Irish family clans would converge at the church every first Monday in May to hold an "Irish Wake" for their dead, before burial at Calvary Cemetery on Lebanon Pike, and occasionally members of these families return to Nashville to renew their association with St. Patrick's.

114.

Howell House (c. 1870)

1230 Second Avenue South

Judge Morton B. Howell, who was Nashville mayor in 1874–1875, commissioned the building of this two-story brick Italianate-style

St. Patrick's Catholic Church, Gary Layda, photographer, Courtesy of Metro Nashville Historical Commission.

dwelling about 1870. The arched window moldings, projecting bay window with bracketed cornice, recessed central entrance, and symmetrical composition make the Howell House a good representative of the Italianate style as interpreted in Nashville in the post-Civil War era.

115.

Nashville City Cemetery (1822) (NR)
Fourth Avenue South at Oak Street

The City Cemetery is Nashville's oldest extant public cemetery. It began with a four-acre tract, later expanded in 1836 and 1855 to its present twenty-seven acres. The city ceased selling lots in 1878, in an attempt to slow the outbreaks of cholera which periodically swept the city. In 1911, the Women's Federation of South Nashville donated the present stone entrance, walls, and iron gate. For the next four decades, the cemetery received little attention until a mid-1950s restoration cleared the grounds, repaired roads, installed lights, and restored damaged tombstones. In past decade, Metro officials have developed a conservation master plan and an interpretive plan for this vital Nashville landmark.

City Cemetery documents the early settlement patterns of Nashville, when this area was considered on the outskirts of town. It also contains an architecturally significant array of nineteenth century gravestone art, ranging from simple stones of folk design to gravemarkers designed by architect William Strickland. This final resting place for many significant Nashvillians includes Nash-

Nashville City Cemetery, Courtesy of Metro Nashville Historical Commission.

ville founders James Robertson, Charlotte Reeves Robertson, and Ann Robertson Cockrill, six-term Tennessee governor William Carroll, Confederate Generals Richard Ewell and Felix Zollicoffer, politician George Washington Campbell, sea captain William Driver, and original Fisk Jubilee singers Mabel Lewis Imes and Ella Sheppard Moore. The City Cemetery is unique in its diversity. Catholics and Protestants as well as whites and African Americans have been buried within its walls. Still an active cemetery, City Cemetery sees a few interments each year where family ownership of a plot can be proved.

116.
Fort Negley (1862-64, 1936-37, 2004-07) (NR)
Fort Negley Boulevard and Chestnut Street
James St. Clair Morton, engineer
J. D. Tyner, restoration engineer
Moody Nolan, Inc., visitors center architect

Fort Negley is the largest remnant of the various Union fortifications that once surrounded Nashville during the Civil War. The designer was Federal Army engineer James St. Clair Morton, who was influenced by both German and French fortification plans. Federal soldiers and large numbers of African American contraband laborers completed the approximately 600 by 300 feet fort in 1862. It was polygonal in shape, with sets of blockhouses and two large casements of iron and earth to protect large cannons. The fort also contained an extensive system of underground magazines and storage spaces. In all, it consumed 62,500 cubic feet of stone and 18,000 cubic yards of dirt. During the Civil War, units of the U.S. Colored Troops manned the fort.

Federal troops remained at Fort Negley until 1867. After they left, it became a gathering place for the initial Nashville Den of the Ku Klux Klan, who used it in 1869 for their last public demonstration. Nathan B. Forrest led Klan members to the fort where they burned their robes and "officially" disbanded.

In 1928, the city Park Board acquired the deteriorated fort site. During the late 1930s, the Works Progress Administration funded a partial restoration as part of its dual interest in creating public parks and in preserving significant historic properties. Engineer J. D. Tyner was in charge of the restoration and the fort became a city museum. But with the end of the New Deal and the outbreak of the World War II, the restoration of the fort was never fully completed.

Many people viewed the fort as a symbol of the military occupation of Nashville during and after the war. For others, the fort represented, as historian Bobby L. Lovett explained, "the uneasy alliance between the Union Army and local blacks in their successful campaign to preserve the Union and destroy slavery."[3] As one of the last remnants of the Battle of Nashville open to the public, Fort Negley is significant today as an example of Civil War-era military construction techniques, a place of African American history and identity, and as a relic of WPA historic preservation efforts.

Not until recent times have historians and preservationists again turned their attention to Fort Negley. It reopened to visitors in 2004 and a visitor center was added in 2007. The fort's highest points provide some of the best vantage points to view Nashville's architecture and its development over the last 150 years.

Fort Negley, Gary
Layda, photographer,
Courtesy of Metro
Nashville Historical
Commission.

117.

Adventure Science Center (1973, 2002–08)

800 Fort Negley Boulevard
Brush, Hutchison and Gwinn, architects
Gresham, Smith and Partners, architects, 2002 renovation
Tuck Hinton Architects, 2008 Sudekum Planetarium addition

The Adventure Science Center, known for many years as the Cumberland Science Museum, is located on the north slope of St. Cloud Hill at the base of Fort Negley. It evolved from the old Nashville Children's Museum, which was once located on Rutledge Hill at the Literary Department of the University of Nashville.

The earth tones of the building blend into the natural landscape of St. Cloud Hill as the facade's design plainly displays the interior's functions. For example, the projecting twin brick towers contain interior staircases and a vast array of glass lights the large open exhibit spaces. A 2002 renovation designed by Gresham, Smith and Partners added 9,000 square feet for a lobby entrance and meeting space. The expansion was funded by engineering societies, firms, and individuals across the state. The latest addition is the pyramidal Sudekum Planetarium (2008), designed by Tuck Hinton Architects.

118.

Fall School (1898) (NR)

1116 Eighth Avenue South
Wayne Morrison, architect, 1981–82 renovation

The oldest extant building from Nashville's old public school system, Fall School is named in honor of P. S. Fall, a Nashville businessman and former member of the city Board of Education. With the balanced facade, pilasters, terra cotta trim, and pedimented entrance characteristic of Renaissance Revival architecture, the school was a stylish, modern addition to the city's public buildings. The three-story atrium, lighted by an octagonal glass cupola topping its hipped roof, is the delight of the otherwise functional interior. On the atrium's first floor is a colonnaded court surrounding a bronze nautical-themed fountain.

The building served as a school until 1970. In 1981–82, it was adapted into offices, with careful renovation of the original materials and spaces. In 2009 it opened as the Church of Scientology Celebrity Centre Nashville.

119.

Eighth Avenue South Reservoir (1887–89) (NR)

Eighth Avenue South, south of Edgehill Avenue
J. A. Jowett, engineer

Located on the site of Fort Casino, a Union Civil War fortification, this fifty million gallon reservoir has an elliptical shape,

Eighth Avenue South Reservoir,
Metro Nashville Historical,
Commission

with a major axis of 603 feet and a minor axis of 463 feet. Reportedly, some of the stones came from Fort Negley. A limestone and red brick Romanesque-style gatehouse stands on the north side wall. The reservoir is considered an engineering landmark, even though part of its southeast wall failed in 1912, spilling some twenty-five million gallons of water onto the nearby state fairgrounds. Property damage was extensive; fortunately no one died in the accident.

Woodland in Waverly Historic District (NR, HZD)

Nestled between commercial and highway development is the Woodland in Waverly Historic District. Most of the dwellings here date to the first three decades of the twentieth century. Some are on a large scale of multiple stories with high-style architectural detailing while others are more modest in size, materials, and ornament.

With its two and one-half story brick construction, adorned with Ionic column portico, wood balustrade, and hipped dormer windows, the house at 746 Benton Avenue (1907) is an outstanding example of Colonial Revival style. Of particular interest is the row of bungalows (mostly built in the 1920s) on Roycroft Place. The name "Roycroft" means "craft of kings" in French, but the reference is most clearly associated with the Roycrofters of New York State, a loosely knit association of artists, craftspeople, architects, and designers, who worked in East Aurora, New York, in the early 1900s. Led by businessman and writer Elbert Hubbard, the Roycrofters specialized in Arts and Crafts decorative arts and architecture. The developers of this street used the name Roycroft as an instant way of identifying the types of houses they wanted to sell. With the diagonal braces under the eaves, tapered porch posts, and clipped gable porches, the houses of Roycroft Place show how the bungalow idea was translated and marketed to a southern middle-class neighborhood.

121.

Waverly Place Historic District (NR)

Established in 1887–88 by the Waverly Land Company, Waverly Place is another streetcar suburb distinguished for its mix of Victorian dwellings and early twentieth century styles of domestic architecture such as the American Four-Square and bungalow. J. A. Jowett, the engineer of the Eighth Avenue Reservoir, was the suburb's designer and he prepared a plat that utilized the rolling terrain and natural contours of this section of Nashville to best advantage. It was the only Nashville suburb to break the common grid pattern of street development until the 1950s.

The name Waverly Place refers to an estate that existed here in the mid-nineteenth century. It was the antebellum home of A.W. Putnam, who wrote an important history of Middle Tennessee in 1859.

122.

Sunnyside Mansion (circa 1850s, 1920s) (NR) and Sevier Park
3000 Granny White Pike

Located along an old antebellum turnpike route, and set within the boundaries of Sevier Park, is Sunnyside Mansion. This two-story five-bay central hall house is graced by a two-story portico of Greek Revival and Italianate styling. Italianate brackets run the length of the facade's cornice; four square, recessed paneled Doric piers support the projecting classical pediment. In 1849, Mrs. Mary Benton, the widow of Jesse Benton, Jr., purchased the property and began construction of the dwelling. Fighting during the Battle of Nashville took place near here and the house briefly served as a hospital.

In the 1920s, owner Colonel Granville Sevier, a relative of the Bentons, gave the dwelling a Colonial Revival-styled renovation, adding one-story brick wings to the central block and making several interior improvements. The colonnaded one-story stone building near the drive served as Sevier's private office. Nashville's Park Board purchased about twenty acres around the house

Sunnyside, Metro Nashville Historical Commission.

in 1945 and opened the property as Sevier Park in 1948. In 2003, the Metropolitan Historical Commission moved its offices here.

Woodbine United Methodist Church (1915)
2625 Nolensville Road

This restrained Gothic Revival-styled red brick building on a limestone foundation replaced an earlier frame church that had served the congregation since circa 1875. The facade's center section balances three different architectural treatments: the stone triple arches of the entrance doors; the single stone arch over the Gothic stained glass window; and the battlements of the roof line. Of particular note are the many original stained glass windows, especially the stained glass transoms of the recessed entrance. Located on a busy part of Nolensville Road populated by Hispanic businesses, this historic building documents the ever shifting populations of South Nashville.

Airdrie (c. 1800, 1910) (NR, LL)
3210 Avenal Avenue

This country estate began as a log dwelling, thought to have been built by early settler William Dickson circa 1800. By the mid-nineteenth century, the Buell family had developed the simple farmhouse into an elegant antebellum plantation. The frame house took on its current appearance in 1910, after Nashville architect George Norton, whose sister resided there, restored and modernized the house and gardens in a Classical Revival fashion.

A two-story portico, of four Doric columns supporting an unadorned entablature, creates a commanding facade. The main two-story block of the house is flanked by matching one-story wings, which were added during Norton's renovations.

MIDTOWN NASHVILLE

Key Map

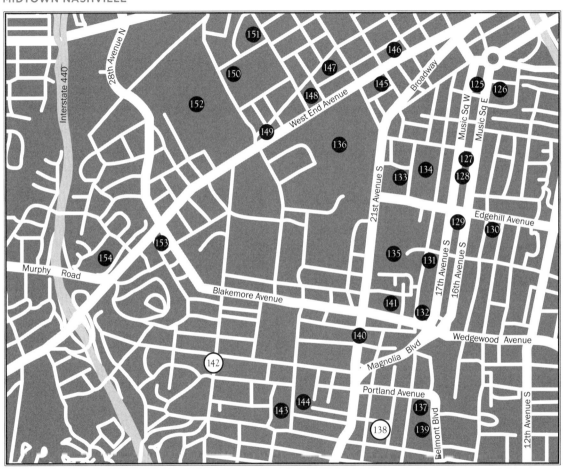

Interstate 440

28th Avenue N

151

150

152

149

146

147

148 West End Avenue

145

Broadway

125

126

Music Sq W

Music Sq E

136

127

134

128

133

21st Avenue S

Edgehill Avenue

129

130

135

131

Murphy Road

154

153

Blakemore Avenue

141

132

17th Avenue S

16th Avenue S

140

Wedgewood Avenue

142

Magnolia Blvd

Portland Avenue

143 144

137

138

139

Belmont Blvd

12th Avenue S

0   1000'   2000'   4000'

Midtown Nashville
Music Row, Vanderbilt, Belmont-Hillsboro, and West End

Streetcars at the turn of the century, then automobiles in the twentieth century, have subtly but permanently shaped Nashville's West End. Before the Civil War, turnpikes connected area farms and plantations to downtown Nashville. Outside of the great manor house of Belmont plantation, and other dispersed residences and outbuildings, little remains of the antebellum rural landscape; almost everything else, especially the open spaces, was sacrificed or subdivided in the forty years after the Civil War.

The West End became a place where Nashvillians created their self-proclaimed "Athens of the South" in an educational sense with such new schools as Vanderbilt University, Roger Williams University, George Peabody College for Teachers, Scarritt College, Lipscomb University, and Belmont University. Athens also was recreated in a physical sense by Nashville's embrace of classical architecture in the construction of the great Parthenon and the Peabody campus.

The new colleges proved irresistible lures for suburban development, especially as streetcar transportation allowed Nashville business people to live "out west" but still commute downtown. The streetcar tracks would hardly be laid before developers were building the first houses along the lines. Significant portions of this suburban explosion—with excellent examples of popular domestic architectural styles from the late nineteenth and early twentieth centuries—remain in the Belmont-Hillsboro and Hillsboro-West End districts.

New businesses also shaped Nashville's West End, especially along Sixteenth Avenue South. Beginning in the 1950s, music publishers and record companies took American Four-Squares and

Studio B, Metro Nashville
Historical Commission.

other common suburban houses and turned them into offices and recording studios for the booming music industry. Soon Nashville had a new nickname, "Music City, U.S.A." to add to the earlier "Athens of the South."

Gracious homes that once stood along West End Avenue, between the Broadway intersection and Centennial Park, were demolished to make room for hotels, gas stations, offices, and restaurants that catered to the new automobile culture. The colleges continued to demand more space as did the rapidly expanding health care industry. Broadway, Twenty-first Avenue South, and West End Avenue became heavily travelled highways to newer suburbs even farther to the west. Finally in the early 1980s, the construction of I-440 destroyed even more homes and physically divided Nashville's urban west side into two sections.

As blocks of homes and offices around evolved into Nashville's "Music Row" during the 1950s and 1960s, the architecture of the city's music industry emerged. Like the music it produced and recorded, Music Row's architecture was contemporary, but had traditional features. At the original Country Music Hall of Fame and Museum (1967, demolished in 2002), architect W. S. Cambron used modern materials within the profile of a rural barn. From 1957 to 1995, Music Row evolved into a distinct, special place.

125.

RCA Studio Buildings (1957, 1965) (NR)
1611 Roy Acuff Place and 30 Music Square West
Bill Miltenburg, designer
W. B. Cambron, contractor RCA Studio B

This unadorned 1957 one-story buff concrete block Studio B is one of the most important recording spaces in American music history. When Chet Atkins became RCA Music's Director of Operations in 1957, he told his bosses that the label's recording facilities in Nashville were inadequate, and he convinced them to build offices and a recording studio to the plans of recording manager Bill Miltenburg. Built by Dan Maddox for $37,515, Studio B opened in November 1957; recording engineer Bill Porter made crucial interior changes to improve acoustics in 1959; and an addition was built in 1961.

RCA added Studio A in 1965 and together the complex became home to a thousand hits—it produced an estimated 60 percent of the Billboard Country Music Chart. The artists recording here include the Everly Brothers, Roy Orbison, Willie Nelson, Waylon Jennings, Dolly Parton, Bobby Bare, Charley Pride, and Ernest Tubb. It was one of the most important studios for Elvis Presley. The complex also is closely associated with the development of the "Nashville Sound," a pop-influenced approach to country music that gained popularity in the 1960s. Some of the leading artists associated with the Nashville Sound, including Atkins, Boots Randolph, Floyd Cramer, Anita Kerr,

and the Jordanaires, recorded their own records and served as session musicians here.

RCA sold the studios in 1977. Studio B serves as studio and student laboratory and as a museum. Studio A still hosts recording sessions and provides offices for the music industry.

126.

Warner Reprise Nashville (1994)
20 Music Square East
Tuck Hinton Architects

In the mid-1980s, the country music industry expanded. The format gained new fans and more nationwide popularity. The architecture of Music Row changed too, in tune with the times, as it became more progressive, and adventuresome. Tuck Hinton Architects's modernist design and massing for the new Nashville headquarters for Warner Reprise Records expresses these themes well. This 45,000 square foot building utilizes Tennessee fieldstone, cut limestone, and gray brick to create an indigenous building for an industry grounded in the roots of American culture.

127.

Belmont Church (1914, 1987–88)
68 Music Square East
Floyd and Corbin Architects, 1987-88 renovations

At the corner of historic Sixteenth Avenue South and Grand Avenue is the Classical Revival-styled Belmont Church. Constructed

RCA Victor Studios Building,
Carroll Van West.

of yellow brick and resting on a limestone foundation, the original building was in temple form, with Doric columns at its gable end entrance; stained glass windows lit the interior. In 1987–88, the firm of Floyd and Corbin Architects expanded and adapted the building with the addition of a four-story, 38,000-square-foot facility of compatible design. It includes offices, classrooms, and an auditorium capable of seating one thousand people.

1013 Sixteenth Avenue South (circa 1890)

The Victorian era roots of the Music Row area are documented in this vernacular interpretation of Queen Anne style. Converted to commercial use with an award-winning renovation in 1976, the building has served as a bank and Music Row offices.

Church of the Advent (1910)
1200 Seventeenth Avenue South

Originally constructed as an Episcopal church, this stone Gothic-styled sanctuary was later converted into offices and work space for the YMCA's "Urban Village" project before its acquisition by the Tennessee Performing Arts Foundation in 1977. Retaining the church's exterior features and such critical interior elements as the beautiful stained glass windows, the foundation renovated the church into offices and a theater. Following the opening of the Tennessee Performing Arts Center downtown, the ministry of Tony Alamo acquired the building for its use. In 1995, the church

was remodeled into a modern recording studio. Belmont University purchased it in 2001 and operate Ocean Way Studio today.

White Way Laundry Building (1931)
1200 Villa Place
Hart Freeland Roberts, architects

Built as an ultra-modern laundry and dry cleaners handling up to twenty thousand pieces a week from many west Nashville households, the White Way Cleaners now houses an array of retail shops and eateries. The building's formal architectural features presented an appealing progressive image, a perfect way to attract the middle- and upper-class patronage the laundry needed. Originally built by Foster and Creighton Company in 1931, the business proved so popular that the construction company built four more additions over the next nine years. The many expansions, however, did not detract from the success of its contemporary commercial design. White Way is the centerpiece of a new mixed-use development known as Edgehill Village.

Little Sisters of the Poor Home for the Aged (1916–17) (NR)
1400 Eighteenth Avenue South
Barnett, Haynes, and Barnett, in association
with Christian Asmus, architects
Manuel Zeitlin, 1999–2000 renovation architect

Influenced by the earlier Cathedral of the Incarnation, the Little Sisters Home for the Aged is a more restrained interpretation

Phillips Memorial Hall (Disciples of Christ), Photograph by Carroll Van West, MTSU Center for Historic Preservation, National Register Collections, Tennessee Historical Commission.

of Renaissance Revival style. Key stylistic elements include its hipped slate roof with hipped roof dormers, the stone belt course and rounded arch windows of the first floor, the pediment and Tuscan columns of the entrance, and the glazed yellow brick of the main three floors. The chapel features a barrel vault ceiling, Ionic pilasters with egg and dart molding, stained glass windows, and a glazed tile floor.

The Little Sisters of the Poor is a private Catholic relief organization, which opened its first Nashville facility in 1904. The 1916 poor house and retirement home cost $123,000 and was designed to hold one hundred residents. The Little Sisters limited residents to those over sixty-five with little to no income; it was a white-only segregated facility until the 1960s. Closed in 1968, the building was later converted into a nursing home. From 1999–2000, the building was transformed into offices for Bertlesman Music Group (BMG). Vanderbilt University acquired it in 2014.

132.

Sharp-Crabb House (1911)
1701 Eighteenth Avenue South
Robert S. Sharp, architect

Stepped gable ends characterize the Dutch Colonial Revival style of this two-story brick residence, designed by Nashville architect Robert S. Sharp as his own home. The interior, however, blends different design ideas, from the beveled glass, oak floors, and varied windows of Craftsman style to the English tile fireplaces and chestnut woodwork of the Colonial Revival.

In 1928, Dr. Alfred L. Crabb acquired the dwelling. Crabb was a popular mid-twentieth century southern writer, who often used Nashville locations and subjects in his fiction and his studies of history and people. Crabb's books include *Dinner at Belmont* (1942), *Journey to Nashville* (1957), and *Nashville: Personality of a City* (1960).

133.

Thomas W. Phillips Memorial Hall, Disciples of Christ Historical Society (1956–58)
1101 Nineteenth Avenue South
Hoffman & Crumpton, Pittsburgh, architects
Hart, Freeland and Roberts, architects

This late interpretation of the Gothic Revival was designed by Pittsburgh architects Kenneth R. Crumpton and Roy Hoffman, with local firm Hart, Freeland and Roberts overseeing the construction in Nashville. B. D. Phillips and T. W. Phillips, Jr. of Phillips Gas and Oil Company donated the money to the Disciples of Christ Historical Society to fund the library and archives building as a memorial to their father, Thomas W. Phillips. The Phillips brothers chose Crumpton and Hoffman as the primary architects as a condition of their gift; the firm previously had designed the Phillips Gas and Oil Company building as well as B. D. Phillips' residence.

The limestone building reflects the spirit of medieval architecture, incorporating the "masterful, original works in stone and stained glass that were filled with religious and educational symbolism and were created by local, professional artists Puryear Mims and Gus Baker. This symbolism was based on historic as well as new iconography developed by the Society's Arts and Inscription Board Committee under the leadership of Eva Jean Wrather."[2]

134.

Scarritt-Bennett Center (1924–28) (NR)

1908 Nineteenth Avenue South
Henry C. Hibbs, architect

Scarritt-Bennett Center, Gary Layda, photographer, Courtesy of Metro Nashville Historical Commission.

The most intimate collegiate landscape in Nashville is the original campus of Scarritt College for Christian Workers, designed by architect Henry C. Hibbs during the mid-1920s, and now known as the Scarritt-Bennett Center. With native Tennessee Crab Orchard stone and Indiana limestone, Hibbs designed a modest, yet inspiring, Collegiate Gothic campus, which is the best example of that architectural style in Nashville, and rivaled in Tennessee only by the campus of Rhodes College in Memphis. In 1929, Hibbs' work received the prestigious AIA Gold Medal.

The Susie Gray Dining Hall, with a main dining hall in the style of those at Oxford University in England, was the first Scarritt building to open in 1927. The following year came the Belle Harris Bennett facility, which was named in honor of the school's founder. The Bennett complex interconnected the Administration Building, the Social Building, and Wightman Chapel. The chapel's soaring Gothic tower was instantly the campus's landmark, its 115 feet representing the tallest building in Nashville at the time of its construction. Hibbs in 1940 designed the Gibson Memorial Dormitory and ten years later, at the time of his death, his firm Hibbs, Clinton Parrent, and Terrill Hall had just finished the design of Bragg Hall. Terrill Hall maintained a close relationship with Scarritt over the next two decades, designing Fondren Hall (1951) and Cadwallader Hall (1962), and serving as an associate for Laskey Library (1968).

In the pointed arches, bay windows, exquisite stonework, stained glass windows, cloisters, parapets, buttresses, limestone surrounds, and ribbed vaulting typical of Gothic designs of the Middle Ages, Hibbs and his partners created an elegant architectural landmark that still conveys an atmosphere of repose, comfort, and serenity.

The United Methodist Church in 1892 established Scarritt in Kansas City, Missouri, as an institution for the training of women missionaries. In 1924, it moved the school to Nashville in order to affiliate with George Peabody College for Teachers, where it became training grounds for both male and female Christian workers. The college later concentrated its efforts in graduate instruction in Christian education and church music. Due to low enrollment, Scarritt Graduate School closed in 1988. The Women's Division of the United Methodist Church bought the property and reopened the campus as the Scarritt-Bennett Center in 1989. It is a not-for-profit conference, retreat, and educational center.

Peabody College, Carroll Van West, photographer.

135.

Peabody College of Vanderbilt University (1914–1968) (NHL)

Twenty-first Avenue South at Edgehill Avenue

When classes opened in 1914, the George Peabody College for Teachers was one of the most important developments yet to take place in Southern education. The college's mission was to prepare teachers to uplift the rural South through education. The college's first president, Bruce Payne, consciously replicated, yet modernized, the University of Virginia's campus plan of a landscaped mall surrounded by classical buildings because he believed that classical architecture created a perfect inspirational environment for future teachers.

Boston architects Ludlow and Peabody developed the master plan and their Social and Religious Building (1913–15), with its monumental Corinthian colonnade and dome, served as the symbolic, and architectural, heart of the campus. From the vantage point of the Social and Religious Building, the Ludlow and Peabody plan was an open quadrangle, with the mall pointing to the north. The firm surrounded the mall in 1913–15 with the Psychology, Industrial Arts, and Home Economics Buildings, all in red brick and in Classical Revival style, with the Ionic order predominating. In 1918–19, Edward Tilton also chose the Ionic order for his new library design.

Major changes occurred on the campus during the 1920s. The New York firm of McKim, Mead, and White added the Administration Building and the University School in 1925 as well as the Cohen Fine Arts Building three years later. Interestingly, in the late 1890s the University of Virginia itself had commissioned McKim, Mead, and White to renovate and update the original Virginia campus. Other buildings from the 1920s include Henry C. Hibbs's east and west dormitories (1921–24) and New York architect Raymond Hood's Graduate Dormitory (1929). In 1953, Nashville architect Granbery Jackson, Jr., contributed the campus's last Classical Revival building, appropriately named the Bruce Payne Building.

The first major building to break Peabody's classical mold was the Student Center (1950), designed by Nashville architects Warfield and Associates. In 1968 came two additional contemporary buildings. The Nashville firm of Warterfield and Bass designed the Human Development Laboratory while Nashville architects Bob Street and Ed Street designed the Mental Retardation Laboratory.

In the twenty-first century the college landscape changed significantly with the addition of The Commons residential complex (2006–2008), which renovated five historic dormitories and added five new dorms. The Commons Center, by architects Bruner/Cott of Cambridge, Massachusetts and the Nashville engineering firm of Smith Seckman Reid, received a Gold level LEED certification for its environmentally sustainable design as well as a Facility Design of Excellence award from the Association of College Unions International.

The Peabody campus is a monumental collegiate landscape, a physical embodiment of the city's claim to be the "Athens of the South." The college merged with Vanderbilt University in 1979, but its original campus, designated a National Historic Landmark in 1966, maintains its design integrity and identity.

136.

Vanderbilt University
West End Avenue and Twenty-first Avenue South

Vanderbilt University opened its doors in 1875 as a Methodist-sponsored institution, not as a denominational college. (The connection between church and university ended in 1914.) Carefully landscaped grounds and picturesque Victorian Gothic buildings distinguished the original campus; the 1878 university *Register* listed 306 different trees and shrubs; the campus today is recognized as a national arboretum.

The Old Gymnasium (1880), at West End and Twenty-third Avenue North, was designed by Nashville architect Peter J. Williamson. Four brick towers, exhibiting the influence of Second Empire style in their tall, colorful slate roofs, are set at 45 degree angles at each of the building's four corners, creating a very picturesque effect on what is otherwise a rectangular brick building. During the 1970s, the gymnasium was restored as the university's Fine Arts Building.

Architect Peter J. Williamson was a native of Holland, who immigrated to Wisconsin where he joined the Union army and rose to the rank of major during the American Civil War. Afterwards, he settled in Nashville and served as a partner in the firm of Dobson and Williamson. Another Williamson design at Vanderbilt is the former Science Hall, now Benson Hall.

In 1886–87, Vanderbilt engineering dean Olin H. Landreth designed the West Side Row of student dormitories. The Mechanical Engineering Hall (1888–89) is a Romanesque-influenced design from the drafting table of Nashville architect William C. Smith. The first building in Tennessee to be constructed specifically for the teaching of engineering, the Mechanical Engineering Hall has been incorporated into the Post-Modern styled Owen Graduate School of Management building. The Victorian Gothic-styled Kirkland Hall dates to 1874–75, but thirty years later, in 1905, a disastrous fire left only the shell of the original twin-tower administration building. In its reconstruction, supervised by architect J. Edwin Carpenter, only a single tower, now the campus's most recognized landmark, was repaired and left standing.

The university today reflects the 1905 campus plan of George Kessler, who changed the prevailing architectural style from Victorian Gothic to the popular Collegiate Gothic, best seen in the stone masonry of Furman Hall (1907). In the mid-1920s, new donations and a new campus plan by Charles S. Klauder of Philadelphia left a legacy of restrained Collegiate Gothic style in the Alumni Memorial Hall, Neely Memorial Auditorium, along with Buttrick, Garland, and Calhoun Halls.

In the late twentieth century, the university added several impressive new buildings. Noted international architectural historian and designer Peter Blake renovated Neely Auditorium. The firm of Brush, Hutchison, and Gwinn completed the Vanderbilt Divinity School (1957–59). The abstract Gothic profile of the chapel is noteworthy as is the firm's treatment of the nave, in which a repeating pattern of square and rectangular stained glass windows puncture the walls. The brick bell tower, with its tall metal spire, is a modern adaptation of the Tower of the City Hall of Stockholm.

On the heels of its success with the Divinity School, the firm of Brush, Hutchison, and Gwinn next designed the Vanderbilt Law School (1961), a 85,000 square-foot three-story brick building, which includes a courtyard and wide hallways next to lecture rooms so students could gather and debate. At the end of the decade came the new Sarratt Student Center (1968–71), designed by Nashville architects Bob and Ed Street. While modern in design and conception, Sarratt Center is also a casual, friendly space, blending well into the university's historic fabric as it manages to carve out its own special niche. With its inviting entrances, earth tones, diversity of spaces, sculpture court, fountain, and ingenious integration of site and building, it avoids the typical repetitive character of institutional buildings. The work of several regional artists—Puryear Mims, Morris Parker, Gary Gore, and Michael Taylor—was also integrated into the building's design; the end result of all of these components is a logical and satisfying solution to for a 1970s student center.

The late twentieth century witnessed another period of campus expansion, including the new Owen School of Management building, the Postmodern blending of Victorian and Prairie School styles at Wilson Hall (the Psychology building), and the Eskind

Biomedical Library, designed by Davis, Broady & Associates of New York in association with Thomas, Miller and Partners of Brentwood. The Eskind Library features a 49-foot high glass tensile curtain wall, which is the nation's first self-supported tensile curtain wall. Other renovations and expansions include a compatible yet modern wing at Calhoun Hall (1995), by the Nashville firm of Everton Oglesby Askew Architects.

137.

Belmont Mansion (1853–1859) (NR) and Belmont University
1900 Belmont Boulevard
Adolphus Heiman, architect

Belmont was the most splendid antebellum estate in Nashville, the home of Adelicia Acklen, purportedly the richest woman in the South at the time of the death of her slave trader husband, Isaac Franklin, in 1846. She began to acquire the land that would eventually comprise what she called "Belle Monte" in January 1849, before her marriage to Colonel Joseph Acklen in May. The construction of the estate probably was underway by 1853. There is no certain date when the house was finished; family records indicate the Acklens were in residence by 1855, at least.

Four years later, they engaged engineer and architect Adolphus Heiman to substantially enlarge and enliven what had been the family's "summer villa" into an overwhelming mansion of Greek Revival proportions with Italianate sensibilities. By 1860, Belmont had thirty-six rooms and 10,900 square feet of living space, with one-story east and west wings, which were heavily adorned with ornamental cast iron, flanking the main two-story hipped roof central block. Its richly appointed Grand Salon of fluted Corinthian columns, chandeliers, paintings, and statuary created the city's most elegant private ballroom. Heiman further enhanced the interior by adding cornices with dentils and modillions; colored glass transoms and sidelights; and Italianate windows. A pair of colossal two-story fluted composite columns highlighted the south facade's entrance, which, in turn, was flanked by projecting four-column one-story porticoes. A flat entablature, balustrade, and pilasters tied the composition together.

Belmont Mansion was the centerpiece of elaborately landscaped grounds, in the manner of a villa from the Italian Renaissance. Visitors were suitably impressed, as recorded in this description from Mother Frances Walsh of the Dominican sisters:

> On leave taking a scene of sylvan loveliness greeted the view; such a dazzling array of art and nature, commingling so as to beautify each other, was arranged as by the hand of a master artist. Here and there were statuary, marble and bronze, placed in groups or singly. Fountains, costly vases and flowers of the richest hues intermingled in endless profusion. There were summer houses and grottos of all devices, some so dainty that they might be fitting haunts of wood-nymphs or water-sprites.[3]

The Italianate-styled 105-foot-high water tower, marble fountains, and cast-iron gazebos remain in the gardens south of the mansion, but other parts of the grounds, such as the zoo, deer park, and bear house, have disappeared. These landscape elements were lost to subdivision and the growth of the educational institutions housed on the property since its transformation into the Belmont Junior College for girls, later Ward-Belmont College, and now Belmont University.

In 2003, Belmont's built environment changed significantly with the opening of three related buildings, the Beaman Student Center, the Curb Event Center, and the Maddox Grand Atrium, designed by Earl Swensson Associates of Nashville and built by Hardaway Construction Company of Nashville. Five years later, Earl Swensson Associates added the Troutt Theater to the campus. The classicism reflected in the new buildings complements without overwhelming the campus's nineteenth and twentieth century architectural traditions.

138.

Belmont-Hillsboro Historic District (c. 1890-1940) (NR, CZ)

The Belmont-Hillsboro neighborhood runs the gamut of early twentieth century domestic architecture but maintains the lot size, massing, and materials common to middle-class houses of one hundred years ago. Twenty blocks of the neighborhood, between Twenty-first Avenue South to the west, Belmont Boulevard to the east, Magnolia Boulevard to the north, and I-440 to the south, were listed in the National Register of Historic Places in 1980.

The roots of the neighborhood were not middle-class, but lay in the great plantations of the antebellum era, specifically the estates of Adelicia Acklen of Belmont fame and of Colonel A. B. Montgomery. At 1806 Cedar Lane is the only surviving remnant of the Montgomery plantation, a two-story brick, central chimney outbuilding, which may have been used as a smokehouse. The first large subdivision came in 1890–91, after the death of Adelicia Acklen; an advertisement in the *Nashville Evening Herald*, May 10, 1891, bragged: "its location cannot be equaled; its scenery cannot be approached; its healthfulness cannot be questioned." Yet, sustained development was delayed until after 1901, when the Belmont Land Company established a streetcar line along Belmont Boulevard. The greatest concentration of houses dates from 1905 to 1920, with a second period of building along Wildwood and Primrose avenues coming in the early 1940s.

An impressive degree of architectural consistency characterizes the district. A persistent trend is the American Four-Square style—two stories high, brick or frame construction, and hip-roof. Examples include dwellings at 2807 Oakland and 2511 Belmont Boulevard. Famous music producer "Cowboy" Jack Clement operated his home studio at 3405 Belmont Boulevard, a Tudor Revival style house. An example of the Prairie style, a regional interpretation of the famous midwestern houses of master American architect Frank Lloyd Wright, is at 2616 Belmont Boulevard.

The most common house, however, is the bungalow. From the use of gable roofs, shingles, stone, and stucco, local builders were clearly influenced by the house designs in the popular magazine,

The Craftsman. New York furniture maker and Arts-and-Crafts devotee Gustav Stickley published the magazine during the early 1900s. Local builders took designs and inspiration from this and other popular architectural and construction magazines and, in turn, created what can be called a manufactured vernacular style that marks almost every American town and city.

The 1920s witnessed a revival of earlier architectural styles in American suburbs and that taste for Colonial and Tudor Revival cottages of stone and brick is amply documented along the neighborhood's streets. Apartment living also became more common in the post-World War I years. The Ivy Lodge (1920 Portland Avenue) and The Clair (2804–6 Belmont Boulevard) are Tudor Revival, a style associated with many early apartment complexes in the city.

Hillsboro Village, Metro Nashville Historical Commission.

139.

Sterling Court Apartments (c. 1915)

2101-2109 Belmont Avenue

Perhaps the most outstanding example of an early apartment complex in the Belmont-Hillsboro district is the Craftsman-influenced Sterling Court Apartments. A low stone wall, complete with Craftsman-styled trolley shelter, and a landscaped lawn with large mature trees separates the apartments from the street. Thus, Sterling Court takes on the appearance of a domestic oasis apart from, yet directly connected to, the frantic pace of life in a busy city. It was a very popular address for the city's professional class in the first half of the twentieth century.

140.

Hillsboro Village (c. 1920–2014)

Twenty-first Avenue South between Blakemore Avenue and Acklen Avenue

The commercial heart of the Hillsboro neighborhood began in the 1920s when grocery stores, drug stores, a post office, and dry cleaners opened along both sides of Twenty-first Avenue South. Streetcars running down the middle of the street brought eager patrons to the many different stores. By the end of the 1920s, at least nineteen businesses were located in the district.

A focal point was the Hillsboro Theater, a Spanish Revival-tinged silent movie house that had the city's largest stage when it opened in 1925. The Children's Theatre of Nashville and WSM's Grand Ole Opry radio program both used the ample stage in the 1930s. In 1937, the building became the Nashville Community Playhouse; then in 1966 it once again became a movie theater, renamed as the Belcourt Cinema. It faced a uncertain future in the late 1990s but has emerged in the 21st century as a popular neighborhood theater, named Belcourt Theatre, regularly used for concerts, performances, and movies.

Many family-owned businesses have operated in Hillsboro Village. Due to their quality and the human scale of the village's commercial setting, several have become favorite Nashville haunts. In the late 1990s, redevelopment introduced revival-styled mixed-use buildings that added apartments and new retail stores to the village with considerable recent construction.

141.

Blakemore Avenue District (c. 1920-c. 1940) (CZD)

Blakemore Avenue, between Nineteenth Avenue South, and Twenty-first Avenue South

Conservation zoning has become an important tool to protect the architectural character of Nashville's historic neighborhoods. The Blakemore district developed between 1920 and 1940 and contains only six properties, representing the city's smallest

conservation district. The dwelling at 1904 Blakemore, renovated by architect Manuel Zeitlin in 1995–96, is a good example of the American Four-Square style and represents the district's architectural quality.

142.

Hillsboro-West End Historic District (c. 1910-c. 1940) (NR, CZ)

In 1908, developers turned to land further west and established the Hillsboro-West End neighborhood, with most houses being constructed from 1910 to 1943. Once again, the expansion of streetcar lines—in this case the Nashville Railway and Light Company extension of tracks to Blair Boulevard—spurred rapid development. The new suburbs again replaced earlier farms and residences; one that survived is the Gothic Revival-styled Glen Oak (1854).

The district is bounded by Twenty-first Avenue South and West End Avenue, from Blakemore Avenue to I-440. Almost one thousand contributing historic buildings are located within these boundaries, making it Nashville's largest residential National Register historic district.

Hillsboro-West End has been home to its share of famous Nashvillians. The Agrarian writer Donald Davidson lived at 410 Fairfax; George D. Hay, the "Solemn Ol' Judge" of the Grand Ole Opry, resided at 3303 Orleans. Fannie Mae Dees lived on Capers Avenue and became famous in the 1960s for her protest against short-sighted development in the area. At 2400 Blakemore Avenue is Fannie Mae Dees Park, which features the mosaic sea

Hillsboro-West End Historic District, Calvert School, Carroll Van West, photographer.

serpent sculptures of artist Pedro Silva of Chile. In general, this was a middle-class neighborhood, where clerks, managers, government employees, small retailers, and blue-collar workers daily took the streetcars, or later drove their own automobiles, to work in the city.

The bungalow style predominates in Hillsboro-West End. Tudor Revival cottages also are numerous. Complete with its stone corner tower, the house at 2704 Woodlawn Avenue is an

outstanding example of the style. The dwelling at 2812 Belcourt is an interesting English cottage design and half-timbered gables mark the home at 2816 Blair Boulevard. The district also contains representative examples of American Four-Squares, Colonial Revival, and the largely unadorned one-story rectangular house style of the late 1930s and early 1940s known as the Minimal Traditional house. But unlike the nearby Belmont neighborhood, the impact of the automobile is clearly seen in the Hillsboro-West End district, not only by the number of historic detached garages but also by the lack of rear alleys in the street plan.

The New Deal left its mark on the neighborhood in the 1930s when the Public Works Administration funded Eakin School (1936), designed by architects Tisdale and Pinson in the PWA Modern style. Between 2006 and 2008, the historic school was converted into the Martin Professional Development Center. Both Eakin School/Martin Center and the adjacent Cavert School (1928) were designated local landmarks in 2001.

143.
Glen Oak (1854) (NR)
2012 Twenty-Fifth Avenue, South

The Reverend Charles Tomes, the English-born rector at the downtown Christ Church Episcopal, built this two-story multi-gabled Gothic Revival dwelling in 1854. Two years earlier, Tomes had engaged the New York firm of Dudley and Wills to design Holy Trinity Church; he may have taken the design ideas for his own home from these noted church architects.

Glen Oak, Gary Layda, photographer, Courtesy of Metro Nashville Historical Commission.

The many Gothic details of Glen Oak include a three-story square frame Gothic tower, topped by an ogee-shaped dome and a steeply gabled roof. A one-story veranda, of carved posts with attached vergeboard decoration, wraps around the primary elevations. Gothic-inspired carved vergeboard with a quatrefoil inset design enlivens the gable eaves. Original wood floors, three marble mantels, and wood molding highlight the interior.

Once a fifteen-acre country estate, Glen Oak now sits on a one-half acre lot within the Hillsboro-West End historic district.

144.

St. Bernard Convent and Academy (1905, 1924)

2021 Twenty-first Avenue South

Thompson, Gibel, and Asmus, architects

Established by the Catholic Sisters of Mercy, St. Bernard Academy dates to 1868. For the next thirty years, the Sisters operated the school at three different Nashville locations, but in about 1900 they closed the school until a new West Nashville campus was built. The Academy operated in this four-story red brick building until 1989, when the school closed. The Sisters of Mercy constructed a new convent in Donelson in 1990–91.

The Academy is typical of the simplified Victorian Gothic often found in school buildings and other institutional structures of the late nineteenth century. A stone cornice, Gothic dormers, and stone quoins add architectural flavor to what is otherwise a functional building. The symmetrical bands of triple windows on the second and third floors allowed adequate lighting into classrooms; the Gothic dormers of the fourth floor illuminated the twenty-eight bedrooms found there. In 1924, a north wing containing a beautiful two-story chapel was constructed.

In the 1990s, developers converted St. Bernard into a multi-use facility, with classrooms, apartments, and offices. The former chapel has become a reception and banquet room.

145.

Cathedral of the Incarnation (1914)

2001 West End Avenue

Asmus and Norton, architects

Fowlkes and Associates, 2002 renovation

The inspiring Italian Renaissance of the Cathedral of the Incarnation (1914) is one of the few remnants of the upper-class neighborhood that once existed on West End Avenue, before the automobile, retail development, and roadside architecture transformed the street into a busy commercial area. The yellow brick, red tile roof church is highlighted by a tall brick bell tower (1910), modeled after St. Martin's of the Hill in Rome. The cathedral design has been described as Lombardian Romanesque and came from different sources. Nashville Bishop Thomas S. Byrne approved the basic design from architect Aristide Leonard; Nashville architects Asmus and Norton took these ideas and produced the final building.

The cathedral is of a basilica design. Fluted Corinthian columns and Scalioli pilasters support a fifty-seven-foot coffered ceiling. Its innovative beam ceiling—among the first of its type in the United States—is decorated in gold leaf while the baptismal font is a miniature replica of the baptistry designed by Michelangelo for St. Peter's Cathedral at the Vatican in Rome. The Daprato Statuary Company of Chicago, a firm which specialized in ecclesiastical interior design, executed the paintings, altars, statues, and other interior decoration. In 1987, the Nashville diocese renovated the interior, adding crystal, beveled glass in the clerestory windows.

West End United Methodist
Church, Metro Nashville
Historical Commission.

146.

Gilbert Mansion (1908) (NR)

1906 West End Avenue

Joseph Lightman, architect/builder

The Gilbert Mansion is a rare turn-of-the-century remnant of the architecturally impressive homes once found in abundance on West End Avenue. Built by Nashville stone mason Joseph Lightman, the house is an excellent example of the American Four-Square, with Craftsman style influences, topped by a clay tile hipped roof. The interior contains mahogony paneled wainscoting executed by the Edgefield and Nashville Manufacturing Company. Now used as an office, its owners expanded the building with a rear addition.

147.

Elliston Place Soda Shop (1939, circa 1950)

2111 Elliston Place

Behind the black cararra glass and neon sign of this popular Elliston Place eatery, which has been in business at least since 1939, is a largely intact Art Deco interior, which was installed in the post-war years, probably the early 1950s. After the construction of the Art Deco interior of the Tennessee Theater in 1952, this interior design again became popular, for a brief time, in Nashville. The counter, white and green floor tiles, red vinyl of the booths, and even the individual juke boxes reflect the modernist styling of Art Deco.

148.

West End United Methodist Church (1927–1950)

2200 West End Avenue

Donald Southgate, architect

The city's last great monument in twentieth century Gothic Revival ecclesiastical design, the West End United Methodist Church is the work of Nashville architect Donald Southgate. Like Scarritt College, the church complex utilizes Tennessee native Crab Orchard stone and Indiana limestone for its elegant exterior finish. Southgate's design also reflected the early campus architecture of Vanderbilt University, which is across the street. The four-story Religious Education Building was finished first, in 1929, but Southgate's soaring Gothic sanctuary was not opened until 1940. The D'Ascenzo Studios of Philadelphia produced its seven leaded art glass windows; the Gothic wooden pews provide seating for over one thousand people.

In 1949 Southgate and his associate John Preston completed McWhirter Hall and in the following year, they designed the Memorial Cloister that unites the north facade of the complex along West End Avenue. John Preston would become one of the leading architects of the city's suburban explosion of the 1950s and 1960s.

Although built in stages, the unity of the design conveys a sense of purpose, reflecting an institution of strength and permanency. Southgate's achievement is clear; as he promised the congregation in 1927, his West End Methodist would be a "pleasing, beautiful and spiritually inspiring" building "in its use of that great medium known as Gothic architecture."[4]

Centennial Medical Center, AIA Middle Tennessee.

Firestone Building (1931)
2410 West End Avenue
Chris Magill Architects, 1984-85 renovation

The Firestone Building, which was renovated into a drugstore in 1984–85, is a good 1930s example of roadside commercial architecture. Located at the prominent intersection of Elliston Place and West End Avenue, the Firestone Building was perfectly positioned to take advantage of the increasing amount of automobile traffic in West Nashville.

Its Art Deco styling, topped by a large electric Firestone sign, made the building an eye-catching, three-dimensional billboard as it also met the functional needs of a full-service gas station and garage. The building's canopy-covered gas pumps and service bays were accessible to traffic on both streets. The Firestone Tire Company designed this Nashville store, as well as others in major American cities, as part of a national advertising and expansion campaign in the late 1920s and early 1930s.

150.

Thomas F. Frist Centennial Sportsplex (1987-90)
225 Twenty-fifth Avenue North
Thomas, Miller and Partners, architects

Standing on a large landscaped lot across the street from Centennial Park, the Sportsplex contains multiple recreational facilities, including the city's public ice skating rink. In 1992, the complex was named in honor of Thomas F. Frist, a leading Nashville doctor who was a founder of the HCA health care corporation. In 1998–99, the National Hockey League's Nashville Predators built a second ice rink, for use as a practice facility and training center, that is also open to the public for skating lessons and hockey leagues.

151.

Centennial Medical Center (1992-94)
230 Twenty-fifth Avenue North
Earl Swensson Associates, architects

Centennial Medical Center is a flagship hospital for the HCA health care corporation. By 1991, the firm of Earl Swensson Associates had completed 111 major hospital and medical office building projects nationwide; it used its experience to design this Nashville facility. A concrete, steel, and glass tower centers the building, flanked on either side by multi-story wings. A canopy wraps around the primary facade, uniting the different units into one coherent expression. In its materials, spaces, and aesthetics, Centennial's interior avoids the sterile, repetitive, institutional quality once common in hospital interior design, creating design precedents now found in scores of hospitals across the nation.

The Parthenon and Centennial Park,
Carroll Van West, photographer.

152.

The Parthenon (1920–1931) (NR, LL)
and Centennial Park (NR)

Russell E. Hart and William B. Dinsmoor, architects
Belle Kinney, Leopold Scholz, George Zolnay,
Alan LeQuire, sculptors
Gresham, Smith and Partners, 1986–90 renovation
Quinn-Evans Architects; Tracy Coffing,
conservator; Orion Building Corporation;
Western Waterproofing Company, 1994–2001
exterior restoration
Gustafson Guthrie Nichols, architects,
Centennial Park Master Plan, 2010

The original Nashville Parthenon (1895–97) stood on this site in Centennial Park as the heart of the state's Centennial Exposition. It housed fine arts exhibits and proved so popular that fair organizers decided to leave it in place after the exposition closed in 1897. The original Parthenon of brick, wood, and stucco, however, was not built to last. By 1920, city officials decided to build a full-size replica of the ancient Greek temple as a lasting fine arts center and as a memorial to the city's reputation as the "Athens of the South."

Classics scholar and architect William B. Dinsmoor of New York worked with Nashville architect Russell E. Hart on the design; Foster and Creighton Company was the general contractor. Nashville sculptor Belle Kinney and her husband Leopold

Scholz, along with original Nashville Parthenon sculptor George Zolnay, were commissioned to produce accurate reproductions of the Greek figures that once adorned the pedimented entrances of the temple. Kinney and Scholz traveled to the British Museum in London to study and copy the famous Elgin marbles, taken from the ancient Greek temple.

Key to the building's success was the development of an aggregate concrete finish, designed to resemble marble, since the city lacked funds to rebuild the replica in its original marble. John J. Earley of the Earley Studio of Washington D.C., fresh from his spectacular success in concrete design at the Church of the Sacred Heart in D.C., created the colored concrete necessary for the Parthenon. He used Potomac River gravel, crushed ceramic tile, and quartz in his concrete mix. In its archaeologically correct dimensions and the mere ambition of rebuilding it, the reconstructed Parthenon is an impressive achievement. "It is nearly impossible not to like the Nashville Parthenon," concluded *New York Times* architectural critic Paul Goldberger, "this carefully detailed, well wrought replication of classicism's most celebrated building is utterly well intentioned, without the tiniest hint of cynical commercialism."[5]

A forty-two-foot high statue of Athena, by Nashville sculptor Alan LeQuire, was unveiled in the temple interior in 1990. Like the exterior sculptures by Zolnay, Kinney, and Scholz, Athena too is a historical replica, but made of a mixture of fiberglass and a gypsum cement mixture to simulate the original ivory. In 2002, the Parthenon Patrons raised funds to complete the long-planned gilding and ornamentation of Athena.

By the 1980s, roof, statuary, and various architectural elements of the Parthenon had deteriorated badly. Beginning in 1994, Metro Government committed a total of twelve million dollars to repair and restore the building. The restoration process proved highly complex, requiring methods and skills rarely called for in historic preservation. Orion Building Corporation managed the project; a team comprised of architects, a conservator, Western Waterproofing Company, and various artists also contributed to the successful restoration.

The Parthenon dominates the landscape of Centennial Park, which became a city park in 1903. Since then, city officials and civic groups have added other historical monuments and public facilities. The James Robertson monument honors the Nashville founder and his wife Charlotte Reeves Robertson. The John W. Thomas Memorial (1907), sculpted by Enid Yandell, recognizes the contributions of this turn-of-the-century railroad magnate. Sculptor George Zolnay's World War I memorial was sponsored by the Nashville Kiwanis Club in 1923. The park also contains a marker locating the Nashville terminus of the Natchez Trace. More than twenty other contributing historic structures and features define the Centennial Park landscape, including Wilbur Creighton, Sr.'s, concrete bridge (1910), the Rustic-styled picnic pavilion (1942, 1957), and the classical styled Centennial Art Center (1932, 1962, 1972). This latter building also documents the impact of Jim Crow

segregation on the park's history and landscape. Originally built as the park's swimming pool, city officials in 1962 closed the building and filled in the swimming area rather than integrate the pool. Ten years later, the building was converted into the arts center.

The end of Jim Crow at Centennial Park soon meant, however, that the park was a place for everybody and in the decades since it has become the city's center to celebrate diversity, community, and culture. Several art, theatre and music festivals occur throughout the year.

153.
The Westboro (1914–1923)
3101 West End Avenue
C. K. Colley, architect

This classically-inspired apartment complex is a West End landmark. Designed by Nashville architect C. K. Colley, The Westboro reflects both Classical Revival and late Gothic Revival styles. Prominent Jewish businessmen and cultural leaders lived here, including Bessie Pritz, the only woman practicing architecture in Nashville in the 1920s.

154.
West End Office Buildings
West End Avenue, Thirty-first Avenue North to Murphy Road

The combination of the 1920s Blackstone Apartments, several modernist-styled office buildings from the 1960s to 1980s, and a large landscaped area of large mature trees and a stone wall create one of Midtown's most distinctive places. In 1893, the West End Land Company established a trust, which donated "lawns, roadways, strips of land, and ornamental spots of ground" for the use and benefit of the owners of what was then a row of elegant mansions. Once called Acklen Park for Joseph H. Acklen, the company president and owner of one of the houses, the property is still held in trust.

WEST NASHVILLE

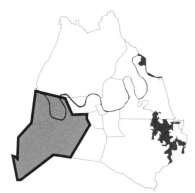

Key Map

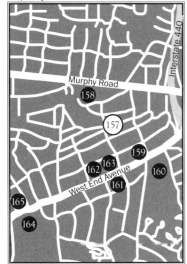

Richland-West End Detail

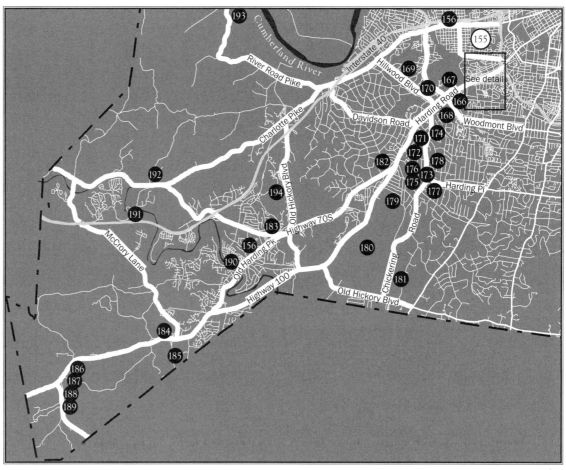

0   1½ mi   3 mi   6 mi

West Nashville
Sylvan Park, Richland-West End, Bellevue to the Natchez Trace

Nashvillians today recognize West Nashville as containing different, yet related, areas. The most prominent is Belle Meade, which was carved from a nationally renowned prize-winning thoroughbred horse farm that once totaled over 5,000 acres. Today elements of the plantation's nineteenth century landscape remain—stone fences, the nearby railroad tracks, open spaces—but they do so within a suburban context that developed rapidly after the creation of the Belle Meade Land Company in 1906. From that point until the onset of the Great Depression in the 1930s, Belle Meade became a suburban enclave, with persistent rural overtones, for Nashville's business and professional elite. In 1938, residents even incorporated themselves as the city of Belle Meade, a separate place within the larger urban landscape of Nashville.

Two other suburban neighborhoods—Richland-West End and Sylvan Park—also developed in the early twentieth century. Richland-West End has the city's best collection of highly stylized bungalows, often with various Classical Revival embellishments in the large, wrap-around front porches. Sylvan Park reflects a more middle-class setting, with homes ranging from small Queen Anne-influenced cottages to brick and frame bungalows.

Compared to the impressive country estates and grand suburban homes of Belle Meade and other West Nashville neighborhoods, the western corner of Davidson County was largely rural, with farms located near the waters of the Harpeth River and crossroad hamlets along the turnpikes and country roads. A few farms such as the Smith Farm remain from the early settlement years.

Syvlan Park, Metro Nashville Historical Commission.

Bell's Bend is a rural landscape nestled along the Cumberland River. The South Harpeth Church of Christ, Newsom's Mill, and the Harpeth school (later Harpeth Civic Club) were among the nineteenth century institutions that served rural people.

Then came the railroad in the late nineteenth century and in the 1920s, the Memphis-to-Bristol Highway, to create small villages and commercial areas. The construction of Interstate Highway I-40 during the 1960s made permanent already developing divisions in the landscape. Between the interstate and the railroad tracks near the old village of Bellevue are concentrations of suburbs and extensive commercial development. Suburban sprawl is moving farther to the west, along both the Old Harding Pike and Highway 100, but once both roads cross the Natchez Trace Parkway at Pasquo, the countryside emerges once again. Portions of the modern Bellevue suburbs were among the hardest hit areas during the May 2010 flood.

Nashville's architecture and history have been shaped by its often close relationship between rural and urban life. The grand mansions, the exclusive suburbs, open spaces, farms, and churches of West Nashville nurture an important source of the city's distinctive character.

155.

Sylvan Park Neighborhood (c. 1902-c. 1950)
Colorado, Nebraska, Nevada, and Park Avenues

Sylvan Park contains an impressive array of turn-of-the-century to early twentieth century domestic architecture, including Queen Anne-influenced frame cottages, American Four-Square houses, and bungalows. Although initial development began around 1902, home building came slowly; many of the extant dwellings were constructed between the two world wars. The house at 4703 Park Avenue is a Classical Revival-influenced Victorian brick house while an excellent frame Queen Anne-style cottage is at 4404 Nebraska Avenue. An American Four-square house is at 4510 Colorado Avenue. Two representative bungalows from the 1920s are at 4209 Nebraska Avenue and 4400 Nebraska Avenue. A Cape Cod cottage, a popular middle-class house style of the immediate post-World War II era, is at 5200 Nevada. A landmark church building is the All Saints Southern Episcopal Church at 4513 Park Avenue; the stone Gothic-styled church was built in 1932.

156.

First American National Bank,
West Nashville branch (1961)
5100 Charlotte Avenue
John A. Preston Associates, architect

This striking, gold-domed building opened as the West Nashville branch of the Nashville-based First American National Bank. Designed by Nashville architect John A. Preston, it features a domed roof of gold anodized aluminum inspired by Buckminster Fuller's patented geodesic dome design. At the time of its grand opening, the bank was described in the *Tennessean* of December 19, 1961 as the "only such [bank] design in the South and one of three in the nation." With its sleek, modernist style, drive-in banking access,

First American National Bank, Metro Nashville Historical Commission.

and plenty of room for parking, the building was designed to provide complete banking services for the growing West Nashville suburbs.

John A. Preston was a respected and prolific late twentieth century Nashville architect, with residential, commercial, and institutional designs. He studied and worked with Donald W. Southgate as a draftsman and designer from 1946 to 1953, the year he received his architecture certificate. He soon branched out on his own, designing an addition to the Madison High School in 1954, and the Inglewood Baptist Church in 1955 as well as an addition to the Fidelity Federal Savings and Loan building. In 1956 he established the firm of John A. Preston Associates. Prior to the commission for the First American West Branch Bank, Preston had designed the Learner Lab Building (1960) at Vanderbilt University. The firm took on multiple projects for the Seventh Day Adventist Church in Madison, including a new church building in 1970–71 and a large International-style addition to the Madison Hospital in 1972.

157.

Richland-West End Historic District (c. 1905–1930) (NR, CZ)

From 1905 to 1930, the Richland-West End neighborhood developed along West End, Richland, Central, and Westbrook Avenues between Park Circle and Wilson Boulevard. It originally was a homogeneous white community of middle to upper-middle class merchants and professionals. Protective covenants maintained not only its residential character but also forbade the industrial and commercial use of most lots, producing today a street grid of comfortable homes, and churches. Skillfully crafted homes were built in varied sizes, from different materials, and of diverse architectural styles. Landscaped medians along Richland Avenue, an influence of the turn-of-the-century City Beautiful Movement, gave the neighborhood a distinct sense of scale and balance.

In 1905, the Richland Realty Company purchased a large portion of the antebellum estate of John B. Craighead, whose circa 1811 house still stands at 3710 Westbrook Avenue. Development was underway by the following year, but most of the neighborhood took shape from subdivisions between 1910 and 1913. Many dwellings are bungalows; Westbrook and Princeton Avenues have many good examples. Near West End, along Richland Avenue, the bungalows are often adorned with elements of classicism, from stone quoins and Palladian windows to classical column porches and entrances. Brick is the primary construction materials and many homes have tile roofs.

The American Four-Square, with classical embellishments, is prevalent on Richland and Central Avenues. Dwellings built in the 1920s and later were often designed in Colonial Revival or Tudor Revival style.

158.

Craighead House (c. 1811) (NR)
3710 Westbrook Avenue

Craighead House, Carroll Van West, photographer.

West End High School, Gary Layda, photographer, Courtesy of Metro Nashville Historical Commission.

A three bay symmetrical facade dignifies this Federal style home. With its exterior end chimneys, Flemish bond brick facade, and two-story size, the Craighead House is a perfect example of the hall-parlor dwelling of the early settlement era. The initial residents were John B. Craighead, son of famous Nashville educator and religious leader Thomas B. Craighead, and Jane Erwin Dickinson Craighead. After the death of his wife Jane, Craighead married Lavinia Robertson Beck, the daughter of Nashville founders James and Charlotte Robertson. Charlotte Robertson lived here until her death at the age of ninety-three in 1843.

159.
Welch Library (1907)
3606 West End Avenue

Originally a Colonial Revival-influenced American Four-square dwelling built by businessman Edward M. Neal, this impressive stone house, with its projecting classical entrance and hipped clay tile roof with dormer windows, served as the Welch Library of Free Will Baptist Bible College, now Welch College. The college opened its doors in 1942. At its West End Avenue location, the college maintained a campus of new buildings and preserved historic homes from the early twentieth century. In 2007, the college purchased land in Sumner County, and officials in 2015 announced the sale of the historic campus.

160.
West End High School (1935–37) (NR)
3529 West End Avenue
Donald Southgate, architect

Donald Southgate's Colonial Revival design for West End High School was a major, yet completely successful, exception to the modernist designs for public schools and buildings often funded by the Public Works Administration in Nashville during the New Deal. Its soaring 122-foot high cupola with clock is one of West Nashville's best known architectural landmarks. With its horizontal three-story central block serving as a focal point for a large landscaped city lot along busy West End Avenue, the school was meant to be, and is, an impressive statement of the place of public education in twentieth century American culture.

The traditionalism of the school's exterior, however, masked a progressive educational institution, stocked with the latest in technology and hardware. The school initially had thirty-five classrooms, with eight designed for science classes. It had a large library, cafeteria, gymnasium, and a modern auditorium, complete with a 63-by-28-foot stage.

Washington Hall, Gary Layda, photographer,
Courtesy of Metro Nashville Historical Commission.

161.

Washington Hall (1912–14)

3700 Whitland Avenue

A unique example of Adamesque Revival style in Nashville, Washington Hall was built by Judge John B. Daniels. Businessman, senator, and newspaperman Luke Lea lived here from 1936 until his death in 1945. In the facade's octagonal dome and one-story pedimented portico, the stone and brick house represented a conscious attempt to replicate Thomas Jefferson's Monticello in a modern manner. Its construction came at the same time that the George Peabody College of Teachers—which reflected the influence of Jefferson's design for the University of Virginia—was also under construction in Nashville. The gardens were designed in a Colonial Revival fashion, complete with boxwoods and magnolia trees.

162.

West End Synagogue (1947–50)

3814 West End Avenue
Percival Goodman, New York City, architect

This brick and stone synagogue reflects the post-war expansion of Nashville residents, and their social and cultural institutions, into the southwestern corner of the county. The building is a successful regional interpretation of International style, with its horizontal bands of brick and concrete, its flat roof, a breath-taking open interior, and a central courtyard.

The West End Synagogue is home to Congregation Adath Israel, which dates to 1876. The congregation received its first full-time rabbi in 1897 and five years later, it dedicated a new synagogue on Gay Street downtown. This historic building was demolished in the post-war Capitol Hill Redevelopment Plan; the congregation purchased this West End property and built the present synagogue.

The historic cemetery for Congregation Adath Israel is located on Cass Street in North Nashville, with the cemeteries for Sherith Israel Congregation and Congregation Ohabai Sholom adjoining it. Each cemetery contains significant examples of gravestone art, which reflect Jewish traditions and craftsmanship.

163.

The Gladstone (1923) (NR)
3803 West End Avenue
Charles A. Ferguson, architect

Real estate developer Morris Fisher built The Gladstone to meet the increasing demand for up-scale apartments along West End Avenue. Its large, multi-paned windows, the use of limestone and brick, and the half-timbering apparent in the gables make it an excellent example of Tudor Revival style, as adapted to a three-story apartment building. Ferguson (b. 1869) was an active Nashville architect in the first third of the twentieth century. Before the commission for the Gladstone Apartments, for example, he was the designer of Pearl High School (1916–17), the Langsford House on Gallatin Pike (1916), and an apartment complex for Thomas F. Murray and Company in 1917.

164.

Montgomery Bell Academy (1927)
4001 Harding Road
Tuck Hinton Architects, 1991–98 renovation and expansion

On a rise facing Harding Road is the distinguished historic campus of Montgomery Bell Academy, which for decades has been a respected private school for boys. The school is named in honor of its first major benefactor, Montgomery Bell, who amassed a fortune from antebellum-era iron mines and mills in adjacent Dickson County.

In 1915, a year after the opening of the Belle Meade streetcar line, the school moved from Rutledge Hill to Garland Tinsley's "Totomoi," a Georgian Revival estate on Harding Pike. Here the academy prospered as a country day school, which had the best features of boarding schools without separating the boys from their families.

In 1922, fire destroyed most of the original buildings. The new campus of three-story red brick buildings, each graced with porticoes of classical columns, conveyed Classical Revival style, in keeping with the earlier style of "Totomoi." At the heart of campus was the Isaac Ball Memorial Hall, the main administration building. Various other buildings were constructed in the post-World War II decades as attendance increased and new programs were introduced.

From 1991 to 1998, MBA commissioned Tuck Hinton Architects to develop a Master Plan in addition to designing a new Fine Arts Building, which contains classrooms, cafeteria, and a six

hundred-seat auditorium. By the end of the century, new brick classroom buildings and facilities joined with the earlier historic buildings to create the modern MBA campus.

165.

Overbrook Mansion (1911–13, 1992) (NR)

4210 Harding Road

Everton Oglesby Askew, architects, 1990s renovation

Built by Nashville capitalist Joseph Warner, this two-story brick, stuccoed, and painted white mansion is the historic focal point of the Dominican Campus of Nashville and is called the White

House by the Dominican Sisters of St. Cecelia. Its graceful seven-bay facade balances the first floor's fanlighted double doors with three recessed double doors and one-over-one windows on the second floor. The dentilled cornice is topped by a balustraded parapet and a slate roof with gable dormers. The central hall plan interior retains many of its original Colonial Revival features, including paneled wainscoting, heavy crown molding, and pocket doors. The entrance hall's large dogleg staircase and tall mantel with paired Tuscan columns remain majestic and impressive.

In 1923, Warner sold the house and extensive grounds to the Dominican Sisters, who established Overbrook School at the mansion in 1936. Seven years later, the house was converted into a convent and was used for that purpose until 1989. At that time, the Sisters commissioned Tuck Hinton Everton Architects to prepare a master plan to guide future building and preservation at the Dominican campus, which includes Overbrook Mansion, Overbrook School, St. Cecilia Academy, and Aquinas Junior College. Nashville architects Everton Oglesby Askew carried out renovations of the Overbrook Mansion in the late 1990s.

166.
Belle Meade Theater (1939–40)
4301 Harding Road
Marr and Holman, architects

This Art Moderne landmark was one of the city's most popular, and spectacular, movie theaters of the mid-twentieth century. The combination of bright neon lights and streamlined exterior Georgia marble walls with metal casement windows turned the theater into a virtual three-dimensional advertisement for the entertainment business. The theater opened on May 1, 1940; on that same day, the adjacent Moon Drug Company opened its doors and remained in business until 1997. The theater's elaborate external and internal lighting system was by the Federal Electric Company of Chicago and Nashville's Braid Electric and Deaderick Electric companies. In 1991, the theater closed and was converted into a retail space.

167.
Imperial House Apartments (1961)
111 Bosley Springs Road
Earl Swensson Associates, architects

An early Nashville project of Earl Swensson Associates, this twelve-story concrete and steel high-rise apartment complex, with projecting individual balconies, reflects the "contemporary" style

Imperial House Apartments, AIA Middle Tennessee.

aesthetic and effectively introduced modern apartment design to the city. It is one of the city's great modernist buildings from the Space Age of the early 1960s.

168.

Lynmeade (1913)

105 Lynwood Boulevard
J. Edwin Carpenter and Russell Hart, architects

Lynmeade's French Chateauesque style—marked by decorative iron balconies, steep tile roof, and French interior design—was one of the last Nashville commissions by architect J. Edwin Carpenter before he left his native Tennessee to build his career in New York City. Carpenter designed the twenty-room mansion for his brother John Carpenter, who became rich in the phosphate industry of Maury County.

In 1951, the house was left to Vanderbilt University, which used it for a time as the official residence of Chancellors Harvie Branscomb and Alexander Heard. Clearly visible at the point where Harding Road enters the eastern end of Belle Meade, Lynmeade has long been a residential landmark for this elegant suburb.

169.

Richard and Margaret Martin House (1956) (NR)

825 Kendall Drive
R. Bruce Draper, architect

Nashville has few domestic designs that reflect the architectural ideas of famed American architect of Frank Lloyd Wright; the Martin House, commissioned by Dr. Richard Martin and his wife Margaret in 1956, may be the best example. Bruce Draper, born in Gainesboro, Tennessee, in 1927, was a student at the University of Chicago when he took a tour of the campus's Robie House (1909), one of Wright's best Prairie-style homes, as part of a class requirement. The tour changed his career—Draper gave up studies in meteorology and moved to Wright's Taliesin Fellowship in Wisconsin to study with Wright from 1948 to 1950.

The Martins worked closely with the architect in the design of this two-story brick and weatherboard multi-plane roof dwelling, a good example of the "Usonian" house design that Wright advocated for the American middle class from the late 1930s to the end of his career in 1959. Draper's use of large glass windows and the open floor plan centered around a huge fireplace conveyed well Wright's ideas of how a house and its environment should mesh together to create living space.

The Martin House was Draper's first important independent Nashville commission, although he had worked as a designer with Marr and Holman earlier in the decade. Most of his early commissions came from the Cumberland Plateau, where he designed a shirt factory (1955) and elementary school (1957) in his native Gainesboro, the Citizens Bank Building (1956) in Lafayette, and several elementary schools in Wilson County in 1958–59. In 1963, Draper designed the Nashville's First Unitarian Universalist Church at 1808 Woodmont Boulevard in a similar Wright fashion as found at the Martin House.

170.

Cliff Lawn (1910–11)

101 Hillwood Drive

Marr and Holman, architects

Nashville merchant Horace G. Hill, Sr., commissioned this early design from the firm of Marr and Holman. Like other mansions of the time, the house blends elements from various early American architectural traditions in a massive composition that harkens to the Classical Revival of ten years earlier while individual design elements are more closely related to the emerging fashion for the Colonial Revival. For instance, the entrance's semi-elliptical fanlight, dormer windows, stone lintels, and lunette in the portico pediment belong to the Georgian and Federal periods. The paired Ionic fluted columns, especially the four two-story columns at the east gable end, reflect Greek Revival traditions.

The interior design is firmly Colonial Revival, with hand-carved pediments over the doorways and a stairway copied from one taken from the John Hancock house in Boston, as preserved at the Metropolitan Museum of Art in New York. Landscaped gardens in a Colonial Revival style are also extant.

171.

Braeburn (1914)

211 Deer Park Drive

Christian H. Asmus, architect

Six fluted Corinthian columns, supporting a classical entablature topped by an ornate balustrade, dominate the facade of this gracious Colonial Revival stone house. Braeburn is Scottish for "Hill Above the Creek." As one of the first completed Belle Meade residences, it established a tradition of Colonial Revival domestic architecture that later owners followed in the design of their residences. Ida E. Hood and Susan L. Herron, the founders of Belmont College and the Ward-Belmont College for women, built Braeburn as their retirement home. Its landscaped grounds were once part of the deer park of Belle Meade plantation.

172.

Belle Meade Plantation (c. 1820, 1853, 1870s) (NR)

5025 Harding Road

While beginning the work of directing his family and slaves in the building of Belle Meade Plantation in 1807, John Harding resided with his family in a log dwelling, which was later expanded to a dog-trot, meaning two single-pen cabins connected by a single gable roof with an open breezeway between the cabins. Quickly turning Belle Meade into a prosperous antebellum plantation of over one thousand acres and fifty slaves, Harding built a two-story brick Federal style house by 1820. The family later established,

Belle Meade Plantation, Gary Layda, photographer, Courtesy of Metro Nashville Historical Commission.

along today's Jackson Boulevard, a deep park that by 1854 held about two hundred deer and fourteen buffalo. Bob Green, a former slave, directed the plantation's development of prize-winning breeds of horses.

The Greek Revival appearance of the manor house may date to 1853–54 when John Harding's son William Giles Harding probably designed and directed his slaves in making major exterior and interior changes. Stucco was placed over the original brick to give the dwelling a white masonry look. Slaves also added a two-story portico of six limestone columns, topped by a pediment with carved stone finials and a shell and scroll pattern. The interior was updated with new mantels, woodwork, wallpaper, and furniture. Belle Meade was now an antebellum showplace with few equals in Middle Tennessee.

After the plantation recovered from the ravages of the Civil War, Harding expanded the manor house again in the 1870s. During the 1880s came new architectural landmarks in a Victorian styled stable and carriage house. The stable is a huge two-story frame barn, with its primary facade marked by triple Gothic gables and two Queen Anne-influenced cupolas.

In 1886, William H. Jackson inherited the more than 5,300-acre plantation. Jackson continued alterations of the house's interior as he further enhanced the national reputation of the stock farm. When Belle Meade sold for subdivision in 1904, it was the largest and oldest thoroughbred farm in the country.

The manor house remained a private home until 1953 when the state acquired it as a historic site. The following year, the Association for the Preservation of Tennessee Antiquities opened the property as a historic house and plantation museum.

173.

Belle Meade Boulevard (1909-10)
Ossian Cole Simonds, architect

This is one of Nashville's best known streets. In 1909, the Belle Meade Land Company commissioned architect Ossian Cole Simonds, one of the leading landscape architects in the country, to design its new subdivision, then called Belle Meade Park. To open the old plantation fields for new house lots, Simonds designed several new streets, the most important being a road to connect Harding Pike to the Lower Franklin Road, about three miles away. A noted cemetery designer, Simonds produced a curving street plan that adapted to the natural contours of the landscape. His plan was never fully realized, however, because the land company encountered financial difficulties. By December 1910, Luke Lea and a group of local investors controlled the land company. Lea approached the Nashville Street Railway and Light Company to build a four-mile-long streetcar track from the end of its line at Wilson Boulevard to what is now Percy Warner Park. Lea even promised to underwrite the cost of the line extension and to provide a macadam boulevard twenty feet wide on both sides of the streetcar line. This streetcar line later became the route of today's Belle Meade Boulevard. As fine homes, apartments, churches, and parks were built along the elegant drive over the next two decades, the boulevard became the centerpiece of the Belle Meade neighborhood.

174.

Immanuel Baptist Church (1954)

222 Belle Meade Boulevard
Edwin A. Keeble, architect

With its soaring tower serving as an ecclesiastical landmark on
Belle Meade Boulevard, the Immanuel Baptist Church is one
of Edwin Keeble's most gracious interpretations of classical
architecture. Established in 1887, the congregation held services
at Stonewall and Hayes Street before building a new sanctuary at
Seventeenth and Broadway in 1913. The congregation moved to
Belle Meade in 1954.

175.

Belle Meade Country Club (1914–16)

815 Belle Meade Boulevard
Edward E. Dougherty, architect

The clubhouse of the Belle Meade Country Club effectively
expresses such elements of Colonial Revival style as columns,
dormers, shingles, gambrel roofs, limestone and brick chimneys,
and balustrades, which give individual charm to what otherwise
would be a long and repetitive facade. Dougherty's design bor-
rowed ideas from famous Southern resorts, like the Greenbrier
in the Virginia Appalachians, places that Belle Meade residents
already knew and enjoyed. Colonial Revival style proved very
popular for southern country clubs, in general, since the modern

Immanuel Baptist
Church, Metro Nashville
Historical Commission.

southern elite could equate their success and lifestyle with that of the planter class of the colonial and antebellum eras.

Belle Meade Links Triangle (1925–1950) (NR, CZ)

Harding Place, Westover Avenue, Blackburn Avenue, Windsor Drive, and Pembroke Avenue

Begun in 1915, the Belle Meade Links District occupies approximately 43 acres, immediately adjacent to the Belle Meade golf course, from which it derives its name. The pattern and orientation of the streets represents a significant departure from the grid pattern common in the early twentieth century. Early developers deliberately made the neighborhood park-like, with careful attention to curving roads, many trees, and the inclusion of three parks, complete with fully developed landscape plans, within its borders. Unlike many of the houses in the City of Belle Meade, this district reflects the Small House Movement of the time. From 1919 to 1942, the Architects' Small House Service Bureau advocated for and published designs for model "small homes," similar to those of the district, where the homes were mostly built between 1925 and 1938. The Bureau pushed Colonial Revival, Tudor Revival, and Bungalow designs in their many publications. Later homes from the 1940s and 1950s in the district include Cape Cod cottages and Minimal Traditional house designs.

Gardner-Warner Place (1917)

4415 Harding Road
Thomas A. Gardner, architect

Gardner, a local architect and partner of Edward Dougherty, built this creative interpretation of Colonial Revival domestic architecture as his personal dwelling. Its horizontal massing is similar to long, rambling Virginia manor houses of the early 1700s, but the dwelling's low hipped roof and overhanging eaves suggest that Gardner's design was also influenced by the Prairie house style. The Robert Warner family later acquired the property as their Belle Meade residence.

Auburn (1931)

4410 Howell Place
A. Herbert Rogers, architect

The general design of this neo-Greek Revival mansion was inspired by a circa 1812 house, also named Auburn, which stood in Natchez, Mississippi. The four colossal Ionic columns and denticulated pediment of the two-story portico are certainly associated with Deep South plantation architecture. The interior design, executed by local craftsmen, is of special value. The main hallway has a dramatic free standing staircase, reaching from the first to second floors. Carved pineapples, columns, shell designs,

Auburn, Metro Nashville Historical Commission.

and a library paneled with cypress combine to produce a refined statement of Colonial Revival decorative arts.

179.

Cheekwood (1929–32, 1971) (NR)

1200 Forrest Park Drive

Bryant Fleming, Ithaca, New York, architect

R. Neil Bass, Nashville, architect

Cheekwood, built for the Leslie Cheek family in the Depression Era, holds a significant place in the twentieth century architec-

tural history of Nashville. Its setting reflects architect Bryant Fleming's love for the eighteenth-century English country house. He successfully translated to a southern suburban setting the eighteenth-century tradition of an irregular garden design where every element seems to be rooted in nature, be they the various water features, the statues, the rock-lined walks and pools, or the attractive shapes of ornamental metal, all centered on the opulent manor house. Perhaps Cheekwood's best example of this is at the northwest gardens, where ornamental metal balustrades by Philip Kerrigan, Jr., combine with stone walls, stone steps, stone pedestals, two lead Roosters, two iron urns, and a marble Cherubic Bacchus urn to create a place of incongruity, surprise, and variety.

Cheekwood is also important to the history of decorative arts and interior design in Nashville. The various English and European antiques were combined with the outstanding craftsmanship of local masters such as metal master Philip Kerrigan, Jr.; Harold V. Hopton, whose Nashville firm executed the plaster work; and Leo Barthle of Memphis, who led the carpenters who carved the mansion's exquisite woodwork. Kerrigan's work is particularly impressive. Cheekwood was his first major commission and there he made a lasting friendship with Fleming, who expanded the young craftsman's understanding and appreciation of nature and historical European traditions in ornamental metal. They worked together on many other commissions after Cheekwood. Contemporaries also praised Kerrigan's Cheekwood designs for their revival of the ornamental metal arts in the city in particular and in the South in general.

Cheekwood, Carroll Van West,
photographer.

Kerrigan's work provides an important visual link between the gardens and house. To Fleming, the house should not only extend into the gardens, but the gardens should extend into the house, fusing the two components into one coherent design. In Fleming's conception of Cheekwood, the landscape and not the mansion was the focal point of the design, a reality admitted early in written accounts about Cheekwood. In the *Tennessean* of April 20, 1952, writer Louise Davis observed that "it is easy to believe that the house was made to grace the gardens."

In 1959, Walter and Huldah Cheek Sharp deeded the estate to the Tennessee Botanical Gardens and Fine Arts Center, which converted the mansion into an art museum. Despite the change in function, many interior decorative features remain intact and visible, enhanced by a sensitive restoration to the manor house carried out in the late 1990s.

Although contemporary in design, the Botanic Hall (1971) by Nashville architect Neil Bass relates well to the overall Cheekwood landscape. Its style reflects the spirit of New Formalism while its concrete exterior mimics the masonry of the manor house. The hall's interior curvilinear plan creates large spaces for public meetings and displays as well as incorporating vistas from the surrounding landscaped gardens. As appropriate for a botanical center, nature remains within reach in this modern setting.

180.

Warner Parks (1927–1938) (NR)

Belle Meade Boulevard, Old Hickory Boulevard, Highway 100
Edward Dougherty, Bryant Fleming, Works Progress Administration, architects

With over 3,100 acres, the Warner Parks together comprise one of the largest municipal parks in the country. Most of the land was acquired and developed over twenty years. In 1927, Luke Lea of the Belle Meade Land Company donated 868 acres for the creation of a city park, named for his father-in-law Percy Warner, at the end of Belle Meade Boulevard. Three years later, Edwin Warner donated $20,000 for future land acquisition. Under his guidance as a park board member (1927–39) and board chairman (1939 to 1949), the park grew to near its present size. In 1937, 606 acres of undeveloped land were named Edwin Warner Park in his honor, but despite the dual names, the two adjacent parks are operated as a single entity.

Lea and the Warner family commissioned two architects to design the park's initial features. Edward Dougherty designed the Beaux Arts-style gate at the Belle Meade Boulevard entrance in 1932. At that same time, Bryant Fleming designed the multi-tiered allee that climbs 875 feet up to the park's first major hill. But most development came under the New Deal's Works Progress Administration. The work crews constructed a golf course, seven limestone entrance gates, two limestone bridges, thirty-seven picnic shelters, and miles of limestone retaining walls, roads, bridle paths, and trails. Using the design of sportsman William I. DuPont, Jr., the federal agency even constructed a riding academy and the famed Iroquois steeplechase course from 1936 to 1941. The steeplechase course and two golf courses may be reached from Old Hickory Boulevard.

The expenditure of so much WPA time, effort, and money, at what was initially a park for the Belle Meade elite, became extremely controversial. But as more and more Nashvillians acquired automobiles after World War II, the park became accessible to most whites; integration of public facilities in the early 1960s finally opened the park to all Nashvillians. Despite the controversy at the time, the WPA's projects left an impressive legacy of Rustic-styled park architecture and landscape features, from the entrance gates, shelters, and bridges to the trails and paths now enjoyed by many Nashville families. In 2000, the Friends of Warner Parks completed a new facility, the Warner Parks Nature Center.

Within the park is an important example of early Nashville domestic design, the Hodge House, which began as a log cabin c. 1797 and then had a two-story log addition c. 1811. The home was later covered with weatherboard. When the park was developed in the 1920s and 1930s, the Hodge House became a park employee residence. In 2008, a careful restoration of the house was finished and the dwelling is now periodically open for tours.

Small World, Tuck Hinton Architects.

181.

Small World (1992–93)
1644 Chickering Road
Tuck Hinton Architects, architects

Across the road from the rustic-styled limestone gates of Percy Warner Park, framed by a forested hillside, is one of the city's most remarkable examples of Postmodern domestic architecture. Sculptural effects taken from Art Deco, Art Moderne, and International styles, as well as twentieth century decorative arts, mesh together in an imaginative and expressive manner. The various

West Meade, Gary Layda, photographer, Courtesy of Metro Nashville Historical Commission.

materials, textures, shapes, and colors created an instant domestic architectural landmark, one in sharp contrast to the adjacent open, bucolic spaces of Percy Warner Park.

182.
West Meade (1886) (NR)
6204 Old Harding Pike

This Second Empire-influenced, three-story red brick country house was home to Howell E. Jackson, attorney, jurist, U.S. Senator, and U.S. Supreme Court Justice. Its mansard roof, iron cresting, and irregular shape are typical Second Empire characteristics. The interior is based on a traditional central hall plan, but it features such Victorian details as louvered shades, carved newel post, and eight-foot high pocket doors between two large parlors. In 1944, Ronald and Margaret Price Voss acquired the home and made changes, including the removal of some iron cresting from the exterior while adding marble mantels, ceiling woodwork, and white wainscoting in the interior.

The property was once part of the Belle Meade thoroughbred horse plantation. In 1880, General William G. Harding gave 2,600 acres to his daughter Mary Elizabeth Harding, who married Howell Jackson. Twentieth-century suburbs and modern roads now surround the old manor house.

183.
Devon Farm (c. 1798) (NR) at Ensworth School
Hicks Road off Tennessee Highway 100

Settled by Virginia planter Giles Harding circa 1798, Devon Farm was initially centered around a one and one-half story Flemish bond brick house. In 1816, his son Morris Harding inherited the homeplace and married Fanny Davis. As his family and his farm began to expand, c. 1820, Harding enlarged the house. Within a two-story, common bond brick wing expansion of the original dwelling, he added a large parlor, bedroom, entrance, and classically influenced columned porches. This new wing, with its central hall linking the 1798 house and the addition, became the dwelling's primary entrance. Called Oak Hill, the house reflected Federal style, with the two different sections blending into a unique L-shaped vernacular house.

In the late nineteenth century, owner Edward D. Hicks, II, renamed the property Devon Farm to emphasize his business of breeding English Devon cattle. In 1976, this still productive family farm was listed as one of two Tennessee Century Farms in Davidson County. By the end of the century, however, most of the farm land was sold for residential development. In 2001 the house and 127 acres was acquired as the site of Ensworth High School, which was designed by architects Graham Gund of Cambridge, Massachusetts, in association with Hastings and Associates.

Smith Farmhouse, Carroll Van West, photographer.

184.

Smith Farmhouse (c. 1815–1825, c. 1840, c. 1874, c. 1920) (NR, LL)

8600 Highway 100

Located to the immediate west of the Pasquo entrance to the Natchez Trace Parkway, the Smith Farm is recognized as a Tennessee Century Farm, one of only five in Davidson County. The Smith Farmhouse began in 1815 as a one and one-half story single-pen log cabin, built by storeowner and farmer James H. Smith. About ten years later, the log cabin was expanded into a three-bay dogtrot dwelling, with limestone chimneys at the gable ends. During the prosperous decades after the depression of 1837, the Smith family, like many Middle Tennessee farmers, chose to improve their log home in a classical style. They cut weatherboards to cover the original logs while a wooden porch of Doric columns was added to the facade.

Little happened to the house for the next thirty years. As prosperity returned to Tennessee agriculture in the 1870s, the dwelling received an architectural update, this time in vernacular Victorian style, probably by Walter S. Smith who acquired the property in 1874. Walter Smith replaced the heavy Doric column porch with a veranda of decorative turned posts, sawn brackets, and a spindle frieze. The last changes probably came circa 1920 during the "Better Homes, Better Farms" movement, which urged Colonial Revival-styled improvements to Tennessee farmhouses. Charles Benjamin Smith owned the property at this time. He centered a dormer window on the roof and installed a new multi-light entrance door with sidelights.

Compared to the many spectacular rural residences in this collection, the Smith Farmhouse might seem too commonplace to recognize. But the significance of this rural dwelling actually lies in its very commonplace character. Homes like these, which expanded over time, often in step with changes in agricultural production and philosophies, were once dominant elements of the rural landscape. As family farmers have disappeared in the last half of the twentieth century so have their houses. Those that survive today deserve careful recordation and preservation.

185.

Natchez Trace Parkway (1938–96)

National Park Service and Figg Engineering Group, Tallahassee, Florida

The Natchez Trace Parkway (1938–1996) is a federal recreational highway that traces its beginnings to the New Deal of Franklin D. Roosevelt. Parkways of long, landscaped stretches of limited access road were popular design concepts in the 1920s and 1930s. One of the longest was this landscaped drive from Natchez, Mississippi, to Nashville. Congress established the Natchez Trace Parkway in 1938 and work crews from the Civilian Conservation Corps and the Works Progress Administration began its construction almost immediately. But before the parkway was complete, demands for men and material during World War II stopped construction; after the war, Congress lost interest in this type of large

Old Harpeth School, Gary Layda, photographer,
Courtesy of Metro Nashville Historical Commission.

public works project. Future construction was funded in a piece-meal fashion and the last section in Tennessee, from Highway 96 in Williamson County to Highway 100 at Pasquo, opened in 1996.

186.

Old Harpeth School (c. 1880)
8407 Old Harding Road

The one-story rectangular-shaped Harpeth school was built c. 1880. Twentieth century public schools often follow standardized

architectural plans, but remaining school buildings from the late nineteenth century are rarely standardized in any manner, save for their building materials (typically frame) and size (usually one story in height). This building is notable for its off-centered gable entrance, with the eaves decorated with Eastlake-influenced detailing. Four square wooden piers, decorated by a spindle frieze, support the oversized center gable, which breaks the monotony of the facade's repetitive window bays.

The consolidation of rural schools in the twentieth century transferred the school's students to more modern and progressive schoolhouses, but rural families continued to use the building as a local community clubhouse, until its sale in 2005.

187.

Beech Grove (c1850, 1920) (NR)
8423 Old Harding Pike

Beech Grove is an excellent example of how West Nashville farms adapted and changed from the 1850s to the 1950s. Thomas Jefferson Allison inherited the farm in 1835 and c. 1850 he hired local carpenters Thomas Jones and Caleb Lucas to build an expansive two-house, central hall I-house on a hill overlooking the property. The new house matched his status as an important, politically connected member of the planter class. He owned 1,150 acres and 22 slaves and also operated a gristmill, store, and blacksmith shop. By the end of the decade, Allison owned 43 slaves. The Civil War and Reconstruction eras changed those fortunes as the farm's proximity to the railroad, the Harpeth River, and local turnpikes brought foragers and armies. Emancipation meant that his slaves left and what had been an antebellum plantation became a middle-class Tennessee farm.

The farm's barns, cribs, and chicken coop document how the family rebounded in the first half of the twentieth century. Allie Morton, a granddaughter, and her husband Sam transformed the farm from cotton and grain production to one yielding dairy products, eggs, breeded livestock, and burley tobacco. Allie Morton also made significant changes to the house, adding a Colonial Revival portico and Craftsman-styled interior features, and modernizing with plumbing and electricity.

188.

Johnson-Linton House House (circa 1880)
8722 Old Harding Pike

Built at an unknown date in the late nineteenth century, the symmetrical five-bay Johnson-Linton House is an excellent example of the vernacular dwelling type called the "upright and wing" house, with Italianate-influenced paired brackets decorating the cornice.

189.

South Harpeth Church of Christ (1845)
8727 Old Harding Pike

The unadorned original brick church of the South Harpeth Church of Christ, distinguished by its gable end entrance of two symmetrically placed doors with plain stone lintels, has served a local Church of Christ congregation for over 150 years. In the mid-twentieth century, members connected a new sanctuary to the older building. Adjacent to the church is an outstanding example of a nineteenth century rural cemetery, with representative gravestone markers from the early settlement period to more recent times. The hand-laid limestone wall dates to the construction of the brick church, about 1845. Together, the church and cemetery

South Harpeth Church of Christ, Gary Layda, photographer, Courtesy of Metro Nashville Historical Commission.

document the religious life and settlement patterns of rural Davidson County.

The church location dates to 1812 and the congregation is the oldest Church of Christ in Davidson County. Among the early ministers were Tolbert Fanning, William Anderson, J. C. McQuiddy, James A. Harding, and David Lipscomb.

190.

Thompson-Dunlap House (1910–12) (NR)

7544 Old Harding Road

For almost sixty years, this vernacular Gothic style building was home to Bellevue Methodist Church until the congregation moved to a new building in 1969. In the mid-1970s, owners converted the church into a residence, retaining such historic Gothic exterior features as the tower and lancet windows. Due to suburban expansion in the 1990s, however, the original rural setting of the church has disappeared.

191.

Newsom's Mill (1862) (NR)

Newsom's Station Road, Harpeth River State Park

Water-powered mills were once common in Davidson County. Typically frame structures, most were abandoned by 1900 and the very few that survive today are often nothing more than industrial ruins. Newsom's Mill, handsomely constructed in hand-dressed limestone in 1862, is the only mill left in the Big Harpeth area of

Newsom's Mill, Metro Nashville Historical Commission.

Davidson County and is an excellent example of mid-nineteenth century stone masonry. Builder Joseph C. Newsom took the limestone from the Newsom Quarry, about one mile south of the river. The mill house measured approximately thirty-eight by forty-six feet and was at least forty feet in height. The mill dam was rebuilt in concrete in 1907. The turbine-powered complex remained largely intact until a fire in 1960 destroyed the wooden roof and flooring.

Around the mill was once a small rural trade center, which expanded in size and importance as a railroad stop—called

Newsom's Station—in the late nineteenth century. In 1905, James Ezzell acquired the property and used mill power to operate the Ezzell Mill and Stone Company from circa 1912 to 1930.

In 1974, the Tennessee Department of Conservation acquired the property and developed it as a historic site about the state's mill industry. The park has informative interpretive markers about the mill's history and the process of nineteenth century milling.

192.

Hows-Madden House (circa 1830, 1880, 1920) (NR)

7401 Huntwick Trail

This impressive rural dwelling is a significant example of a frame two-story five-bay I-house, first constructed circa 1830 but expanded with a one-story frame addition circa 1880. Then circa 1920, at about the time of the construction of the Memphis-to-Bristol Highway that passes in front of the property, the owners altered the original portico by creating a projecting second-story room and adding decorative millwork to the central cross gable of the facade.

193.

Dozier Farm (circa 1842, 1955) (NR)

8451 River Road Pike

This brick two-story symmetrical three-bay house, with central hall plan, has the key characteristics of a folk house type called the I-house. In 1955, the owners expanded the dwelling with brick one-story wings and a two-story Colonial Revival portico.

Dozier Farm, Carroll Van West, photographer.

The farmstead has several historic outbuildings, including a mid-nineteenth century log dwelling, a log corn crib, and a circa 1935 tenant house. Near the dwelling are two chicken houses—typically a farm production space managed by the farm wife and children—from the 1930s.

Hindu Cultural Center of Tennessee, Metro Nashville Historical Commission.

194.

Hindu Cultural Center of Tennessee (c. 1990)

521 Old Hickory Boulevard

Muthiah Sthapathi, Chennai, India, architect

The Hindu Cultural Center, designed by noted temple architect Muthiah Sthapathi of India, reflects the architectural traditions of the Chola dynasty, which reigned in south India from 850 to 1200 AD. Its statement of traditional Indian design makes an important contribution to the city's architectural diversity.

195.

Belle Vue (c. 1800, 1802, 1820) (NR)

7306 Old Harding Road

As different owners made their marks on this distinguished vernacular dwelling during the first two decades of the nineteenth century, Belle Vue became one of the most interesting antebellum plantation houses in West Nashville. John Garrett built the original log house before 1800; two years later, Thomas Harding expanded the dwelling by adding a two-story frame hall and parlor section.

In about 1820, Abram and Betsy Demoss created Belle Vue's present appearance by expanding the two-bay hall and parlor wing with a larger three-bay frame wing. The central bay of the new five-bay facade became the home's entrance hall. They named the new home "Belle Vue" in honor of the family's early log homeplace.

The Belle Vue of 1820 had a unique profile. Combining the sections of 1802 and 1820 did not produce a strictly symmetrical facade; the windows of the 1802 wing, for instance, were six-over-six lights while the windows of the 1820 wing were twelve-over-twelve lights. The gable roofs of the two sections were not joined; indeed, the 1820 wing was about four feet higher. But a new four column portico, with Palladian-influenced pediment, stood over the central hall entrance, overlapping partially the facade of the older 1802 section. This one design solution gave the dwelling an appealing appearance of balance and grace.

In addition to farming, the Demoss families operated a gristmill, sawmill, store, and a granary in this rural community. When the railroad came in the 1850s, a new post office and rail station were established. They were given the name of Bellevue, in recognition of the early Demoss settlements.

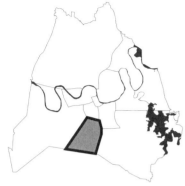

Key Map

SECTION VII
Southwest Nashville

Southwest Nashville is best defined by its primary roads–Hillsboro Road, Granny White Pike, and Franklin Road. All of these routes were originally part of the antebellum turnpike system that substantially improved Nashville's connections to surrounding county seats and country estates. Along parts of the roads are remnants of historic dry-laid stone walls, which are now treasured as an almost lost folk art tradition.

The picturesque region has two noteworthy architectural trends. First, it is a place of many country estates, some larger than others but all distinguished by large, landscaped lots. A few are remnants of mid-1800s farms and plantations, a landscape built by and shared by prominent white plantation owners and their African American slaves more than 150 years ago. Most properties, however, were built between 1910 and 1930 when developers and architects turned farms into suburban communities such as Oak Hill, Green Hills, and Forest Hills.

Next, the region is a showcase for early twentieth century domestic architecture, especially the Colonial Revival style, as interpreted by key Nashville architects. The new mansions possessed the Palladian entrances, dormer windows, brick construction, and symmetrical facades of their colonial predecessors, but they did so to an exaggerated degree, producing a swagger and boastfulness in character with the optimism and confidence of the times. The region also contains a range of apartment complexes from the mid-twentieth century, such as the National Register-listed Woodmont Terrace, a c. 1940 complex on Woodmont Boulevard influenced by "Garden City" planning principles, designed by Nashville architects Warfield and Keeble.

Woodmont Christian Church, Metro Nashville Historical Commission.

Woodmont Christian Church (1947–49)
3601 Hillsboro Road
Edwin A. Keeble, architect

With its majestic steeple stretching 220 feet high, the Woodmont Christian Church interprets traditional southern church architecture in a modern yet respectful manner. Although the height of the steeple was designed, in part, to compensate for the church's sunken site, it also made the church an instant Green Hills landmark. Ornamental details are understated in both the exterior and interior. In fact, the simplicity of the large central nave conveys Gothic solemnity as well as any twentieth century Nashville church.

Functionalism is commonly an important aspect in any Keeble design. Woodmont Christian Church's admired white color, in fact, resulted from the architect's decision to use utility brick, to save the congregation money, and to cover it with a new cement-based paint called Thoroseal. The original treatment lasted until the late 1960s when the church was repainted.

197.

Hunter's Hill (1928)
5401 Hillsboro Road
Dougherty and Gardner, architects

Behind stately stone and iron gates, on top of a steep hill overlooking the once rural countryside, stands this two-story gray

Hunter's Hill, Metro Nashville Historical Commission.

stone Tudor Revival manor house. It has a projecting central entrance with a second story bay window and decorative turret, flanked by three bay wings. Hunter Hill's masonry construction and battlements convey the image of a medieval English abbey.

Many architectural delights distinguish this Tudor Revival design. Paired Gothic arched windows are encased in stone archways; at the tip of the windows for the living room, library, and dining room are glass medallions depicting different hunting

Deepwood, Gary Layda, photographer, Courtesy of Metro Nashville Historical Commission.

scenes. This decorative glass is the work of Owen Boniwit. The interior replicates the materials and appearance of a medieval castle and includes an octagonal library with a vaulted ceiling.

Nashville businessman Guilford Dudley, Sr., and his wife, suffragist and socialite Anne Dallas Dudley, originally built the mansion. The name Hunter's Hill derives from the fact that fox hunters often gathered here before and after the hunt. Later suburbs now cover their old riding grounds.

198.

Deepwood (1936)

5335 North Stanford Drive
Edwin A. Keeble, architect
Tuck Hinton Architects, 1989–91 expansion

In the United States, the International style was rarely the pure expression of modernist functionalism associated with the work of European masters Walter Gropius, Ludwig Mies Van Der Rohe, and Le Corbusier. Like the earlier European precedents, the American version of the International house was typically rectangular, built of concrete and steel, white in color, and with a flat roof. But here the homes often blended elements of Art Deco and Art Moderne into the general context of International style, thus producing distinctive domestic environments.

Deepwood, by Nashville architect Edwin A. Keeble, is an excellent example of this mixing of modernist elements. From the roadside, it appears to have the flat, white concrete walls

typical of the style, but actually the walls are of brick and stucco and have been painted white. Interior curved walls clearly belong to the streamlined Art Moderne tradition as do the glass block windows and the projecting three sided bay extension of the living room. Located on a rural, forested hillside, the house's materials, style, and color are in jarring contrast to its surroundings as if Deepwood's industrial-driven aesthetics were challenging nature itself.

199.

Longleat (c. 1900, 1930–32) (NR)

5819 Hillsboro Road
Bryant Fleming, architect, 1930–32 renovation

Architect Bryant Fleming transformed this circa 1900 Renaissance Revival house, originally built for J. Wilson Forsyth, into a gracious Colonial Revival mansion for Thomas J. Tyne, a Nashville insurance executive. To the main facade, Fleming added three dormers on the roof, matching the three bays of the main block; a projecting two-part portico; and flanking one story wings. His new interior design incorporated many opulent features. A marble Adamesque mantel, with Wedgewood medallions, was placed in the drawing room while the new dining room had its own Adamesque mantel, along with a carved wood and plaster ceiling, with gold leaf detail, from a Sicilian archbishop's palace. Fleming commissioned Kerrigan Iron Works to design decorative ironwork for the front entrance as well as iron balusters for the

Longleat, Gary Layda, photographer, Courtesy of Metro Nashville Historical Commission.

main stairway. Victor Perllman of Chicago produced the crystal wall sconces of the dining room. Fleming also redesigned the estate's landscaping, constructing a grassy front terrace with stone retaining walls and steps, flanked by lion statues and metal lamp posts.

5880 Fredericksburg Drive (c. 1985)
Robert Anderson, architect

From the early 1970s to the 1990s, Nashville architect Robert Anderson designed several modern residences along Laurel Ridge and Fredericksburg Drives. Wood is the primary material of these houses. Easy to shape in imaginative and creative ways, wood reflected the surrounding forested environment while its light weight made the houses easier to construct and adapt to the naturally steep contours of the lots.

Anderson's residential designs are good Nashville examples of how dwellings can be related to the natural environment, a key trend in twentieth century domestic architecture.

201.

Henry Compton House (c. 1819, c. 1840, c. 1939)

1645 Tyne Boulevard

Henry Compton was a quartermaster under General Andrew Jackson's command during the War of 1812. He probably built the first part of the house soon after acquiring the land in 1819. During the antebellum era, this dwelling evolved from an unadorned log house into a larger, almost ungainly frame residence, with such Greek Revival elements as the six square Doric piers of the shed roof front porch. In 1939, William Blackie acquired the house and restored it in a Colonial Revival fashion.

202.

Woodmont Terrace Apartments (1938) (NR)

920 Woodmont Boulevard
Warfield and Keeble, architects

Residential developments were few and far between during the Depression decade, but the construction of Woodmont Terrace in 1938 was a sign that Nashville had weathered the worst of the depression and was growing again. Apartment complexes in Nashville were not uncommon in the first third of the twentieth century, but certainly in the second third, from 1933 to 1966, more apartment houses were designed and built in Nashville than in all of the decades before, a trend that accelerated even more in the last third of the century.

The earlier New Deal public housing project at Cheatham Place in north Nashville, where Francis B. Warfield had been part of the PWA design team, influenced Woodmont Terrace. Like at Cheatham, these houses are two-story brick buildings with restrained Colonial Revival details, dispersed among a landscaped property of ten acres. Woodmont Terrace was Nashville's first private development to mirror the early twentieth century garden apartment movement, where green space was part of the overall design. The original complex had eleven apartment houses with six garages; the houses remain but the garages are gone, save for one that was converted into a clubhouse/fitness center.

203.

Washington-Draughon House (c. 1870)

3702 Granny White Pike

This rare Middle Tennessee example of a Victorian farmhouse now stands in the middle of modern surburban homes near Lipscomb University. Frank McNairy built the original one-story frame house, which is now the rear ell of the house. In the 1870s, Thomas A. Washington added a two-story gable front and wing brick section. The gables of the front facade suggest a Gothic

Lipscomb University, Carroll Van West, photographer.

Lipscomb University and Avalon (1903–2010)

3901 Granny White Pike
George D. Waller, architect, 1930s
Brush, Hutchison and Gwinn, architects, 1960s
Tuck Hinton Architects, 2001–2010

David Lipscomb and J. A. Harding established the Church of Christ-affiliated Nashville Bible College in 1891. First housed at several different downtown locations, the school moved to a new campus on Lipscomb's former farm along Granny White Pike in 1903. At that time, Lipscomb's home, Avalon, was constructed. The design of this two-story brick residence, attributed to Lipscomb's wife, Margaret Zellner Lipscomb, features a one-story square Doric pier wrap-around porch. Next to Avalon stands the Lipscomb log cabin, a single pen dwelling once owned by David Lipscomb in the Bell's Bend area that was moved to the campus in 1985.

After David Lipscomb's death in 1917, the institution changed its name to David Lipscomb College. It gained university status in 1988. In 1930, Nashville architect George D. Waller remodeled Harding Hall and designed Elam Hall and Sewell Hall in the Classical Revival style. Classicism remains the dominant motif, even in buildings constructed since 1950. A good representative example is the Science Building and McFarland Hall, designed by Brush, Hutchison and Gwinn in 1966.

Lipscomb was Nashville's first university to complete an institutional overlay, or master plan, for its future growth and impact on influence while the windows and bracketed porch reflect Italianate styling. John R. Draughon, founder of Draughon Business College, later acquired the home.

Girl Scout Council
of Cumberland Valley,
Tuck Hinton Architects.

the city, an important step considering how the university is nestled into Nashville's twentieth century suburbs. Tuck Hinton Architects completed the plan and during the first decade of the twenty-first century, the firm designed several key new buildings, including the Allen Arena (in partnership with Berger Devine Yaeger of Overland Park, Kansas), the Ezell Center, the Beaman Library, and the Hughes Center, all of which are clearly modern in look and feel but also blend into the historic campus environment in their size, massing, and reliance on red brick and classical-derived details.

205.

Girl Scout Council of Cumberland Valley (1990)
4522 Granny White Pike
Tuck Hinton Architects

The administrative headquarters for Girl Scouting in south-central Kentucky and Middle Tennessee is located in this rambling, creative design that combines modern office spaces with references to regional architectural traditions. The building

Dyer Observatory, Metro Nashville Historical Commission.

contains a museum display about the history of the Council and the Girl Scout movement.

206.

Arthur J. Dyer Observatory (1953) (NR)
1000 Oman Drive
Clarence T. Jones and R. Bruce Jones, architects

Completed in 1953, Vanderbilt University's Arthur J. Dyer Observatory was built under the guidance of well-known astronomer

Carl K. Seyfert. Arthur J. Dyer of the Nashville Bridge Company provided significant funding for the observatory and was an integral part of the development campaign. Chattanooga architects Clarence T. Jones and his son R. Bruce Jones designed the observatory; the elder Jones had designed an observatory at the University of Chattanooga (now the University of Tennessee, Chattanooga) with Public Works Administration support in the 1930s.

The east façade of the Classical Revival brick observatory is dominated by the central entry rotunda, which contains the original telescope on the second level. Dyer Observatory continues to operate as an important facility for research and graduate training, and is regularly open for school tours, lectures, observation nights, and other public programming.

207.

McCrory-Mayfield House (c. 1798, 1960) (NR)
1280 Old Hickory Boulevard

This log dwelling began as the circa 1798 two-story, central hall-plan home of Thomas McCrory. The original three-bay house is built of chestnut logs, notched with half-dovetail joints. William B. Carpenter purchased the property in 1837 and his daughter, Mary E. Carpenter Mayfield, next acquired the home. Circa 1869, the dwelling passed into the Mayfield family by inheritance and it remained within the family until 1939.

In the middle decades of the twentieth century, the house was modernized with the addition of interior baths, electricity, and new log additions for a modern kitchen, additional baths, bed-

Longview, Gary Layda, photographer, Courtesy of Metro Nashville Historical Commission.

rooms, a dining room, and utility rooms. A Greek Revival-styled portico also was constructed. These additions give the dwelling its present three-part appearance as a historic, yet modernized Frontier Revival landmark.

208.
Longview (c. 1840, c. 1880, 1906) (NR)
811 Caldwell Lane

This grandiose Beaux Arts-style mansion, complete with a massive projecting two-story central portico of four fluted Ionic columns,

actually has antebellum roots. The house began circa 1840 as a four-room one-story brick cottage, owned by Henry Norvell and his wife Laura Sevier Norvell, the granddaughter of Tennessee frontier hero and first state governor John Sevier. After James E. Caldwell acquired the property in 1878, he converted the cottage into a two-story Italianate house in the early 1880s.

The house acquired its current appearance in 1906, when the Caldwells completely renovated the dwelling, with major changes including the three-story Beaux Arts facade, a conservatory, an attic story, a two-tier chandelier in the dining room, a winding

Glen Leven, 2009, Carroll Van West, photographer.

staircase in the living room, and a huge entrance hall highlighted by Ionic columns. Two Gothic-styled nineteenth century out-buildings—an office and a stone springhouse—are to the rear of the dwelling. The Caldwells practiced progressive agriculture and a 1923 history of Tennessee called Longview, "the pride and admiration of Middle Tennessee."[6]

209.

Glen Leven Farm (1856-57, 1890) (NR)

4000 Franklin Road
A.E. Franklin, builder

The story of Glen Leven Farm is wrapped into the history of Nashville transportation from 1830 to the 1960s. Tennessee's first state-chartered turnpike, the Franklin Turnpike Company (1829), passed through the middle of the farm. During the 1850s, the tracks of the Nashville and Decatur Railroad passed through the farm's east side. In 1909–1909, the Nashville Interurban Railway entered the farm along the old turnpike route; it, in turn, was replaced with U.S. Highway 31 in the 1920s. Then came the almost crippling impact of Interstate I-65 along the farm's east side during the 1960s. Through it all, Glen Leven Farm survived and today represents a unique rural landscape in the middle of a city but also a powerful document of how transportation has shaped the Nashville built environment.

The manor house dates to 1857–1858 when prosperous plantation owner John M. Thompson, son of one of Nashville's first settlers, Thomas Thompson, built a two-story brick central hall plan house, with an impressive two-story Greek Revival portico of four Corinthian columns supporting a classical pediment. Thompson was an ardent Confederate, for which he was assessed (fined) $500 by Military Governor Andrew Johnson in 1862. Union General Gates P. Thruston (one of the state's leading archaeologists after the war) occupied the house during 1862 and 1863. Before the battle of Nashville, Confederate officers and troops came to the farm. During the fighting, both armies moved through the property and once the battle was over, Glen Leven served as a Union field hospital. Fifty-nine white U.S. soldiers and 32 members of the U.S. Colored Troops were buried at the plantation; their bodies were later moved to the National Cemetery in Madison. .

In 1876, John M. Thompson, Jr., inherited the house; two years later he married Mary McConnell ("Conn") Overton, the daughter of John Overton at the neighboring Travellers' Rest plantation. The Thompsons turned the farm into one of the county's major livestock centers, and in 1887–88 they joined other partners to create The Hermitage Stud. At around the same time, the Thompsons updated the mansion with an Eastlake-styled porte-cochere on the north elevation and a more up-to-date East-lake styled interior. They also added architecturally distinctive show barns, one of which still exists.

The house remained in the Thompson family until the late 1960s, when music executive Shelby Singleton briefly acquired it before selling it back to a Thompson descendant, Susan West, in 1971. She lived in Glen Leven and farmed the land until her death in 2006. West left the house and surrounding 65 acres to the Land Trust for Tennessee with a perpetual easement upon the property and protections for the historic farm.

210.

Father Ryan High School (1991–94, 2001–08)
700 Norwood Drive
H2L2 Architects and Planners, Philadelphia
Gresham, Smith and Partners, Nashville

Father Ryan High School, Gary Layda, photographer,
Courtesy of Metro Nashville Historical Commission.

For over seventy years, Father Ryan High School was a Collegiate Gothic landmark. A private Catholic school, Father Ryan outgrew its space on Elliston Place by 1991. Church officials decided to build an entirely new campus to the west, off of the Franklin Pike and along Interstate Highway I-65, one that would be much larger, reflect the ideas, curriculum, and technology of late twentieth century education, and have better access to the interstate and the west Nashville suburbs. Placed within landscaped grounds are various classically style-influenced classroom buildings and structures.

In the fall of 2001, administrators began the second construction phase of the campus plan, adding a new library, fine arts center, amphitheater, and other facilities. The major Nashville-based firm of Gresham, Smith and Partners designed the classically inspired Performing Arts and Media Center and in 2008 it designed the Jim Carrell Alumni Athletic Complex.

211.

Far Hills (The Governor's Residence) (1929–31)
882 Curtiswood Lane
Hart Freeland Roberts, architects

This elegant Colonial Revival mansion, originally named "Far Hills," was built for the family of W. Ridley Wills, an insurance executive for the Nashville-based National Life and Accident Insurance Company. A two-story seven bay Georgian style central block dominates the north facade, from which the family and visitors could enjoy wonderful vistas of the countryside to the south. The stone quoins and entrance arcade are reminiscent of fine colonial Virginia mansions. The curved main staircase, with wrought-iron balusters, belongs to the Adamesque tradition of interior design. The large parlors were ideal for the many parties and receptions hosted by the family. Throughout the mansion, the skill and abundant detail of the interior design reflected Russell Hart's earlier training in classical architecture, gained from his years at the Ecole des Beaux Arts in Paris during the early 1900s.

In 1948, the State of Tennessee acquired the mansion for use as the official Governor's residence. From 2003 to 2009, First Lady Andrea Conte (wife of Governor Phil Bredesen) directed a privately funded restoration of the building, which included the construction of Conservation Hall, a 2,800 square foot underground meeting space. Conte enlivened the interior with the installation of new art works from Tennessee artists. For example, Gloria Felter and Shelia Rauen designed quilted wall hangings. The restored residence is available for meetings and events and is periodically open for public tours.

Far Hills, Tennessee Historical Commission.

212.
Robertson Academy Elementary School
(1933, 1936, c. 1955)
835 Robertson Academy Road

The history of Robertson Academy dates to 1806, making it the oldest school in Davidson County. The first building was constructed from logs in 1806 and stood in the Blackman Road area. The present school dates to 1933, when a five classroom building was constructed. Three years later, the Works Progress Administration erected the auditorium/gymnasium. During the 1950s, four additional classrooms, a cafeteria, and kitchen were added to the original building. The architecture of the one-story brick building reflects the standardized plans utilized in rural Tennessee schools during the 1920s and 1930s.

Oak Hill, Carroll Van West, photographer.

213.

Oak Hill (1930, c. 1950)
First Presbyterian Church (1956–57)
4815 Franklin Road
Warfield and Keeble, architects

A two-story fluted Ionic portico with classical pediment, quoins, and beautiful decorative iron work from the Kerrigan Iron Works are the distinguishing features of Oak Hill's seven-bay central block. This monumental example of Colonial Revival domestic architecture for the John H. and Susan Glenn Cheek family was under construction at the same time as Cheekwood Mansion. Different in its materials (red brick) and in its reliance on overstated classical exterior elements (the Ionic portico), Oak Hill was an impressive mansion, overlooking the Franklin Road countryside. Nashville architects Francis Warfield and Edwin A. Keeble moved on from this success to design other elite homes throughout the region during the 1930s.

In 1949, First Presbyterian Church acquired the mansion and fifty-five acres for its new suburban home. At first, it used the dwelling for its services. But the congregation in 1956–57 constructed a large Colonial Revival church building, which stands adjacent to the mansion.

214.

Shedd House (c. 1990)
801 Tyne Boulevard
Edwards and Hotchkiss Architects

This Postmodern interpretation of a Tudor country house mixes modern building materials like polystyrene, split-face concrete blocks, glass blocks, and cedar siding with lofty, inspirational interior spaces to create a residence that is both contemporary and traditional.

Located at Tyne Boulevard and Franklin Road, a prominent corner in southwest Nashville, the house has become a modern domestic architectural landmark in Nashville.

Shedd House, Metro Nashville
Historical Commission.

Holy Trinity Greek Orthodox Church, AIA Middle Tennessee.

215.

Holy Trinity Greek Orthodox Church (1991–92)

4905 Franklin Road

Don Stoll, architect

This brown brick and concrete building, dominated by its central octagonal dome, is an example of Byzantine Revival style, influenced by the design of the historic Agios Sostis Church in Athens, Greece. The recessed entrance is flanked by two smaller octagonal domes, topped by a metal seam roof. The combination of elements and materials reflects a contemporary interpretation of traditional Greek Orthodox ecclesiastical architecture.

Holy Trinity Greek Orthodox Church was established in Nashville in 1917. The church moved from Sixth Avenue to this 13.5-acre suburban location in 1986 and the congregation met in a community center until the new sanctuary was completed in 1992.

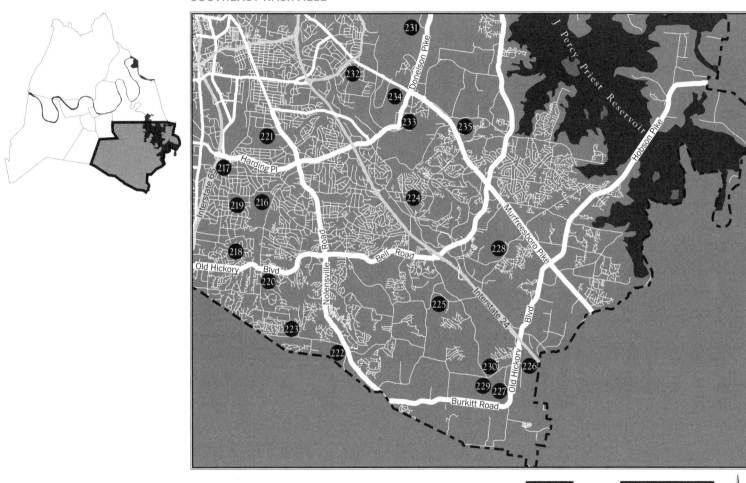

J Percy Priest Reservoir

Donelson Pike

Hobson Pike

Murfreesboro Pike

Interstate 65

Harding Pl

Interstate 24

Road

Bell Road

Nolensville

Old Hickory   Blvd

Old Hickory

Blvd

Burkitt Road

231
232
234
233
235
221
217
224
219 216
228
218
220
225
223
222
230 226
229 227

0   1½ mi   3 mi   6 mi

Southeast Nashville

A persistent myth about Nashville is that its rural past has been discarded, paved over, and forgotten. Too much has been lost in the name of progress, but the southeast corner of Davidson County retains significant vestiges of the nineteenth century rural landscape. From the years of early settlement, there are Federal-styled brick homes, multiple pen log cabins, and distinguished heavy braced frame dwellings. This was not a place of great antebellum plantations, but the distinctive I-houses of the rural middle class stand along old turnpike routes. Churches, schools, and cemeteries remain to document the nature of nineteenth century rural life.

These country places have survived within a rapidly developing modern commercial and suburban landscape created, in large part, by new transportation routes. In the 1920s came the concrete lanes of the original Dixie Highway as it left downtown and headed toward Chattanooga. Near its route the WPA built the city's first modern airport, Berry Field, in the 1930s. The four-lane U.S. Highway 41 arrived in the post-World War II years, followed twenty years later by Interstate I-24.

Suburbs, new factories, commercial strips, and shopping malls were constructed adjacent to the new transportation systems. The resulting pressure for even more development has been profound, though there are important reminders of the rural quality of much of area's landscape.

Brentwood Hall (Ellington Agricultural Center) (1920–27)
Marr and Holman, architects

As one of the most powerful capitalists in early twentieth century Nashville, Rogers Caldwell was known as the "J. P. Morgan of the South." In 1920, he commissioned Marr and Holman to design a red brick replica of Andrew Jackson's Hermitage as the mansion of his new horse farm along Edmonson Pike. Like the Hermitage, the dwelling has a two-story central block flanked by one-story wings. The massive portico has six fluted Corinthian columns lifting the entablature and pediment. The central entrance hallway, like the Hermitage, featured a circular staircase and the walls were covered with imported hand-painted French paper.

The secondary buildings of the estate were largely Colonial Revival in design, including servant quarters, a six-car garage with stepped gable ends, a frame farm office with portico, and a brick, Greek Revival temple-style guest house. Because of his great delight in raising fine racehorses, Caldwell built two magnificent horse stables, both complete with dormers and cupolas.

During the Great Depression, Caldwell's financial empire collapsed, taking with it millions in state funds. To reclaim some losses, state officials attempted to wrest away Brentwood Hall. The courts eventually ruled in the state's favor, but Caldwell continued to live at the estate until 1957. Four years later, the state converted the 207-acre property into the Ellington Agricultural Center. The house became offices for the Tennessee Department of Agriculture. One stock barn now serves as the Tennessee Agricultural Museum.

Travellers Rest (1799–1812; 1828; 1885) (NR)
636 Farrell Parkway

John Overton was a leading Jacksonian politician, state Supreme Court justice, and prosperous planter, who, along with Andrew Jackson and James Winchester, founded the city of Memphis. The evolution of his country estate, Travellers Rest, mirrors his rise in political prominence during Tennessee's Jacksonian era.

In 1799, Overton directed master carpenters David Cummins and Frederick Binkley in the construction of the first Travellers Rest, a two-story, hall and parlor plan, heavy braced frame house. The interior's finely carved parlor mantel, chair rails, and wainscoting are attributed to Cummins and Binkley. By 1812, Overton had built additional rooms to give the dwelling a symmetrical five-bay facade and an interior central hall plan. Overton expanded the dwelling again in 1828 by building a two-story brick wing with a gallery. This rear wing was extended again in 1885–87.

During the Civil War, the property served as headquarters for Confederate General John B. Hood during the Battle of Nashville in December 1864. Some of the battle's bloodiest fighting took place on the nearby Peach Orchard Hill.

In 1954, the National Society of Colonial Dames of America in Tennessee acquired the house, remaining outbuildings, and three

acres of the original plantation, saving it from demolition by the Louisville and Nashville Railroad who wanted the property for an expansion of its adjacent Radnor Yards. Nashville architect Charles W. Warterfield, Jr., directed the first restoration project, which was completed in 1966. A fire in 1969 led to a second restoration, directed by Nashville architect Clinton E. Brush, III, in 1970. An exhibit on the plantation's slaves opened in 2015.

218.

Alford-May-Granbery House (c. 1807)
631 Hill Road

The three-bay symmetry of this two-story Federal residence is matched by the precise interior balance of twenty by twenty foot rooms flanking the central hall. Its construction date is uncertain, but its restrained Federal styling and Flemish bond brick facade suggest that it was probably built by John Alford after he acquired land on the west fork of Mill Creek in 1807. Alford had moved to Davidson County from central Virginia and the house is similar in appearance to many rural middle class dwellings from that region.

Alford lived here until his death in 1837, when the property passed to James F. May, who was also managing the Overton plantation at Travellers' Rest in that year. May possibly erected the house circa 1837. In 1909 William Granbery acquired the home, which remained in the family for over seventy years.

219.

Hogan House (c. 1795)

407 Landon Drive

This one and one-half story double-pen log dwelling, with external gable end limestone chimneys and half-dovetail notching, dates circa 1795, when Daniel Hogan moved his family from Robertson County to a new 640 acre farm along the west fork of Mill Creek. In 1819, John Hogan acquired his father's homeplace. From then until his death in 1859, Hogan lived at the family farm and he probably added the vernacular Greek Revival style front porch.

220.

Oglesby School (1898) (NR)

5724 Edmonson Pike

With its bracketed cornice and cut-away gable entrances, this turn-of-the-century frame school building is more architecturally distinctive than other extant rural schools from that era. One reason for its distinctiveness was that it was originally built as a private academy, not a public school. It opened in 1898 as the private Mary Lee Academy, named for its first teacher Mary Lee Clark. The county acquired it in 1906 and changed the name to Ogilvie, in honor of the land donor Benton H. Ogilvie. The school later took the name of Oglesby. During the New Deal, while so many

Oglesby School, Metro Nashville Historical Commission.

new Nashville and Davidson County schools were being built, the Oglesby School received repairs and landscaping, including the stone wall at the front of the building. It remained a public school until 1943 when it became a community center for this rural Edmonson Pike neighborhood.

221.

Grassmere (Nashville Zoo at Grassmere) (c. 1810, 1876) (NR, LL)

3725 Nolensville Road

Michael C. Dunn built this elegant five bay Flemish bond brick house circa 1810. Family members added the Italianate-styled veranda, tiered central portico, bracketed and denticulated frieze, and segmental arched windows to the facade between 1875 and 1881. Interior alterations included the creation of dual parlors and the installation of Victorian woodwork and walnut burl doors. The family named the renovated house "Grassmere," adapting the name from a village in the poem, "Home at Grasmere," by English poet William Wordsworth. Behind the house are historic structures often found at nineteenth century estates, including a tenant house, smokehouse, and two cemeteries.

In 1964, Dunn descendents Elise and Margaret Croft left the house and surrounding acreage to the Cumberland Science Museum for the development of a wildlife park after their deaths. Park development began in 1986. Ten years later, the museum transferred the park and house to Metro Government, which leases the property for operation by the Nashville Zoo.

Grassmere, Metro Nashville Historical Commission.

222.

Wrencoe (c. 1860)

6439 Nolensville Road

A massive entablature, supported by four large square Doric piers, gives a commanding Greek Revival facade to what is otherwise a smallish two-story three bay double house. Jeremiah Primm is credited with building the house between 1858 and 1860. In the 1870s–1880s, a small rural village developed around the farm. Owner Constantine Williams operated a mill, blacksmith shop,

Locust Hill, Metro Nashville Historical Commission.

and general store. When a post office was established at the store in the mid-1880s, Williams named the village Wrencoe. The village is gone, but the farmhouse has retained the historic village name.

223.
Ogilvie House (c. 1832, c. 1870)
6700 Holt Road

This excellent example of a two-story frame I-house, with exterior gable end brick chimneys and limestone foundation, sits near the east fork of Mill Creek. William Holt likely added the Victorian mill work of square posts and sawn brackets to the one-story porch in the 1870s. Behind the Ogilvie House is a log slave dwelling, which may date to the early nineteenth century.

224.
Locust Hill (c. 1800) (NR, LL)
834 Reeves Road

One of most distinguished early brick homes in Davidson County, this two-story, Flemish bond brick, three-bay Federal house was under construction by 1800. Its hall and parlor plan interior exhibits a high degree of craftsmanship, featuring mantels and chair rails carved by North Carolina craftsmen and interior decorative painting resembling mahogany and green marble in the second floor master bedroom.

In 1965 historic preservationist John Kiser acquired the property and began its restoration. Eight years later, the house received the Metropolitan Historical Commission's initial award for restoration excellence. In 1989, Locust Hill became the first locally-designated historic landmark.

225.
Gillespie House (1875)
3402 Old Franklin Road

Incorporated into the rear ell of this dwelling is a circa 1797 single-pen log cabin, a significant early example of log craftsmanship in Davidson County. Andrew and Cyrena Turner Gillespie moved here in 1871; between that year and Andrew's death in 1882, they expanded the house into a comfortable country place. The sweeping five-bay facade contains a central double portico with pediment, with folk Victorian details like the second story porch balustrade. Arched windows also distinguish the dwelling's first story from its second story.

226.
Cloudcrest (c. 1830, 1938)
4011 Twin Oaks Lane

On the west side of Hurricane Creek, near the Rutherford County line, carpenter Thomas Johnson built this two-story log house circa 1830. Over one hundred years later, Fannie Taylor and her husband restored the dwelling in Frontier Revival fashion, adding a two-story pedimented portico and modernizing the interior. She renamed the house "Cloudcrest."

227.

Benajah Gray Log House (c. 1805, c. 1870) (NR)
446 Battle Road

Probably between 1800 and 1808, North Carolina native Benajah Gray erected this double-pen log dwelling of yellow poplar and cedar logs, with its unusual combination of a one and a half story log pen and an adjacent one story log pen. The diamond notching of the logs is extremely rare for Middle Tennessee. A one story porch, supported by eight wooden square classical piers, may date c. 1860–70, when son Benajah F. Gray transformed the farm into a thoroughbred horse breeding business. Gray installed new box locks, with Rockingham and porcelain door knobs, on the interior doors while retaining many of the original H-L hinges with hand-wrought nails and leather gaskets. Keeping the original hand-planed beaded poplar board walls, he replaced the poplar moldings, door and window trim, and baseboards. He also constructed a new frame kitchen in the 1870s.

The log house sits in the midst of an interesting collection of three log outbuildings (including a double-pen slave cabin) from the early settlement era, a frame kitchen, and a frame pole barn from the early 1900s. It would be difficult to find a better example of the historical evolution of the middle class farm in Davidson County.

228.

Farview (c. 1840, c. 1874)
5797 Mount View Road

The double porticoes of Farview are oriented to two different nineteenth century roads; one side faces the old Franklin-Lebanon stagecoach road while the other faces the present-day Mount View Road. The first part of the two-story frame house may date to 1840 and was constructed by Richard and Sophronia Wallace. After the Civil War, Josiah Rucker first rented the farm and then bought it in 1874. The folk Victorian porticoes and arched windows were probably installed at this time.

229.

Cane Ridge Cumberland Presbyterian Church (1859) (NR)
13411 Old Hickory Boulevard

This Antioch area landmark is a significant late antebellum remnant of the religious traditions of rural Davidson County. Its gable front orientation, brick construction, and two front doors are typical of nineteenth century vernacular church architecture. Its very simplicity of design embodied the principles of faith, devotion, and humility held by many rural church-goers. A compatible education building was placed at the rear of the sanctuary in the 1970s.

The first Cumberland Presbyterian church at this spot, built in 1826, was a log building. The best known early pastor was

Hugh Bone Hill. The original church cemetery dates to 1826; Revolutionary war veteran Isaac Johnson, who died in 1839, is buried there.

230.

Cane Ridge School (1906)

Cane Ridge Road at Old Hickory Boulevard

A restrained Colonial Revival design, highlighted by the square fluted wooden piers of the recessed entry, marks this one-story hipped roof school building. A pedimented portico centers the five bay facade. Children attended classes here until 1951. Almost twenty-five years later, the adjacent rural neighborhood repaired and restored the building into a community center. The Cane Ridge Community Club, established in 1921, is one of the oldest in the region.

231.

Nashville Metropolitan Airport Terminal (1984–87)

Donelson Pike at Interstate I-40

Robert L. Hart, New York, in association with Gresham, Smith and Partners, Nashville, architects

The huge airport terminals built across the United States in the late twentieth century fulfill the same civic, commercial, and transportation functions possessed by the large urban railroad terminals of the late nineteenth century. They are monuments to civic pride and boosterism, signifying to potential investors and new businesses that the city is a promising and progressive place.

They also embody the latest developments in engineering, designed to meet both modern safety standards, security needs, and the competitive demands of the air travel industry.

The original forty-six gate Nashville terminal contained 750,000 square feet. It centers around an airy, three level public atrium, which is lit by green-tinted skylights. Elevators, stairs, and escalators move thousands of people daily toward their appropriate destinations. Terminal officials worked with local artists and the Metropolitan Arts Commission to use regional art to enliven the lobbies, walkways, and gate concourses. The various elements, proportions, and materials of the terminal create a new type of grand public space, one that speaks strongly to the role of air travel in late twentieth century urban life and culture.

From 2006 to 2011, officials supervised several updates in the airport's parking and access, its security screening section, and its retail and food services areas along the concourses.

232.

Genesco Park Administration Building (1963–65)

1415 Murfreesboro Road

John Charles Wheeler & Associates, architect

The New Formalism style of modern architecture is often associated with the work of Edward Durrell Stone, especially his design for the Kennedy Center in Washington, D.C. and the Legislative Building in Raleigh, North Carolina. In Tennessee, New Formalism is rare, but most often found in public buildings, like the Lawrence County Courthouse (1974) by the Nashville firm of

Cane Ridge School, Metro Nashville Historical Commission.

Genesco, Metro Nashville Historical Commission.

Hart Freeland Roberts. Therefore, the Genesco World Headquarters is a particularly interesting example of 1960s modernist design for a corporate client. When constructed during the mid-1960s, it became a corporate symbol within the urban landscape similar in effect to the Aladdin Building of the late 1940s.

This six-story concrete and steel building of 290,000 square feet was modern in its interior as well as its exterior. Double glazed windows with built-in blinds minimized cleaning. It possessed high-speed escalators, a central monitoring system, large computer room, and a vertical conveyor system for company mail. Although today Murfreesboro Road is difficult to envision as an isolated, undeveloped commercial area, it was exactly that almost fifty years ago. Consequently, Wheeler's project architect, L. Frank Gower, and the rest of the design team, which included the firm of Perkins & Will of Chicago, incorporated commercial services into the building for employee convenience. These services included a credit association, commissary, barber shop, dry cleaners, and large cafeteria.

The State of Tennessee now owns the building and it is the headquarters of the Tennessee Board of Regents, among other state agencies.

233.

Ezell-Shriver House (1888)
652 Old Ezell Road
Ken Adkinsson, architect, 1994–95 renovation

Henry Clay Ezell had this two-story brick vernacular Queen Anne residence built as the centerpiece of a large late nineteenth century stock farm. It is the ancestral home of developer Houston Ezell and Miles Ezell, Sr., a founder of Purity Dairies. Attorney Berry D. Shriver acquired the property during the Great Depression and modernized it with bathrooms and electricity.

As commercial developments overwhelmed the area in the 1970s and 1980s, the dwelling seemed destined for the wrecking ball. In 1994, Corporate Construction Managers, Inc., purchased the house and restored it as a corporate office building.

234.

Dell Computer Corporation Campus (1999–2000)
1 Dell Parkway
Gobbell Hays Partners, architects

Dell Computer Corporation is an internationally recognized Texas-based corporation that opened a major manufacturing center, one of six international facilities, along Murfreesboro Road in 2000. Dell's modern industrial campus generated controversy in the city because of the number of government inducements used to lure the company to Nashville, the millions spent on infrastructure, and tax breaks granted by the local government. It also led to the destruction of one of the original buildings of the Tennessee Lunatic Asylum, a Gothic Revival landmark designed by Nashville architect Adolphus Heiman. State and city officials, along with the business community, strongly supported Dell's move to the region, wanting to position Nashville and Tennessee in the mainstream of high-tech business development. The campus look is unified by a sleek late twentieth century industrial aesthetic, representing a third type of industrial design tradition, compared to the International style of the Alladin Building and the New Formalism of the Genesco headquarters, found along this busy north-south highway corridor.

235.

Ellis Garage (1929) (NR)
2000 Old Murfreesboro Road
Luther Creech, builder

The construction of the Dixie Highway in the 1920s created, in turn, the need for new buildings and businesses to serve the highway's travelers. In 1929, T. H. Ellis decided to build a service station and garage at the front on his house lot, which faced the Dixie Highway at a prominent rural crossroads. With its Craftsman-influenced canopy, the garage reflected a vernacular adaptation of standardized Gulf Oil Company station design from the late 1920s; Ellis sold Gulf Oil products throughout the life of the business. The garage closed in the early 1990s and recent road expansions and commercial pressure makes for an uncertain future for this piece of roadside architecture.

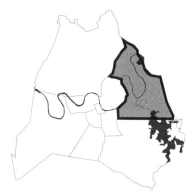

Key Plan

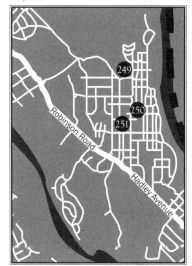

Old Hickory Village Detail

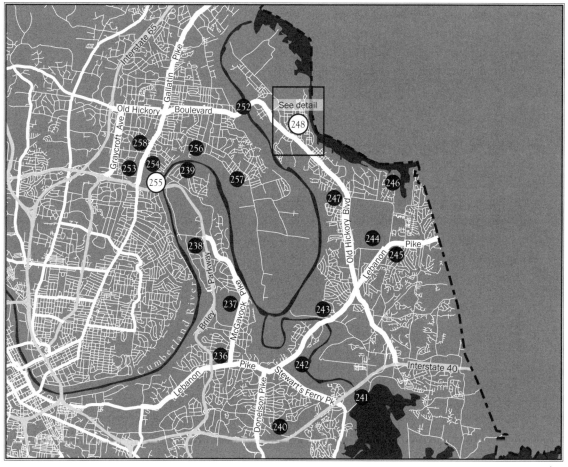

0   1½ mi   3 mi   6 mi

Northeast Nashville

Winding through the northeast corner of Davidson County are the Cumberland River and its tributary the Stones River. The rivers' rich, flat bottomland attracted early settlers, who quickly established productive farms and valuable plantations. The rivers also provided transportation to the Nashville wharves as well as national and international markets at Natchez and New Orleans. The Cumberland and Stones were the lifeblood of northeast Davidson County.

Turnpike and railroad development during the 1840s and 1850s began to change this pattern of dependency. The Louisville and Nashville Railroad passed through this section of the county; after the Civil War, rail connections stretched eastward toward Lebanon.

Throughout these decades, the bottomland continued to yield bountiful harvests. Even into the beginning of the twentieth century, few residents had discarded rural ways of life. The most noticeable exception was at Andrew Jackson's antebellum plantation, The Hermitage, where the Ladies Hermitage Association preserved the property as the city's best known and most visited historic site. Here began the tourism industry that has meant so much to Nashville's modern economy.

Then in the early twentieth century came a huge industrial development. Along Hadley's Bend of the Cumberland River, the federal government and the DuPont chemical corporation agreed to build the largest factory yet in Nashville, and surround it with hundreds of buildings and structures to serve the instant city—first called Jacksonville and soon changed to Old Hickory—they created.

By the mid-century, people had changed the rivers themselves. The U.S. Army Corps of Engineers built Old Hickory Dam and Lake on the Cumberland River in the 1950s. It then built Percy

Belair, 1940, Lester Jones,
photographer, Historic American
Building Survey, Library of Congress.

Priest Dam and Lake on the Stones River in the 1960s. A new era based on industry, tourism, and commerce was underway in the river country of Davidson County.

All sorts of developments, commercial and suburban, crowded along the river banks. In the early 1970s, in fact, downtown's most important tourist spot—the home of the Grand Ole Opry—relocated to the banks of the Cumberland River in northeast Davidson County. In its wake would come the chain restaurants, gift shops, and outlet malls associated with late twentieth century tourism.

Then in May 2010, a record flood of the Cumberland River reminded those who had forgot that the river came here first, and when it was ready to reclaim control, there was little anyone could do, be they the engineers controlling the dams on the Cumberland and Stones rivers or state and city officials hoping that levees could hold the waters. In the fall of 2010, the Grand Ole Opry House and the mammoth Opryland Hotel complex reopened, refreshed and re-energized, but as 2011 began many homeowners knew rebuilding was impossible and Opry Mills shopping mall, the city's largest, had only scattered re-openings, until renovations led to the 2012 rebirth of the city's largest retail space.

236.

Belair (c. 1832, 1842) (NR)
2250 Lebanon Road

Belair was the centerpiece of a thousand-acre Cumberland River plantation, first developed by surveyor and farmer James Mulherin

and later expanded and enhanced by planters Joseph Clay and William Nichol. John Harding of Belle Meade acquired some of the Mulherin tract in the 1820s and gave the land to his daughter Elizabeth, as a wedding present for her marriage to Joseph Clay in 1827. Sometime within the next five years, the couple began the mansion's construction.

In 1842, Joseph Clay sold the house and 1,000 acres to banker William Nichol for $30,000. Nichol added one-story projecting wings, along with a one-story Doric colonnade on the first floor connecting the wings to the central pedimented portico. The result was a three-part Palladian dwelling, with a decided Greek Revival influence, especially in the first story Doric and the second-story Ionic columns of the double portico. The house shared several of the design characteristics of the 1831 Hermitage by David Morrison.

Belair's interior design blends Federal, Greek Revival, and Victorian elements added during periodic nineteenth century interior renovations. Frescoed plaster and dentiled cornices mark several ceilings. Rosewood doors have silver fittings. An Eastlake style mantel is in the library while the dining room mantel is a Richardsonian Romanesque-influenced design.

Nichol established large formal gardens at the house during the 1840s. These are gone today, along with the mansion's once rural setting. The construction of Briley Parkway almost demolished the house during the 1960s. Belair is visible on the east side of the Lebanon Road exit of the parkway.

Two Rivers, Gary Layda, photographer, Courtesy of Metro Nashville Historical Commission.

237.

Two Rivers (1859) (NR, LL)

3130 McGavock Pike

David H. McGavock, a wealthy planter, constructed this valuable example of the transition from Greek Revival to Italianate style in Nashville's late antebellum plantation architecture. The plantation's land came from the Harding family, through the

marriage of Willie Elizabeth Harding to McGavock in 1850. The name Two Rivers comes from the close proximity of the Cumberland and Stones rivers.

The design is attributed to McGavock; the similarities in the facade porticoes indicate that he had been influenced by James Hoggatt's Clover Bottom, although Two Rivers lacks the flamboyance of the earlier mansion. John L. Stewart was the stone mason.

The interior also lacks Clover Bottom's sophistication, although the door jambs, door heads, pocket doors and sixteen inch high baseboards represent accomplished craftsmanship. The double parlors, for instance, have imported Italian marble mantels. McGavock's slaves made the bricks, quarried the stone, and executed all of the construction work and much of the ornamental detail work. The property's National Register nomination, for example, attributes the intricate filigree carvings of the facade veranda to these African American craftsmen.

Adjacent to the mansion is a two-story Federal brick dwelling, with a hall and parlor plan. Evidence indicates that this early dwelling was built by David Buchanan in 1802. After the construction of Two Rivers, it became a slave quarters and dependency.

In the late nineteenth century, the mansion became the focal point of a 1,100-acre estate named the Two Rivers Stock Farm. This prosperous livestock and dairy farm lost many buildings and animals during the tornado of 1933. But the land stayed under cultivation until 1966 when the Metropolitan Government bought the house and 447 acres of land for just under one million dollars. Officials kept the house and fourteen acres for public use as a site for special events. The remaining acreage became the land for the Two Rivers golf course, a city park, and two large school lots.

238.

Grand Ole Opry House (1972–1974, 2010) (NR) and Opryland Hotel (1973–96, 2010)

Briley Parkway at McGavock Pike

Pierre Cabrol, Welton Becket and Associates, Los Angeles, architects

Earl Swensson Associates, Nashville, architects

The owners of the Grand Ole Opry, WSM, and National Life and Accident Insurance Company commissioned the Los Angeles architectural firm of Welton Becket and Associates to design a modern home for the country music institution. Pierre Cabrol, principal architect, produced a massive 48,000 square foot structure of concrete and steel; yet his design has a rural sensibility due to its shingled-like sloping roof and the red brick that wraps around the building. Modern in materials, design, infrastructure, and profile, Beckett's new Opry House (1972–74) also contains lofty, inspirational spaces, in keeping with its role as the secular "mother church of country music." An abundant use of oak paneling and brass trim conveys a simple elegance. The interior has over 1,800 seats on the first floor with an additional 2,400 seats in the balcony. To keep a bit of the old Ryman Auditorium's tradition, padded spaces on long pew-like rows were installed

Opryland Hotel, AIA Middle Tennessee.

instead of individual theater seats. But unlike the Ryman, there are no supporting columns or other visual obstructions. By means of the clearly evident television and radio facilities, the Opry House boldly states its function as an extraordinarily large, but still informal, broadcast studio. President Richard M. Nixon dedicated the building at its opening on March 16, 1974.

The May 2010 flood significantly damaged the building's ground level and below. Repair and restoration began immediately and the Opry House opened for performances in October. The backstage was remodeled and rebuilt; pews on the first floor were replaced. However, the iconic center section of the original Ryman Auditorium stage, which had been installed at the Opry House in 1974, somehow survived the high waters.

The Opryland Hotel complex (1977, 1983, 1987, 1996, 2010) is a fantasyland of a different sort and scale, designed in four stages. The original phase was a collaboration between the Nashville firm of Earl Swensson Associates and Charles Warterfield. The exterior central block of this gigantic neo-Georgian Revival building recalls the Governor's Palace at Colonial Williamsburg. However, the interior—named the Magnolia Lobby—has more in common with the grand old tradition of southern plantation architecture, as symbolized in the dual staircase entrance of the Twelve Oaks plantation in the movie *Gone With The Wind*. The huge chandelier is eighteen feet in diameter.

Since its opening in 1974, Opryland Hotel has evolved into one of the largest hotels and convention centers in the United States. The first major wing was the Conservatory (1983), which contains two acres of gardens, with winding walking paths, set under a huge glass and steel skylight. Next came the Cascades wing (1987), which features huge fountains and man-made waterfalls, again set under a giant skylight and surrounded by walls of hotel rooms. The most recent major section is The Delta (1996), which recalls the architectural diversity and informality of New Orleans' French Quarter and plantations along the Mississippi River.

The hotel received significant water damage during the May 2010 flood, with 70 percent of its common areas and all of its subterranean spaces being flooded. Company officials decided to use the disaster as an opportunity to update the interior and many hotel rooms without changing the basic themes and aesthetics of the hotel. TVS Interiors of Atlanta carried out the assignment in record time and the hotel reopened a mere six months after the flood.

239.

Lock 2 Park and Lock Keeper's House (c. 1890)
2650 Lock 2 Road, Pennington Bend

Lock 2 is one of the series of locks designed for the canalization of the Cumberland River by the U.S. Army Corps of Engineers in the early 1890s. Measuring 52 by 280 feet, the lock exhibits the remnants of fine stone craftsmanship, which has been attributed to the initial project designs of Principal Engineer John W. Walker. After 1892, the entire Nashville project was supervised by Colonel Henry M. Robert, who achieved fame as the author of *Robert's Rules of Order*, the basic parliamentarian guide used in the United States.

Buchanan Log House,
Carroll Van West,
photographer.

240.

Buchanan Log House (1807–08) (NR)

2910 Elm Hill Pike

James Buchanan built this log dwelling, with limestone foundation and chimneys, which served as his residence but also travelers along the adjacent road along the Cumberland River. Buchanan, who married Lucinda East in 1810, had a large family, and by 1820 he had expanded the original house. The two building periods are reflected in the log notching of the home. One section has V-notching, which is usually considered the earliest notch type used in Middle Tennessee, and probably dates to 1807–08 while the other log section has half-dovetail notching, which was more common by 1820.

James Buchanan died in 1841 but his wife Lucinda continued to live there until her death in 1865. After the Civil War, the family of Thomas Neil Frazier occupied the house. Frazier was a controversial state judge during Reconstruction who was impeached and removed from office for obstructing the General Assembly in its attempt to ratify the Fourteenth Amendment to the U.S. Constitution in 1867. His son James Frazier was later elected Governor of Tennessee in 1902 and served the U.S. Senate from 1905 to 1911.

In the late 1980s and early 1990s, a Donelson-based chapter of the Association for the Preservation of Tennessee Antiquities acquired the property and restored it as a house museum.

241.

Percy Priest Dam and Reservoir (1963–70)
Pleasant Hill Road at Bell Road
U.S. Army Corps of Engineers

Percy Priest Dam is one of nine Corps of Engineers' installations along the Cumberland River and its major tributaries, in this case the Stones River, designed for recreation, flood control, and hydroelectric power. First called "Stewart's Ferry Reservoir," the name was changed to honor notable Nashville congressman J. Percy Priest (1900–1956) in 1958.

The concrete and earthen dam is 130 feet in height and stretches some 2,700 feet in length, with the earthen embankment measuring 800 feet at its base. Percy Priest's original powerhouse generated 28,000 kilowatts of power.

As designed, Percy Priest Lake held 652,000 acre-feet of water in a lake of 14,200 acres. The Corps planned for extensive recreational facilities; from the 33,100-acre project area, the Corps developed thirty-three boat ramps, 215 picnic units, 344 camping units, and five commercial boat docks. Nashvillians regularly benefit from the lake's recreational facilities, including the access to the Stones River Greenway and Long Hunter State Park.

242.

Clover Bottom (1858) (NR)
2941 Lebanon Road

Built as the country estate for a Stones River plantation, Clover Bottom was an ornate example of the architectural transition then taking place from the Greek Revival to Italianate style. Its brick construction, central hall plan, two-story rectangular massing, and balanced three bay facade were similar to many other Nashville homes built in the first half of the nineteenth century. But the facade's mixture of a classically-influenced portico with arched spandrels and brackets, paired bracketed cornice, low pitched hip roof, enriched balustrade, and tall thin arched hood windows, highlight its Italianate style. Behind the mansion are two historic slave/tenant dwellings.

The Victorian flavor of the exterior was also expressed inside the dwelling. An elliptical staircase, with Victorian newel post, graces the entrance hall. Interior architraves are heavily molded; five marble Victorian mantels enhance the first floor fireplaces.

The doors, door facings, and door jambs incorporate the design motif of the facade columns.

The mansion initially belonged to Dr. James Hoggatt. After the Civil War, the plantation gained a regional reputation for horse breeding. The name Clover Bottom derives from a famous race track that Andrew Jackson and others once operated along bottomland between the nearby Stones River and the plantation. In 1920, A. F. and R. D. Stanford acquired the property and began to subdivide it. The State of Tennessee in 1949 purchased the mansion and remaining grounds for the campus of the Tennessee School for the Blind, which relocated there by 1955. By the 1980s, the manor house was in great disrepair, but during the early 1990s through the influence of the APTA, it was restored into offices for the Tennessee Historical Commission (THC), which serves as the state historic preservation office. THC maintains the state's records of the National Register of Historic Places and the state's historical and architectural survey.

243.

Stone Hall (1918) (NR) and Eversong Cabin
1014 Stones River Road
George D. Waller, architect

Nashville architect George D. Waller was one of the city's foremost Colonial Revival architects; Stone Hall is an early example of his designs as he transitioned from the Craftsman style of the 1910s into the Colonial Revival movement. The prominent eave, hipped roof, and multi-paned first floor windows are characteristics of Craftsman style while the symmetry and balance of the facade were defining features of the Colonial Revival style. Mason Elly Hayes cut the limestone for the two-story dwelling from local quarries. Waller designed this two-story house for the family of Dempsey and Nora Cantrell, who lived here for several decades. Nora Cantrell had the Eversong log cabin moved to the property to serve as a studio and guesthouse for visiting artists and poets.

Nashville founder John Donelson first owned this land along the Stones River; his descendent, John Donelson, VII, married the Cantrell's daughter Angie, and they lived here in the mid-twentieth century. Metro Greenways acquired the property in 2007 and restored it for use as offices.

244.

The Hermitage (1819, 1831, 1834-36) (NHL)
4580 Rachel's Lane

The best known historic antebellum house in Tennessee, The Hermitage was the plantation estate of Andrew Jackson, Tennessee legislator, judge, war hero, and President of the United States. The architectural evolution of this National Historic Landmark mirrors Jackson's rise to prominence in American history. The Andrew Jackson Foundation leads the site's administration.

The Hermitage experienced three distinct construction phases. The first came in 1819, after Jackson's great success during the War of 1812, when he directed the construction of a brick two story, five bay Federal style dwelling, executed by builder Henry Reiff. Its facade was unadorned, save the semi-elliptical fanlight and sidelights of the entrance door and the flat brick arches over the windows. Jackson also engaged English gardener William Frost to create a landscaped garden, known now as Rachel's Garden, to the side of the new dwelling.

In 1831, while President of the United States, Jackson commissioned architect David Morrison to design a significant expansion of the 1819 dwelling. To the two-story central block, Morrison added flanking one story wings for a dining room and a library. A new two-part Greek Revival portico with pediment defined the main entrance while a colonnade of ten Doric columns covered the first floor of the central block. These alterations gave the facade a three-part Palladian appearance. In the estate gardens,

Morrison also designed a Doric colonnade tomb, topped by a high metal dome, in honor of Rachel, who had died in 1828.

Unfortunately a fire in 1834 severely damaged The Hermitage and destroyed most of Morrison's work. Jackson commissioned carpenters Joseph Reiff and William Hume to rebuild the mansion. Their new design eliminated most of Morrison's facade in favor of a massive two-story Greek Revival portico, with six fluted Corinthian columns of acanthus leaves supporting a wide entablature. The rear of the dwelling received a portico of six Doric columns. Painted white, the restored Hermitage conveyed an almost temple-like appearance, accentuated by the serpentine design of the entrance drive.

The gutted interior also was renovated in a Greek Revival fashion. New mantels decorated with Ionic columns were installed in several rooms. A graceful elliptical grand staircase dominated the central hall. The entry hall was further distinguished by its imported French wallpaper, which portrays the legendary search by Telemachus for his father Odysseus.

Archaeological investigations have focused on locating the property's extensive slave quarters, including the log "Alfred's Cabin," dating to the 1840s, when Jackson owned about 150 slaves. Extant period outbuildings include the brick kitchen, smokehouse, and limestone spring house. To the rear of the

The Hermitage, 1972, Jack E. Boucher, photographer, Historic American Building Survey, Library of Congress.

mansion are two of the original log cabins of the estate. These log buildings document the early life of the ambitious Jackson and his wife Rachel Donelson Robards Jackson from 1804 to 1821. These were restored in the first decade of the twenty-first century with support from the Save America's Treasures program.

Another important building on the estate from Jackson's pre-presidential years is the Old Hermitage Church (1823, restored 1965), a one-story brick building across the Lebanon Road from the main residence.

The Ladies Hermitage Association acquired the house and twenty-five acres from the Tennessee General Assembly in 1889.

Tulip Grove, Gary Layda, photographer, Courtesy of Metro Nashville Historical Commission.

Later state legislatures granted the Association additional lands for the preservation of this significant historical and architectural landmark. The Tennessee Confederate Soldiers' Home, in use from 1891–1933, stood near the current Hermitage entrance gates. A nearby cemetery contains many of the veterans' graves.

245.

Tulip Grove (1836) (NR)
Lebanon Road at Rachel's Lane
Reiff and Hume, builders

This Greek Revival brick home, with a Flemish bond facade, belonged to Andrew Jackson Donelson, nephew of Rachel Jackson, and Emily Donelson, his wife. The house stands directly across Lebanon Road from The Hermitage. Completed in 1836, as carpenters Joseph Reiff and William Hume were finishing their renovations at The Hermitage, Tulip Grove features a tasteful and well balanced two-story Doric pedimented portico of four fluted Doric columns. The entablature has honeysuckle leaves and triglyphs; metal fish-scale shingles were later added to the tympanum of the pediment. Tulip Grove also has an important historic interior. Artist Ralph E. W. Earl marbelized the front plaster walls and grained the hallway door panels. The Greek Revival mantels, derived directly from Asher Benjamin's nineteenth-century pattern books, are exceptional pieces of craftsmanship.

After leasing the property in 1963, the Ladies Hermitage Association restored Tulip Grove. The Andrew Jackson Foundation operates it as a companion property to The Hermitage.

246.

Shute-Turner House (c. 1832–33, 1997)

4112 Brandywine Point Boulevard

This handsome five bay, Flemish bond, red brick Federal residence has prominent stone lintels with cornerblocks over its original six-over-six windows. John A. Shute built the dwelling shortly after his father gave him a tract of land along the Cumberland River in 1832. The Turner family acquired the property in 1877. In the 1990s, the farm was subdivided but the manor house was restored and greatly expanded.

247.

Cleveland Hall (1839–41) (NR)

4041 Old Hickory Boulevard
Reiff and Hume, builders

Stockley Donelson, the grandson of Nashville founder John Donelson and close confidant of Andrew Jackson, commissioned carpenters Joseph Reiff and William Hume to build this two-story five bay country house. A Flemish bond brick pattern graces the facade while American bond was used on the gable ends and rear of the dwelling. Stone lintels with cornerblocks define its six-over-six double-hung windows and four Doric columns support a frieze with triglyphs and pediment. The central hall plan interior has pocket doors between the parlor and dining room, which allowed the Donelsons to entertain large dinner parties. Decorative details abound: hall doorways have architraves with entablatures while

Cleveland Hall, Metro Nashville Historical Commission.

the original mantels express Greek Revival style. Original yellow poplar trim and floors are also extant.

As of the early 1970s, one cedar log slave house stood several hundred yards to the rear of the dwelling, but has since been moved to Belle Meade Plantation. Cleveland Hall in 1976 was listed as one of the Tennessee Century Farms in Davidson County. Several acres still surround the historic house, but during the first decade of the new century a new subdivision, also known as Cleveland Hall, was developed on former farmland.

Old Hickory Historic District, Metro Nashville Historical Commission.

248.

Old Hickory Historic District (c1918) (NR)
North of Old Hickory Boulevard at Hadley Avenue

The city of Old Hickory is a unique part of the county's landscape because it began as an instant city built at the height of

United States involvement in World War I. Several Nashville factories created company housing near their facility elsewhere in Nashville, but nothing had ever appeared to match the scale and numbers of the Old Hickory project.

On January 29, 1918, the DuPont chemical corporation and the federal government agreed to build the largest industrial complex yet designed in Nashville along Hadley's Bend of the Cumberland River. The product was smokeless gunpowder, for use by United States and allied forces during World War I. As planned, the massive factory would have nine units, each with the capacity to produce 100,000 pounds of gunpowder a day. Hundreds of buildings were included within the industrial complex.

Such a gigantic factory demanded worker dwellings to house thousands of employees. For the town plan as well as the design of individual buildings, DuPont followed standardized architectural plans that it already had used in other eastern facilities. The overall look of this new Tennessee town, for example, is similar to another DuPont plant at Hopewell, Virginia.

DuPont quickly designed and constructed a "permanent village," which it first named Jacksonville, in honor of Andrew Jackson, whose Hermitage estate was nearby. By November 1918, the permanent village contained over three hundred dwellings. These were reserved for company foremen, supervisors, and officials. Many homes were utilitarian, but the more substantial ones often had elements from the popular revival styles of the era. Jacksonville also contained a "temporary village" of over five hundred residences. Common laborers lived here, with African Americans segregated into one area while another set of forty-one buildings housed some three thousand Mexicans. A common myth in twenty-first century Nashville is that Hispanic immigration is a recent phenomenon; instead, the modern impact of Hispanic culture in Nashville dates to Old Hickory.

Neither of these residential areas for African Americans and Mexicans remain today. The historic Hadley African American school, built after World War I in 1935, remains intact and is being restored as a community center. Other employees daily commuted to the factories by train and automobile. What had been farmland in an isolated bend of the Cumberland River became a very busy, industrial place, certainly an alien landscape when compared to the still dominant rural ways of northeast Davidson County.

Due to the distance of Old Hickory from downtown Nashville, and the company's desire for security and control, the DuPont village was largely self-sufficient. In addition to the factories and homes, the company constructed a hotel that could serve four hundred people, a hospital, churches, gymnasiums, city hall, police station, first aid stations, fire hall, theaters, bank, commissary, mess halls, and a restaurant. The YMCA built separate buildings for African Americans and whites while the YWCA constructed a facility for women.

Within two months of the November 1918 armistice ending the war, the factory complex closed; by the end of 1919 only five hundred people lived in a place that had claimed as many as 35,000 a year earlier. The town established overnight also had become a ghost town overnight.

In 1920, the Nashville Industrial Corporation bought the complex from the federal government for about $3.5 million; three years later, it sold it to DuPont for conversion into a rayon factory. A cellophane facility was constructed by the end of the decade. DuPont also acquired a large portion of the company town and changed the community name to Old Hickory. The town once again began to grow and new dwellings were constructed. By

1925, the DuPont Rayon Plant was in production; for the next twenty years, the corporation operated Old Hickory as a company town. Not until 1946 did DuPont begin to sell its homes to its employees, ending the tradition of company control over the local built environment. Also in the late 1940s, however, hundreds of original frame "temporary" homes were moved or demolished, often to be replaced by brick Ranch-style dwellings.

Old Hickory is a fascinating place, a perfect location to explore the corporate transformation of the rural South in the early 1900s. Most of the initial community buildings are gone, but in 1984 a survey identified 276 intact historic dwellings in the Old Hickory Historic District, with styles including American Four-Square, Georgian Revival, Bungalow, and Dutch Colonial Revival homes. According to plans developed by the Nashville Industrial Corporation, the prominent house types at Old Hickory were identified by name. The "Davis" was a Dutch Colonial Revival-styled two-story frame dwelling, located primarily along Riverside Drive. Nashville architect Earl Swensson lived for several years in the plant manager's house. Also on Riverside Drive are several examples of the "Ketchum," a frame bungalow design. The "Bay Tree" was similar to an American Four-Square house, with Colonial Revival details, but only two of these were constructed, one at 1202 Riverside Road. The most unique house type in the Village is the "Welford," a six-bedroom Dutch Colonial Revival style house overlooking the Cumberland River.

In its symmetrical three bays and Colonial Revival-styled one-story porch, "The Arlington" reflected the local vernacular. The "Cumberland" was a hipped roof American Four-Square house while the "Georgia" was another Dutch Colonial Revival residence, with a gambrel roof. An extant example of the "Georgia" is 808 Jones Street (1918).

DeBow Street, especially the 900 block, reflects the repetitive, standardized nature of the vernacular house types built for other workers. The pyramid roof cottage was especially prevalent, as represented by the "Denver" house type. The "Haskell" was a two-story frame building similar in appearance to company housing found at railroad and coal towns throughout the country. Smaller, almost totally unadorned worker cottages were represented by the "Florence" and the "Six Room Bungalow" house types. The house at 1402 Clarke Street is an excellent example of the "Florence" house.

249.
Old Hickory Post Office (1934) (NR)
1101 Donelson Avenue
Louis A. Simon, architect

This one-story brick building is an example of the restrained Colonial Revival-styled standardized design that federal architect Louis A. Simon produced in great numbers for the postal service during the New Deal era.

250.

Old Hickory Public Library (1937, 1982)

1010 Jones Street

Built by DuPont in 1937, the red brick library is another restrained example of Colonial Revival style in an Old Hickory public building. It contains extensive historic records about the city and displays an important collection of historical photographs of the town's creation during World War I and its subsequent development in the 1920s and 1930s. The library was expanded and modernized in the early 1980s.

251.

Old Hickory Methodist Church (1928, 1939) (NR)

1216 Hadley Avenue

Once DuPont resurrected Old Hickory in the mid-1920s its employees quickly set out to establish and build new church buildings. DuPont donated certain lots in town for church construction. The Old Hickory Methodist Church is a Classical Revival-styled brick and concrete building that features paired Doric columns supporting a large pedimented portico.

252.

Old Hickory Bridge (1928)

Old Hickory Boulevard

The monumental classicism of the Old Hickory Bridge makes it an appropriate western gateway to the town. As the primary crossing of the Cumberland River, the bridge replaced an original narrow bridge—known locally as the "Swinging Bridge"—built by DuPont in 1918. In the 1940s, a two-lane bridge parallel to the old bridge was built to serve the increasing traffic on Old Hickory Boulevard.

253.

National Cemetery (1866) (NR)

1420 Gallatin Road South

A white marble Doric column gateway, with double iron gates, and limestone walls define one of the most somber landscapes in Nashville. The federal government created the Nashville National Cemetery to hold the graves of the many U.S. soldiers who died in the region during the Civil War. The first burial took place in 1867 and within two years the cemetery had 16,486 burials, representing 741 regiments and twenty-two states. Burials from later wars have brought the number to nearly 35,000 on the cemetery's 64 acres. In 2006, William Tuerk, Under-Secretary of the National Cemetery Administration, dedicated the U.S. Colored Troops National Monument, sculpted by Roy W. Butler. The U.S.C.T. formed during the Civil War and thousands of free African Americans and escaped slaves fought in these units. The monument honors all U.S.C.T. soldiers; 2,133 of whom are buried at the Nashville National Cemetery.

National Cemetery, Metro Nashville
Historical Commission.

254.

Spring Hill Cemetery (c. 1785)

5110 Gallatin Road

The "historical area" within this large urban cemetery is a significant artifact of the early settlement patterns of Davidson County. The oldest known marker is dated 1800. A stone pyramid marks the site of Davidson Academy, established in 1785 by Presbyterian Reverend Thomas Craighead. Craighead is buried here as well as Madison Stratton, for whom the city of Madison is named. Investors purchased the site in 1888 and established the present-day Spring Hill Cemetery.

255.

Tanglewood Historic District (c. 1932–1946) (NR)

4905–4911 Tanglewood Drive
Robert M. Condra, builder

Engineer Robert M. Condra was the principal developer of this complex of log and frame dwellings and outbuildings, including an early outdoor swimming pool that uses water from a natural spring. Such architectural features as natural materials, deep eaves with bracket supports, horizontal orientation, prominent stone chimneys, fieldstone walkways, and ample windows combine to make a distinctive urban statement of Rustic style.

Tanglewood Historic District, Metro Nashville Historical Commission.

256.

Idlewild (1874, c. 1890) (NR, LL)

712 Neelys Bend Road

The county's best extant example of a frame Italianate-styled farmhouse, Idlewild sits on about two acres of land in the Madison community. Through its assymetrical composition, bay window,

Idlewild, Metro Nashville Historical Commission.

central gabled pavilion with arched entrance, bracketed frieze, and hooded paired windows, the two-story dwelling conveys an interesting vernacular interpretation of Victorian architecture. An expansion during the 1890s added a two-story Queen Anne-influenced section with two rooms to the rear. Idlewild's original interior features include pine floors, tall baseboards, heavy window and door moldings, and pine mantels.

The original owner, Robert Chadwell, acquired the initial farm of 210 acres between 1873 and 1874. His son Henry obtained the property in 1906 and farmed it for the next seven years. After that

date, the subdivision of the property began, and by the mid-1900s modern suburban ranch and tract homes surrounded the once rural dwelling.

257.
Gee House (1839)
1248 Neely's Bend Road

This two-story three bay brick dwelling, with stone lintels and a central entrance with transom and sidelights, is all that remains from an antebellum Cumberland River farm. In the early twentieth century, the owners renovated the house with electricity, bath-rooms, and a modern kitchen. To the facade they also added a one-story wrap-around Colonial Revival style porch, with balustrade.

258.
Amqui Railroad Station, Museum and Visitor Center (c. 1910, c. 2010)
301 Madison Street, Madison
Hardin & Barga Construction, restoration contractor

Few historic buildings in Nashville have moved as much as the Amqui Station, first constructed as the Madison depot and rail-road office by the Louisville and Nashville Railroad in 1910. For decades after, the station was at the center of Madison's transportation and commerce but growing reliance on automobile travel and massive suburban growth in this part of the county after World War II soon meant that the station was of little value, it seemed, to Madison's future.

Amqui Railroad Station, Metro Nashville Historical Commission.

In 1979 country music star Johnny Cash purchased the station and moved it to Hendersonville, where it became part of the House of Cash museum. After the death of Cash and his wife June Carter Cash in 2003, a developer purchased the House of Cash and decided to donate the Amqui Station to the city of Madison.

The depot moved back to the city's downtown in 2006. A four year effort ensued to restore the station but also to transform it into a centerpiece for downtown revitalization and its grand opening took place in June 2010.

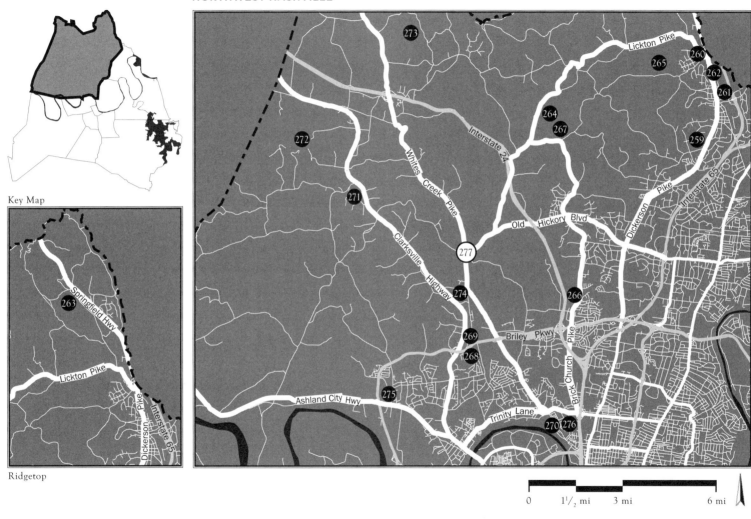

Key Map

Ridgetop

0   1½ mi   3 mi   6 mi

Northwest Nashville

The largest geographic and most rural area of Davidson County is its northwest corner. The Western Highland Rim begins to rise out of the Central Basin of Middle Tennessee at the point where northern Davidson County borders Robertson and Cheatham counties. At places it is a rugged land of steep hills, outcroppings, ridges, untapped forests, and hollows.

Northwest Nashville has its share of modern suburbs and apartment complexes. Industry and commerce are here as well, typically located along the major transportation arteries of Interstates I-24 and I-65, the old Dixie Highway (U.S. 41), and U.S. 41A. But, like the county's southwest corner, Northwest Nashville retains a representative sampling of the open spaces, house types, stores, churches, and schools that defined its history and landscape at the turn of the century.

There are three distinct zones. Tract houses, light industry, and commercial strips in its southern section at Bordeaux are like other working and middle-class neighborhoods of Nashville. The small farms and rough yet beautiful countryside around Joelton and in Bells Bend are almost like another world, similar to the rural landscape of neighboring counties. Here is a place removed from the hustle, bustle, and glare of modern city life, but a place dependent and related to the city's evolution and expansion in these modern times. Goodlettsville is at the center of the third zone, where railroad and highway development brought considerable growth and development in the twentieth century.

Old Stone Bridge,
Carroll Van West,
photographer.

259.

Cartwright House (c. 1810, c. 1850) (NR)

760 Old Dickerson Pike

This frame and log I-house was built in two stages. The first residence of early settler Jacob Cartwright was a two-story half-dovetail notched log house, of a hall and parlor plan. John Beazley was the carpenter. Each floor had two rooms, separated by a log wall, so each side had its own staircase. In about 1850, John Cartwright gave the dwelling a new Greek Revival look, by adding a one-story classical portico, brick chimneys, and Greek Revival-styled mantels. A new two story frame section expanded the dwelling into a central hall plan house. John Cartwright then covered the entire building with weatherboards to give it a uniform appearance.

260.

Goodlettsville Cumberland Presbyterian Church (1902)

226 Dickerson Road

This early twentieth century example of a vernacular Gothic church features a central tower, with high peaked roof, flanked by a gable-end wing and a spacious bay wing. The primary facade has three balanced original stained glass windows in its gable end, with a cupola visually uniting both wings. Later expansions to the facility took place in 1953, 1959, and 1966.

The Goodlettsville congregation dates to 1843 and has met at this location since 1848. Dr. A. G. Goodlett, for whom Goodlettsville was named, was minister here from 1848 to 1853.

261.

Bank of Goodlettsville (1900)

117 North Main Street

Robert Sharp, architect

The Bank of Goodlettsville operated here from 1900 to 1953. Contractor and mason Lee Vecchione was an Italian immigrant who settled in Davidson County and developed a rock quarry. He quarried the stone from the historic Drake property on Lumsey Creek Road and the finished building, including a lot price of $180, cost $3,665.17. The craftsmanship and masonry construction conveyed to local residents the image of a stable, secure place, entirely appropriate, even necessary, for a successful small town bank.

262.

Old Stone Bridge (c. 1837–40)

Dickerson Pike at Mansker Creek

This limestone arched bridge from the old Nashville to Louisville turnpike is a rare example of antebellum engineering. It was probably built in the late 1830s as part of a larger state-funded program to improve and expand turnpikes and roads that began in that decade.

263.

Three Waters (c. 1848)

7723 Old Springfield Highway

William and Narcissa Mathes Connell built this two story I-house on land Narcissa had inherited from her father, Dr. Allen Mathes.

It has a double Greek Revival portico of four square plain Doric columns while the paneled double entrance doors have a transom and sidelights. Historic interior features include a staircase with cherry banister, white ash floorboards on the first floor, and poplar floorboards on the second floor.

John C. Garrett acquired the home in 1956 and gave it the name Three Waters since the property is near Lumsley Creek, Mansker Creek, and a spring. The lot has a circa 1804 limestone springhouse, probably built as part of the original Mathes farm.

264.
Butterworth House (c. 1850)
5387 Lickton Pike

Butterworth House, Metro Nashville Historical Commission.

The John Butterworth House is a poured-in-place concrete house attributed to builder Abner Shaw. The use of poured-in-place concrete for rural domestic architecture was extremely rare in the mid-nineteenth century, but Abner Shaw built this house, and possibly three others in the Goodlettsville area, with that technique. This three bay, limestone foundation dwelling has a two-story double portico of four square piers and a denticulated cornice. Its central hall plan has flanking rooms of equal size, each measuring eighteen by twenty feet.

265.
Drake House (c. 1855)
5508 Brick Church Pike

This vernacular three bay I-house, with its central bay of matching double doors with transom and sidelights, dates to the mid-1850s. It was the comfortable farmhouse of Elias Drake, a cooper and farmer who became a county constable in 1854, and his wife Lucy Cunningham Drake. Several extant period outbuildings indicate the nature of the domestic complex of a mid-nineteenth century Davidson County farm.

266.
Jackson-Wilkerson House (c. 1885)
3500 Brick Church Pike

This rare extant example of Queen Anne architecture in a rural Davidson County setting is easily viewed from Interstate I-24 as the highway passes over Brick Church Pike on its way west to

Drake House, Metro Nashville Historical Commission.

Abner T. Shaw House, Metro
Nashville Historical Commission.

Clarksville. The frame two-story dwelling has several outstanding Queen Anne details, including bay window, Eastlake-influenced porch, and corner turret. The late nineteenth century house also incorporates an earlier building, which may date to the antebellum era, as a rear ell.

267.

Abner T. Shaw House (c. 1850) (NR)

4866 Brick Church Pike

With its rural setting of rolling hills and surrounding fields and forests, the Shaw House conveys the landscape associated with successful middle-class farm families in the late antebellum era. It is a five-bay central hall house constructed of concrete poured in place. Its dominant two-part Greek Revival portico with denticulated cornice and pediment contains a masonic symbol at its point. Underneath its skin of stucco and wood is a concrete house composed of lime cement binding an aggregate of rocks and rubble. Exposed concrete can be seen in the gable ends. The interior retains its original yellow poplar floors and woodwork. The original kitchen, also built of concrete, was later attached as an ell wing to the dwelling.

Surrounding the farmhouse is a valuable collection of period outbuildings, including a stone spring house (c. 1850), v-notched log smokehouse (c. 1850), and gambrel roof stone and frame barn (c. 1915).

Stump Tavern, Metro Nashville Historical Commission.

268.

Stump Tavern (c. 1789) (NR)

4949 Buena Vista Pike

Frederick Stump (1723–1822) was a Revolutionary war veteran and early Cumberland region pioneer of 1779. The following year, he signed the Cumberland Compact, which protected land titles and established the basic government of the Cumberland settlement. During the 1780s, Stump developed his property on White's Creek, operating a tavern and grist mill in addition to farming his land by 1790.

The construction dates of Stump's log house and tavern are uncertain, but they were probably built between the time Stump established the grist mill in 1782 and when he received the tavern license in 1789. They have been traditionally considered the oldest extant dwellings in Nashville.

The Stump House is a two-story cedar log dwelling that exhibits such common German log construction techniques as full-dovetailed notching. The much larger Stump Tavern originally consisted of a pair of two-story cedar log cabins connected in dogtrot fashion. It too has superb craftsmanship in its corner notching. At an unknown time, but likely before Stump's death in 1822, the open breezeway was filled in with logs and a Federal style entrance was added, giving the tavern a symmetrical three bay facade typical for the time.

In the mid-twentieth century, the Stump Tavern was restored in a Frontier Revival style. It was moved about one hundred feet off of Buena Vista Pike to allow for the widening of the road. The one-story portico was added and electricity, kitchen, bathrooms, wood paneling, and central heating were installed.

269.

Ewing House (c. 1823) (NR)

5101 Buena Vista Pike

Another early White's Creek dwelling is this two-story brick Federal style house, historically attributed to Revolutionary war veteran Alexander Ewing, a Maryland native who served as the aide-de-camp to General Nathaniel Greene from 1781 to 1783. Records indicate that the mansion certainly existed by 1835; consequently, the builder may be Alexander's son, Randal Ewing, who owned the property during the 1830s and 1840s. The Ewings located the new family home on land that once belonged to Frederick Stump.

This rectangular five bay Flemish bond brick house rests on a limestone foundation and has paired exterior brick chimneys connected by a parapet wall. The twelve over twelve windows with wood architraves are original as are the fanlight, sidelights, and double leaf doors of the central entrance. The one-story porch, which has rounded wooden columns with dentils and scrolled brackets, dates to the Classical Revival era of the early 1900s.

The interior has two rooms flanking either side of the central hall. "Bulls-eye" type corner blocks are found on the doorway and window surrounds; one of the parlors has a doorway embellished with a pair of columns resting on pedestals. A second floor bedroom contains a rare example of decorative folk art, in this case, a drawing of a running horse that measures approximately 10.5 by 5.8 feet. The artist is unknown, but has been attributed to one of the sons of Randal Ewing.

270.

Lock No. 1 Park (1891–95)
Lock Road, off of White's Creek Pike

In 1889, local merchants and riverboat captains established the Cumberland River Improvement Association in order to lobby the federal government to improve navigation on the Cumberland River. Seasonal fluctuations in the river's level meant that neither merchants nor captains could depend on the Cumberland for year-round transportation. The solution, according to the Association, was a series of locks and dams, to be built by the federal government.

In the 1890s, the U.S. Army Corps of Engineers began to build the necessary engineering structures. The chosen location for Lock No. 1 was an early settlement site, where pioneers built Heaton's Station at a buffalo ford in the river. The lock was finished in 1895 and remained operational until 1952. Ironically, the new system of locks and dams came too late to keep Nashville's steamboat industry alive and prosperous. Annual tonnage in the 1880s had been as high as one million; by the turn of the century, boats carried only 375,000 tons of goods and materials. "The romantic era of the steamboat," observed historian Don Doyle, "gave way to the utilitarian barge that hauled sand and gravel, dredged from the river bottom," which was "one of the few cargoes the railroads could not steal from the river."[7]

Lock No. 1 is a significant historic engineering property that contains the stone foundation of the lockmaster's house, original stone fences and retaining walls, and the river locks themselves. The Metro Department of Parks and Recreation has opened the area as a section of its greenway program.

271.

St. Lawrence Roman Catholic Church (1936)
5655 Clarksville Highway
Frederick Asmus, architect

Nashville architect Frederick Asmus designed this Clarksville Highway (US 41A) landmark during the Great Depression. Built by contractor Edward Ballentine, the Gothic style church features an attractive red brick bell tower, topped by a slender cross, and brick buttresses. White stone trim highlights the central entrance while near the facade's gable point is a stone insert with the statue of St. Lawrence.

272.

Shadowbrook (1929–30)
5397 Rawlings Road

Nestled in the woods and hills near Joelton is this distinctive Tudor Revival country house, built at the beginning of the Great Depression by A. L. and Sophia Rawlings. Carved native Tennessee limestone and approximately one thousand logs of poplar, oak, hickory, and chestnut were used in the construction of the dwelling. Rawlings, who had attended the University of Edinburgh in

Scotland, wanted to replicate a vernacular Scottish cottage in the hills of Davidson County. His wife Sophia Rawlings was an early Davidson County home demonstration agent.

In the early 1980s, daughter Clara Rawlings Davenport acquired the homeplace and restored it as a private residence and a restaurant.

273.

T.J. Wilkinson House (1932) (NR)

7663 Wilkinson Road

C.K. Colley and Son, architect

The Wilkinson House is an important example of Dutch Colonial Revival style in Davidson County. The noted Nashville architecture firm of C. K. Colley and Son designed this home for prominent Joelton resident Thomas Jefferson Wilkinson, who served as a Deputy Circuit Court Clerk and on the Davidson County School Board. The house features a cross-gambrel roof, distinctive of the Dutch Colonial Revival style, and has seen very few changes since its construction in the early 1930s.

274.

Graves House (c. 1850)

3832 Dry Fork Road

Edmund P. and Helen Stump Graves built this frame two-story Greek Revival-influenced central hall house at the place where Dry Fork flows into White's Creek. The couple remained at the farm into the 1900s and the family kept it until 1929. William T. Thompson, Jr., bought the property in 1953.

Jordonia United Methodist Church,
Metro Nashville Historical Commission.

American Baptist College, AIA Middle Tennessee.

275.

Jordonia United Methodist Church (1895)

4225 Cato Road

Dr. David F. Banks, builder

A gracefully executed bell tower of classical columns, topped by a steep pyramid roof with carved balustrade, distinguishes this outstanding example of Victorian rural ecclesiastical architecture. Under the facade's large center gable is an original elliptical stained glass window, symmetrically placed above a balanced row of four original stained glass windows.

276.

American Baptist College and World Baptist Center (c. 1924, 1996) (NR)

1800 Baptist World Center

Dougherty and Gardner, architects

This land has been an African American education center since 1909 when Roger Williams University, which once stood at the site of the present Peabody College of Vanderbilt University, built a new campus here. Closer to African American neighborhoods, located at the end of a streetcar line, and led by an African American administration, the new Roger Williams did well at first, but hard times in the 1920s led to the school's eventual merger with Howe Institute (now LeMoyne Owen College) in Memphis on December 29, 1929.

In 1921 the National Baptist Convention, USA, Inc. (NBC) bought 53 acres here and announced plans to build a new seminary, which would be managed by a governing board representing the NBC and the Southern Baptist Convention (SBC). Griggs Hall (1923–1924), a Classical Revival styled building, opened as the first part of the American Baptist Theological Seminary in September 1924. By 1937 the seminary and the NBC joined the Southern Baptist Convention (SBC) in a unique 50/50 partnership to expand educational opportunities for African American Baptist ministers and students. During the Civil Rights Movement, the seminary trained many important leaders such as Bernard Lafayette, C. T. Vivian, Jim Bevels, and John Lewis. The campus expanded during these years with additional classically styled red brick buildings.

In 1996, the NBC-SBC partnership ended and the college became fully controlled by a new Board of Trustees and served as an independent college for the NBC. Soon thereafter the modern styled world headquarters for the NBC, with its gleaming white spire dominating the landscape, was built adjacent to the historic campus.

277.

Riverside Hospital (c. 1972)
800 Youngs Lane
McKissack and McKissack, architects

Nearby American Baptist College is the historic Riverside Hospital, established and supported by African American congregations of the Seventh-day Adventist Church from the mid-twentieth century until the hospital closed in 1983.

The institution was established in 1927, through the work of Nellie Druillard, and in 1935 the Riverside Hospital Sanitarium was incorporated as a project of the General Conference of the Seventh-day Adventist Church. The creation of the institution was a significant social and humanitarian outreach by the church and its African-American congregations. During the Jim Crow era, the hospital and sanitarium were a relatively small-scale operation, but one of vital importance to local African Americans, who had few medical resources from which to choose. Facilities and programs—including a new hospital building in 1947—greatly expanded in the mid-20th century under the leadership of Dr. Carl A. Dent. After the passage of the Civil Rights Acts of 1964 and 1965, hospital operations were legally integrated, although the great majority of patients, physicians, and staff, who worked at Riverside remained African Americans. The end of the Jim Crow era, however, did coincide with major improvements and expansions of the facilities at Riverside Hospital in 1972, giving the property the appearance it has today. The leading firm of

Whites Creek Historic District, Courtesy of Metro Nashville Historical Commission.

McKissack and McKissack designed and supervised the construction of the new facilities during the 1970s.

Riverside Hospital has an significant association with the career of Dr. Dorothy Brown, who served as Chief of Surgery at Riverside from 1957 to 1983. In the fields of American medical history, Brown was the first woman to receive her medical degree in general surgery from Meharry Medical College and was the first African American woman to become a fellow of the American College of Surgeons. In 1956 she was the first single woman in Tennessee history to legally adopt a child. Ten years later, Brown was elected to the Tennessee General Assembly, the first African American woman elected as a state representative.

278.

Whites Creek Historic District (NR)
Whites Creek Pike and Old Hickory Boulevard

With over twenty contributing buildings dating from the nineteenth to mid-twentieth centuries, this historic district has been considered the best extant historical and architectural rural community in Davidson County, although suburban residential developments in the last twenty years have greatly impacted its rural setting. The district includes businesses, such as the Victorian-era Earthman Store and Saloon (4407 Whites Creek Pike) and the stone Whites Creek Bank and Trust Company (4416 Whites Creek Pike). A wide range of vernacular domestic architecture includes the five-bay Colonial Revival-influenced Bysor-Thompson House (4300 Whites Creek Pike), the Eastlake-influenced Earthman House (4401 Whites Creek Pike), and the Tudor Revival-influenced W. F. Teasley House (7129 Old Hickory Boulevard). The Yarbrough House (3831 Whites Creek Pike) is a two-story weatherboard double-pen house that may have been an inn when initially constructed circa 1835.

Notes

INTRODUCTION

1. Alan Gowans, *Styles and Types of North American Architecture: Social Function and Cultural Expression* (New York: HarperCollins Publishers, 1992), xii.
2. Anita Shafer Goodstein, *Nashville 1780–1860: From Frontier to City* (Gainesville: University of Florida Press, 1989), 201.
3. Don H. Doyle, *Nashville in the New South, 1880–1930* (Knoxville: University of Tennessee Press, 1985), 20.
4. Ibid., 97.
5. Don H. Doyle, *Nashville Since the 1920s* (Knoxville: University of Tennessee Press, 1985), 126.
6. Eleanor Graham, ed., *Nashville: A Short History and Selected Buildings* (Nashville: Historical Commission of Metropolitan Nashville-Davidson County, 1974), 276.
7. John Lomax III, "Music Row," Paul Kingsbury, Michael McCall and John W. Rumble eds. *Encyclopedia of Country Music* (New York: Oxford University Press, 2012), 370.
8. Graham, *Nashville: A Short History and Selected Buildings.*

CHAPTER 1

1. Alan Gowans, *Styles and Types of North American Architecture: Social Function and Cultural Expression* (New York: Perennial, 1993), 349.
2. Jesse Burt, "The Arcade," Nashville Magazine (September 1969): 2.
3. Talbot Hamlin, *Greek Revival Architecture in America* (New York: Oxford University Press, 1955), 60.

CHAPTER 2

1. Michael Cass, "28th Avenue bridge aims to reunify communities," Nashville *Tennessean,* May 25, 2011.

2. Cited in Carroll Van West, *Tennessee's New Deal Landscape: A Guidebook* (Knoxville: University of Tennessee Press, 2001), 136.
3. Federal Writers' Project, Works Progress Administration, *Tennessee: A Guide to the State* (New York: Viking Press, 1939), 203.
4. Ibid.
5. Nashville *Tennessean,* January 24, 1937; West, *Tennessee's New Deal Landscape,* 138.

CHAPTER 4

1. David C. Sloane, *The Last Great Necessity: Cemeteries in American History* (Baltimore: Johns Hopkins University Press, 1991), 75.
2. Bobby L. Lovett, "Nashville's Fort Negley: A Symbol of Blacks' Involvement with the Union Army," *Tennessee Historical Quarterly* 41(Fall 1982): 21.
3. *Nashville Record,* April 17, 1951.

CHAPTER 10

1. St. Ann's Episcopal Church website, accessed December 2, 2010.
2. Melissa A. Zimmerman, MTSU Center for Historic Preservation, "Thomas W. Phillips Memorial," National Register of Historic Places Nomination Form, Tennessee Historical Commission, 2006, Sec. 8–13.
3. Cited in James Patrick, *Architecture in Tennessee, 1768–1897* (Knoxville: University of Tennessee Press, 1981), 153.
4. Orr, *Notable Nashville Architecture,* 15.
5. *New York Times,* March 5, 1989, H-35.
6. John T. Moore and Austin P. Foster, *Tennessee: The Volunteer State, 1769–1923* (Chicago: S. J. Clarke Publishing Co., 1923), 377.
7. Doyle, *Nashville in the New South,* 38.

Sources
and
Suggested
Readings

The Metropolitan Historical Commission, located at the Sunnyside Mansion at 3000 Granny White Pike, developed research files for many of the properties listed in the book. Another invaluable source was the information contained in the Davidson County properties listed in the National Register of Historic Places, which is administered by the Tennessee Historical Commission. Its office is at Clover Bottom Mansion, 2941 Lebanon Road. Other important sources about individual buildings are the Metro Nashville Archives and the Nashville Room of the Public Library of Metropolitan Nashville and Davidson County. The *Tennessee Historical Quarterly* has published many valuable articles about Nashville's built environment. The Tennessee State Library and Archives maintains the valuable African American history source, *Profiles of African Americans in Tennessee*, first published as a book by Bobby L. Lovett and Linda T. Wynn in 1996. The Tennessee Historical Commissions maintains a valuable primary source website about the Civil War era, the *Tennessee Civil War Sourcebook*. Another important website is the American Memory website of the Library of Congress, which maintains records of properties recorded by the Historic American Building Survey.

The suggested readings below were particularly helpful in the preparation of this book; they are not a complete listing of published sources.

Brumbaugh, Thomas B., et al. *Architecture of Middle Tennessee: The Historic American Buildings Survey*. Nashville: Vanderbilt University Press, 1974.

Carey, Bill. *Fortunes, Fiddles, and Fried Chicken: A Business History of Nashville*. Franklin: Hillsboro Press, 2000.

Clements, Paul. *A Past Remembered: A Collection of Antebellum Houses in Davidson County*. Nashville: Clearview Press, 1987.

Creighton, Wilbur F., Jr. *Building of Nashville*. Nashville: private, 1969.

Dorian, Donna, et al. *At Home in Tennessee: Classic Historic Interiors*. Baton Rouge: Louisiana University Press, 2009.

Doyle, Don H. *Nashville in the New South, 1880–1930*. Knoxville: University of Tennessee Press, 1985.

Doyle, Don H. *Nashville Since the 1920s*. Knoxville: University of Tennessee Press, 1985.

Durham, Walter T. *Reluctant Partners: Nashville and the Union, July 1, 1863 to June 30, 1865*. Nashville: Tennessee Historical Society, 1987.

Goodstein, Anita S. *Nashville, 1780–1860: From Frontier to City*. Gainesville: University Press of Florida, 1989.

Gowans, Alan. *Styles and Types of North American Architecture: Social Function and Cultural Expression*. New York: HarperCollins, 1991.

Graham, Eleanor, ed. *Nashville: A Short History and Selected Buildings*. Nashville: Historical Commission of Metropolitan Nashville and Davidson County, 1974.

Kreyling, Christine M. *Classical Nashville: Athens of the South*. Nashville: Vanderbilt University Press, 1996.

Kyrakoudes, Louis. *The Social Origins of the Urban South: Race, Gender, and Migration in Nashville and Middle Tennessee, 1890–1930*.

Chapel Hill: University of North Carolina Press, 2003.

Lovett, Bobby L. *The African American History of Nashville, Tennessee, 1780–1930: Elites and Dilemmas.* Fayetteville, AR: University of Arkansas Press, 1999.

Lovett, Bobby L. and Linda T. Wynn. *Profiles of African Americans in Tennessee.* Nashville: Annual Local Conference on Afro-American Culture and History, 1996.

Orr, Frank, et al. *Notable Nashville Architecture, 1930–1980.* Nashville: Middle Tennessee Chapter of AIA, 1989.

Patrick, James. *Architecture in Tennessee, 1768–1897.* Knoxville: University of Tennessee Press, 1981.

Spinney, Robert. *World War II in Nashville: Transformation of the Homefront.* Knoxville: University of Tennessee Press, 1998.

Waller, William, ed. *Nashville in the 1890s.* Nashville: Vanderbilt University Press, 1970.

West, Carroll Van. *Tennessee's New Deal Landscape: A Guidebook.* Nashville: University of Tennessee Press, 2000.

West, Carroll Van, et al., eds. *Tennessee Encyclopedia of History and Culture.* Nasvhille: Tennessee Historical Society, 1998.

Zepp, George R. *Hidden History of Nashville.* Charleston, S.C.: The History Press, 2009.

Index

Page numbers in **boldface** refer to illustrations.